THE HISTORY OF ANCIENT EGYPT

THE HISTORY OF ANCIENT EGYPT

Nathaniel Harris

CHANCELLOR
PRESS

Publishing Director
Laura Bamford
Executive Editor
Julian Brown
Assistant Editor
Karen O'Grady
Art Director
Keith Martin
Executive Art Editor
Mark Winwood
Design
Glen Wilkins
Production
Dawn Mitchell
Picture Research
Wendy Gay

First Published in Great Britain in 1997
by Hamlyn. Published 2000 by
Chancellor Press, an imprint of Bounty Books,
a division of Octopus Publishing Group Ltd.

ISBN 0 7537 0761 6

Reprinted 2001
This paperback edition published 2003
by Chancellor Press, an imprint of
Bounty Books, a division of Octopus
Publishing Group Limited,
2-4 Heron Quays, London E14 4JP

A catalogue record for this book is
available from the British Library

Produced by Toppan (HK) Ltd
Printed in China

CONTENTS

INTRODUCTION

NO ANCIENT CIVILIZATION AROUSES SUCH PASSIONATE, ALMOST UNIVERSAL INTEREST AS THE EGYPT OF THE PHARAOHS. DESPITE CHANGES IN TECHNOLOGY AND CULTURAL FASHIONS, ONE GENERATION AFTER ANOTHER HAS FALLEN UNDER ITS SPELL. THE GREAT PYRAMID IS NO LONGER THE WORLD'S TALLEST STRUCTURE AND THE VALLEY OF THE KINGS IS UNLIKELY TO YIELD NEW TREASURES TO MATCH THE GOLD-RICH TOMB OF TUTANKHAMUN; BUT ANCIENT EGYPT CONTINUES TO FASCINATE.

One clue to its enduring appeal lies in its otherness. Its ruins and records are awe-inspiring but enigmatic. The kings who ruled it – the pharaohs – were living gods, able to command the building of pyramids or the hewing of deep tombs in desert cliffs. The tombs themselves were filled with everyday necessities, ritual objects and quantities of precious, wonderfully fashioned things, all of which were intended for use in the afterlife – an afterlife that was believed in so devoutly that every reasonably affluent individual arranged to be embalmed after death so that, as a mummy, reanimated, he or she would live on forever. A mythology peopled by animal-headed gods, and a beautiful, bewildering form of picture-writing – hieroglyphs – are among aspects of Egyptian society that make it seem so remote, mysterious and exciting. Fortunately research has revealed a great deal about the everyday lives of the Egyptians, casting them in an unexpectedly ordinary, cheerful light, and helping to overcome the immense distance in time that separates us from them.

For, of course, ancient Egypt was *very* ancient. Its civilization emerged over five thousand years ago from prehistoric settlements along the River Nile, with many of its characteristic features already in place. As a matter of fact civilization had developed even earlier in the Near East, at Sumer in Mesopotamia (roughly modern Iraq). But whereas the ancient Near East was often in turmoil, as peoples and empires rose and fell, Egyptian society endured for three millennia, to all appearances hardly changing. Despite periods of division and disorder, dynasties of pharaohs occupied the throne and, until a very late date, the Egyptian way of life remained largely undisturbed by foreign influences. With the Nile to fertilize it and act as its highway, Egypt was essentially a long green strip, hemmed in by deserts to the east and west, but also protected by them. To the south, beyond the first of six cataracts which disrupted the serenity of the Nile, lay Nubia, known to the Egyptians as the land of Yam or Kush, which was not so much a security threat as a source of valuable raw materials. With the assistance of geography and climate, Egypt was a world in itself, able for centuries at a time to regulate its contacts with the worlds beyond its borders.

Although eventually drawn into Mediterranean power politics, the Egyptians retained their own distinctive culture for some three thousand years. It impressed the Greeks and Romans, as it impresses us, with its antiquity. Yet when the traditional order did finally disappear, accidents of history created a distorted, 'Arabian Nights' image of Egypt as a fabulous land of potent magic and buried treasure. The gradual rediscovery of ancient Egypt is a romance in itself, recounted in the first chapter of this book.

The chronology of the ancient world is uncertain, although there is wide agreement on the order in which most important events in Egyptian history occurred. So it should be borne in mind that all dates given in this book for events before the 7th Century BC are approximate.

Princess Neferti sits at an offering table laden with loaves of bread which will nourish her in the afterlife. She is dressed as a priestess, in a close-fitting leopardskin garment.

1 THE DISCOVERY OF ANCIENT EGYPT

WITH HER GREAT MONUMENTS HALF-BURIED IN SAND AND HER CULTURE AND LANGUAGE FORGOTTEN, ANCIENT EGYPT BECAME THE HAUNT OF LEGENDS AND MYSTERIES. TREASURE SEEKERS INVADED THE GREAT PYRAMID, AND WOULD-BE HEALERS HOPED TO WORK MIRACLES WITH POWDERS MADE FROM MUMMY FLESH. THE DISCOVERY, OR RATHER RECOVERY, OF ANCIENT EGYPT IS A SPLENDID TALE OF ADVENTURE AND DETECTION, BEGINNING WHEN ONE OF NAPOLEON BONAPARTE'S OFFICERS UNCOVERED AN INSCRIBED SLAB OF BLACK GRANITE. THE DECIPHERMENT OF HIEROGLYPHS UNLOCKED THE PAST, AND IN TIME EGYPTOLOGY BECAME A SCIENCE. BUT JUST WHEN SOBER SCHOLARSHIP HAD TRIUMPHED, HOWARD CARTER MADE THE MOST WONDERFUL AND WILDLY ROMANTIC DISCOVERY OF ALL.

EARLY TOURISTS

The Egypt of the pharaohs was was never a 'vanished' civilization. Unlike the Hittites or the Maya, the Egyptians did not disappear so completely that their very existence was unsuspected until archaeologists brought them back to life. But when the traditional culture of ancient Egypt died out, the key to its language was also lost, and only a few aspects of its history were understood. Rich in mighty monuments whose purposes were forgotten, Egypt became a land of fabled mysteries and marvels until pioneering travellers and scholars rediscovered its real past.

Egypt seemed old and a little remote even to people in ancient times. The first substantial foreign account of the country was written by Herodotus, a Greek from Halicarnassus. He is conventionally known as 'the Father of History' because he was the first historian to travel widely, gather evidence and write up interviews with his contemporaries – though it must be said that he made only half-hearted attempts to sort out truth from fantasy. Egypt was under Persian rule when he went there, in about 450 BC, but the traditional culture and customs were still alive. Herodotus acquired most of his information from priests, presumably through interpreters, and subsequent research has confirmed a good many of his statements. However, on occasion he was wildly wrong, and he records some tales so tall (for example, about the pharaoh who put his daughter into a brothel to raise money for pyramid-building) that they must be rated as jokes, invented by his informants to make fun of an inquisitive foreigner.

Herodotus did realize the vital significance of the Nile in Egyptian life, and he also correctly identified the pyramids at Giza as royal tombs; some of the stories he was told about the building of the pyramids, though exaggerated, may preserve a genuine tradition about a time of mass recruitment and severe strains on available resources. But his most important contribution to our knowledge of Egypt was to leave the only extended account of how the dead were embalmed, written at a time when the already ancient techniques of mummification were still being practised.

Though broad-minded, Herodotus felt that almost every Egyptian custom was an upside-down version of what was done in the Greek world; even the Nile flooded at the 'wrong' season. Four centuries later another Greek historian, Diodorus Siculus, took a not dissimilar attitude, adding further details about the practice of embalming and alleging that on occasion the Egyptians practised cannibalism.

Diodorus was a compiler rather than a historian, and none too reliable even as a copyist. A more accurate, if rather dry account of Egypt was written by the Greek geographer Strabo. During his visit in 25 BC, Strabo travelled as far south as the First Cataract, effectively the frontier

Opposite: The Nilometer, essentially a set of steps, was a simple and practical means of measuring the height of the river. This one is at Elephantine, an island on Egypt's southern border.

Left: Symbols of power. The crook and flail were important items of regalia. Royal portraits often show the king holding them crossed over his chest, the flail in his right hand and the crook in his left.

Below: Even in prehistoric times the Egyptians believed in a life after death. This man was buried in about 3200 BC with flint knives and pottery vessels, evidently intended to be useful to him in a future existence.

The Sphinx and the pyramids are the best-known of all ancient Egyptian monuments. This 19th-century view, with the Sphinx still half-buried in sand, is typical of its period in its romantic atmosphere.

separating Egypt from Nubia. There, on the island of Elephantine, he saw one of the devices with which the Egyptians monitored their most precious resource – a 'Nilometer', in the form of a set of steps which served as markers, measuring the rise and fall of the river.

Strabo also examined two colossal stone figures which stood – and still stand – on the west bank of the Nile at Thebes. Dating from the 14th century BC, they represented the pharaoh Amenhotep III, but like many Egyptian monuments they were given Greek names and related to a story from Greek mythology. Baptized as the Colossi of Memnon, they were held to celebrate an Ethiopian warrior-king, the beautiful son of the dawn-goddess Eos, who was slain in the Trojan War. Strabo reported on a mysterious feature of the Colossi that was to make them famous: the more or less musical note 'sung' every day by one of the figures, reputedly when it was struck by the first rays of the rising sun. Strabo suspected that some trickery was involved, but the sound is now believed to have been caused by the action of the sun's heat on a flaw in the stone. The flaw was probably the result of an earthquake that is known to have occurred in 27 BC, two years before Strabo's visit. Some damage evidently became visible, for in AD 199 the singing figure was all too efficiently repaired, and after two centuries of celebrity Memnon fell silent.

Even by Strabo's day, many monuments had become neglected and lay half-buried in sand. But as Egypt was absorbed into the Roman world from AD 30, its exotic character fascinated the conquerors and tourism flourished. The most imposing sights – above all the Great Pyramid – were visited by curious travellers such as the globe-trotting emperor Hadrian, who also carved his name on the figure of 'Memnon'. The Romans found Egyptian culture engaging enough to take over some aspects of it for use in their own increasingly cosmopolitan way of life. When the proconsul Cestius died in 12 BC, a substantial pyramid was raised to serve as his tomb on the outskirts of Rome. At Tivoli, Hadrian built life-size reproductions of Egyptian and other buildings he had seen on his travels. And as the old Roman religion lost its hold, the Egyptian cults of Isis and Serapis were among the 'new' faiths that attracted adherents. Later, Egyptian obelisks were commandeered, transported to Rome and set up in prominent places, anticipating similar arrangements in London and Paris by 1,500 years.

How much of Egypt's traditional culture actually survived the centuries of prolonged contact with the Greco-Roman world is unclear. But the impact of Christianity, which became the religion of the Roman Empire, was decisive. In victory it soon became intolerant, and in 392 the Emperor Theodosius closed the temples and banned the rituals of all other religions. Egyptian learning had already suffered from disasters such as the burning of the great library of Alexandria; the suppression of Egyptian religion, the chief repository of written records, sounded the death-knell for the Egyptian language. In the new dispensation, dominated by ascetics and anchorites, the achievements and values of ancient Egypt were seen as at best irrelevant, at worst satanic.

THE MAGICAL LAND

Egypt remained a part of the Christian world for almost three centuries. Then in 641 it was conquered by Arab warriors who brought with them the new religion of Islam. Egypt became, and has remained, a predominantly Muslim and Arabic-speaking society.

By the time the Arab armies arrived, almost all traces of ancient Egyptian speech and customs seem to have disappeared. Over the centuries that followed, the great monuments came to be seen as magical marvels, akin to those in the tales of *The Thousand and One Nights*. In search of gigantic pearls and emeralds, treasure-seekers tried to burrow into the depths of the pyramids. But those who managed to get in were doomed to disappointment, finding that the tomb robbers had visited them long before and stripped the chambers of all their valuables.

During the Middle Ages, hostility between Christians and Muslims ensured that Europeans would appear in Egypt only as crusaders or occasional pilgrims passing through on their way to the Holy Land; they interpreted anything they saw in Old Testament terms, taking the pyramids to be Joseph's granaries.

This situation began to change after Egypt became part of the Ottoman Turkish empire in 1517. Despite continuing wars, trade expanded and imports into Europe included mummies, which were ground down and made up into cure-all powders and potions. The word 'mummy' comes from *mummiya*, the Persian term for bitumen, a supposedly health-giving mineral substance. The blackened condition of embalmed Egyptians was wrongly believed to result from a soaking in bitumen, and this mistake gave mummies their name as well as their ill-fated popularity as pharmaceuticals. Down to the 19th century

The Nile Delta, teeming with life, as pictured in a Roman mosaic of the 1st century BC at Praeneste. Even other peoples in antiquity marvelled at Egypt's great wealth and distinctive customs.

Stone giants at sunrise. The Greeks called them the Colossi of Memnon, although they were actually twin statues of Amenhotep III. For two centuries a flaw in one of the colossi caused it to 'sing', astonishing visitors.

mummies continued to be so much in demand that, when there was a shortage, suppliers home-cured more recent corpses and passed them off as antique items.

In the 17th and 18th centuries Egypt was visited more and more often by European scholars and travellers. Several of them acted as agents for European collectors, including the kings of France, bringing back art objects and papyri and publishing accounts of their adventures and acquisitions. But although awareness of ancient Egyptian civilization certainly increased as a result of these peaceful activities, much more important breakthroughs were made as side-effects of war and revolution.

The great French Revolution, which began in 1789, plunged France into a long series of conflicts with the rest of Europe. In 1799 the current French government, the Directory, decided to send a large-scale expedition to Egypt, led by the young general Napoleon Bonaparte. Britain was the most unyielding of France's enemies, and control of Egypt would cut Britain's lines of communication with her Indian empire; if all went well, the French army might march overland and sweep the British out of India itself. Despite its plausibility the plan was extraordinarily risky (especially in view of Britain's greater sea power), and it has often been suggested that the Directors were partly motivated by a wish to send their dangerously popular and ambitious general as far away from France as possible.

In hard political terms the results of the expedition were scarcely impressive. Napoleon landed at Alexandria on 1 July 1798 and quickly disposed of the Mameluke rulers of Egypt. But the French fleet was destroyed in Aboukir Bay by a decisive British attack led by Horatio Nelson. Now cut off from France, Napoleon defeated the Turks but failed in a determined attempt to march through Syria. In September 1799, after fourteen months in Egypt, he simply slipped away, returning to France where a promising political situation enabled him to seize power.

The army of occupation that he left behind languished and eventually capitulated to the British.

This apparently uninspired episode had some remarkable consequences. Seen in the light of Napoleon's subsequent European victories and imperial grandeur, the Egyptian expedition became one of the most romantic episodes in his spectacular career. Its impact was strengthened by the appearance of superb new images of the East. Napoleon had taken with him to Egypt a Commission – in effect a task force of scientists, scholars and artists – that spent three years making a comprehensive survey of Egypt's resources, geography, society, natural history and major monuments. The result was a series of detailed, superbly illustrated publications. Vivant Denon, a diplomat and artist loosely attached to the Commission, caused an early sensation when he published his *Journey in Lower and Upper Egypt* (1803), a best-seller filled with vivid, atmospheric illustrations. Then, while Napoleon was still at the height of his power, the Commission began to publish its nineteen-volume *Description of Egypt* (1809-22), perhaps the greatest scholarly achievement of its time.

The heady mix of Napoleonic grandeur and oriental glamour created an immense vogue for all things Egyptian. It was most obvious in interiors and furnishings, where sphinxes and lotus blossoms were combined with classical features to create the dominant Empire style. But it went much deeper than that, creating an ambience from which the passionate, obsessive scholars of the next generation would emerge. Among their works would be the greatest posthumous victory of Napoleon's expedition to Egypt.

UNLOCKING THE LANGUAGE

Down to the 19th century, the only direct written evidence about ancient Egypt – evidence in any language that could be understood – came from a mere handful of sources. Most of these, like the works of the Greek travellers and the Hebrew Old Testament, were by outsiders. An important exception was a history compiled in the 3rd century BC by Manetho, an Egyptian priest who wrote in Greek. His thirty volumes disappeared in antiquity, but fragments quoted by other authors could be pieced together to create a list of Egyptian kings, grouped into thirty dynasties. Despite inconsistencies and obscurities, the list forms the basis for modern chronologies. But so long as the ancient Egyptians' monumental inscriptions and writings on papyrus could not be deciphered, the kings and dynasties remained little more than names.

The courtyard of Edfu, one of the best-preserved Egyptian temples, is shown in this lovely, if romanticized, 19th-century lithograph. In the background stands the mighty pylon (gateway), covered with scenes carved in relief.

The key to the Egyptian past was discovered by accident, when one of Napoleon's officers, Lieutenant Bouchard, began moving quantities of stone to strengthen the defences of a fort near the town of Rosetta, in the Delta. The operations revealed a slab of basalt, inscribed in three different scripts, which Bouchard sent on to the scientific institute established by the French at Cairo. The scripts were Greek, hieroglyphic and demotic (a kind of shorthand Egyptian, more convenient than hieroglyphs for everyday use). The French scholars realized that the three texts might be versions of the same announcement, and that, if so, the presence of a known language – Greek – might at last make it possible to understand the ancient Egyptian tongue.

The 'Rosetta Stone' passed into British hands when the French forces in Egypt capitulated. But the French scholars had taken copies and casts of the original, and it soon became known throughout Europe. Even with parallel texts to work from, deciphering a completely unknown language was a daunting task, especially since its basic principles were unknown. Since the hieroglyphs took the form of pictures, it was tempting to believe that each sign was a symbol (ideogram), representing a thing or idea. The alternative (phonetic) explanation was that the signs represented sounds. Both were plausible, yet neither yielded really satisfactory results.

Contributions to the eventual solution were made by a number of able linguists, notably a Swede, Johan David Akerblad, and the British scientist Thomas Young; but the crowning achievement was that of Jean-François Champollion (1790-1832). Born at Figeac in southern France, Champollion was a child prodigy who had mastered Hebrew, Coptic, Arabic and other Near Eastern languages by the time he reached his late teens; he was also fortunate in having an elder brother, Jacques-Joseph Champollion, himself a formidable scholar, who not only guided Jean-François' studies but oversaw the publication of his work during and after his lifetime.

Right: Jean-François Champollion, the first man to translate Egyptian hieroglyphs. The ancient Egyptian language had died out by the 5th century AD; Champollion's brilliant insights meant that inscriptions and writings on papyrus, indecipherable for well over a thousand years, could be understood.

Far right: The Rosetta Stone, dating from 196 BC. It carries the same announcement in three languages, one of them (Greek, bottom) already known to scholars. This ultimately made it possible to decipher the hieroglyphic (top) and demotic (middle) scripts of the ancient Egyptians.

When he was only sixteen, Champollion delivered a paper at Grenoble on Coptic, the liturgical language of Egyptian Christians, which was mainly written in Greek letters. Champollion asserted (and we now know that he was correct) that Coptic was a descendant, albeit remote, of the ancient Egyptian tongue. Turning his attention to the Rosetta Stone, he worked on the assumption that the hieroglyphs that appeared on the stone within cartouches (lozenge-shaped outlines) received this special treatment because they were the names of kings. Comparing these signs with the royal names mentioned in the Greek portion of the text, Champollion was able to identify them and establish sound values for a number of hieroglyphs. However, his crucial insight was that the signs were not exclusively phonetic, but combined both phonetic and ideographic elements. He announced his early results in his *Letter to M. Dacier* (1822) and *Summary of the Hieroglyphic System* (1824), but these were followed by years of intense labour, including an expedition to Egypt in 1828-9. Before his early death Champollion managed to compile both a dictionary and a grammar of the ancient language, making it possible at last to read the records and enter the minds of the Egyptians.

SCHOLARS AND SCAVENGERS

In the wake of Champollion's great discovery, scholars among his near contemporaries set themselves to record the monuments and inscriptions of ancient Egypt for posterity.

The industry of some pioneers in this field was awe-inspiring. A British scholar, John Gardner Wilkinson (1797-1875), working single-handed, copied and deciphered huge quantities of material. He also produced the first general survey since Strabo to be based on his own observations. His *Manners and Customs of the Ancient Egyptians* (1837) went beyond mere recording; it sought to interpret the surviving pictures and writings vividly enough to recreate a vanished way of life. A revelation in their day, Wilkinson's volumes earned him a knighthood.

Karl Lepsius (1810-84), like Champollion, led a full-scale expedition to Egypt, and the twelve volumes of his *Discoveries in Egypt and Ethiopia* (1849-59) represent a magnificent collective effort on the part of German scholars. As a visual record of ancient Egypt – as far as its remains were then known – Lepsius' work could justly claim to be exhaustive.

Records of this kind were all the more valuable because, even while they were being compiled, the sites from which they originated were being ravaged. In the past, tombs had been looted by the Egyptians themselves, Christian zealots had defaced monuments, and the trade in mummies and the souvenir-hunting of tourists had taken their toll; but the 19th century was the age of pillage on the grand scale. There was no Egyptian law protecting antiquities, and energetic agents and entrepreneurs laid their hands on quantities of objects, large and small, tearing them out of their settings and selling them to wealthy collectors and museums eager to build up their holdings. The casual damage inflicted, and the knowledge sacrificed, make a curious contrast with the dedicated work of men like Wilkinson and Lepsius.

National rivalries encouraged the rapacity of the collectors. The French and British consuls in Cairo, Bernardino Drovetti and Henry Salt, refought the Anglo-French wars, effectively partitioning the ancient city of Thebes between their followers. 'A line of demarcation is drawn through every temple,' wrote one observer, 'and these buildings that have hitherto withstood the attacks of Barbarians, will not resist the speculation of civilized cupidity, virtuosi and antiquarians.'

Drovetti seems to have had the advantage of a closer relationship with the Pasha who ruled Egypt, but Salt had the services of the most

Gangs of labourers transport a colossal head of Ramesses II to the Nile, from which it was shipped to Europe. This watercolour record was painted by Belzoni, who masterminded the operation.

flamboyant of 19th-century explorer-looters, Giovanni Battista Belzoni (1778-1823). The son of a barber, Belzoni was born in Padua, studied hydraulics in Rome, was briefly a novice monk, and then went on the road as a pedlar. In 1803 he surfaced in England, appearing on the stage for ten years or more as 'the Patagonian Samson' and 'the Young Hercules'; over two metres tall, he was so strong that he could raise aloft a heavy iron frame with as many as eleven men standing on it. Moving about restlessly, Belzoni heard in Malta that the Pasha was looking for a hydraulic engineer. He promptly took ship for Egypt and, the Pasha having proved to be an unsatisfactory employer, went to work for Henry Salt as a roving collector of antiquities.

Belzoni's first and most spectacular coup was to locate and remove a colossal head of Ramesses II from the Ramesseum, the king's great mortuary temple on the west bank of the Nile. Belzoni managed to recruit a large labour force and transport the head on rollers to the water's edge, a feat he commemorated in a now-well-known watercolour. Eventually Ramesses – 'Young Memnon' to Belzoni and his contemporaries – was shipped down the Nile and taken by sea to London, where he stands in the British Museum.

Though he had a more sensitive feeling for antiquity than most of his rivals, Belzoni was still a swashbuckler at heart. His accounts of his adventures contain some unintentionally painful episodes, notably his description of blundering about in the darkness of a tomb, grinding mummies to powder with every heavy step.

During his five years in Egypt, Belzoni ranged from the pyramids at Giza to the temples of Abu Simbel, making discoveries and bringing back obelisks, sarcophagi and statues in best strongman fashion.

His showmanship reasserted itself after he discovered the tomb of the warrior-king Seti I; in 1820 he returned to London and hired the Egyptian Hall to exhibit life-sized reproductions of the tomb and its brilliant decorations. This proved to be the high point of his career; his death from dysentry in West Africa, while searching for the source of the Niger, put an abrupt end to an extraordinary life.

Four colossal seated figures of Ramesses II, one badly damaged, guard the king's temple at Abu Simbel in Nubia. Even mountains of sand, built up over thousands of years, failed to bury them.

THE SCIENTIFIC AGE

The idea of conserving Egypt's heritage was slow to take root. Belzoni and his fellow-adventurers gloried in the size of their hauls and, if challenged, claimed that they were rescuing masterpieces which might otherwise be used as kindling or building materials by the natives. When Champollion visited Egypt in 1835, he was horrified by the plundering and destruction he witnessed, and protested directly to the government of Mohammed Ali. Champollion's intervention was effective, prompting the Pasha to issue a decree asserting the state's ownership of antiquities, forbidding their export without permission, and requiring would-be excavators to apply for a licence to dig. Although only sporadically enforced, the decree was a beginning, and it did serve to deter the grossest acts of plunder.

The situation was more rigorously controlled after the advent of Auguste Mariette (1828-81). Formerly a teacher and self-taught Egyptologist in his native France, Mariette came to Egypt in 1850 with a commission to purchase Coptic manuscripts from a monastery. The transaction fell through, and Mariette boldly applied to another purpose the funds which had been earmarked for manuscripts. Fortunately he was triumphantly

Flinders Petrie, the first of the great scientific Egyptologists. Here he is arranging some of his finds of ancient Palestinian pottery for an exhibition at University College, London.

successful. Noticing a sphinx half-buried in the sand, he recalled a passage in Strabo's *Geography* which described the sphinxes lining the sacred way from Memphis to the necropolis at Saqqara. Following this clue, Mariette uncovered underground burial chambers holding sarcophagi with the mummified bodies of generations of sacred bulls, venerated as incarnations of the god Apis.

Mariette's discovery made him famous, and eventually led to his appointment as first director of the Egyptian Antiquities Service. As such he was empowered to clear and excavate sites, collect antiquities, control the activities of foreign archaeologists and collectors, and prevent thefts by foreigners and natives alike. He carried out his brief energetically and, as a natural continuation of the new policy, set up what later became the Cairo Museum, Egypt's first national museum.

In the long run, Mariette's achievement was to make conservation and scientific investigation higher-priority activities than treasure-hunting – although, given the incredible wealth of ancient Egypt, the treasure-hunting impulse was muted rather than eliminated. More organized and scientific concerns also prevailed in Britain, where an unexpectedly important role was played by the popular novelist Amelia B. Edwards. In 1873 she undertook the kind of long, leisurely voyage available to affluent Victorians, turning it into the best-selling copy of *A Thousand Miles Up the Nile* (1877). But the personal effect of her journey was to make her angry about the destruction of monuments and determined to promote a scientific, responsible approach to archaeology. In 1882 she was the principal founder of a deeply respected institution which still exists, the Egypt Exploration Fund (now the Egypt Exploration Society). As its first secretary Edwards travelled and lectured to make converts and raise money to finance a series of historic expeditions.

Easily the most important of Edwards' protégés was William Flinders Petrie (1853-1942), the founding father of scientific archaeology. Cantankerous and supremely confident of his own rectitude, Petrie quarrelled with the Egypt Exploration Fund after working on one of their projects for only two years (1884-6); but Amelia Edwards introduced him to a wealthy patron who financed his subsequent work, and later (1892-1942) Petrie occupied the first professorial chair of Egyptology, founded by Edwards at University College, London.

In a long working life Petrie made a number of major discoveries in Egypt: the Amarna Letters describing the military and diplomatic situation during the reign of Akhenaten (14th century BC); the 7th-century Greek settlement of Naucratis established in the Delta; and the amazing, lifelike encaustic portraits of the dead, painted during the Greco-Roman period. Nevertheless Petrie's greatness lay in the fact that he was not obsessed with large or valuable finds. He placed a high value on everyday artefacts from which the archaeologist could hope in time to recreate an entire way of life. Appropriately enough, the achievement for which Petrie is now most admired is his investigation of Predynastic graves, which revealed Egyptian culture as it existed before the unification of the country and the emergence of the first pharaohs.

Personally eccentric and irascible, Petrie was a model excavator; he worked over the entire site, examined and recorded every item unearthed, however fragmentary, and regularly published his results for the benefit of the scientific community. Such practises are now universal, in large part thanks to Petrie.

With Flinders Petrie, scientific archaeology came of age. But the most glamorous and golden of treasures had not yet come to light.

THE TOMB OF TUTANKHAMUN

The Valley of the Kings is the most celebrated archaeological site in Egypt. Here, the pharaohs of the 18th-20th dynasties were buried in multi-chambered tombs cut deep into the sides of the valley; among them were some of Egypt's mightiest rulers, including Seti I and Ramesses II. Belzoni's discovery of Seti's huge tomb was one of a series of 19th-century finds which yielded figures carved from the rock, wall paintings and many funerary objects. But all the chambers had been stripped of their more valuable contents by tomb-robbers.

The thefts had taken place in antiquity, so promptly that, as early as the 21st dynasty, priests had decided that they must at least prevent the desecration of the mummies, and had removed them, shorn of their finery, to places of safety.

Archaeologist on the move. Flinders Petrie (far left) stands beside the old green bus that carried him for thousands of miles from site to site.

Right: Howard Carter leads a procession of assistants, newspapermen and tourists, accompanied by an Egyptian soldier. An assistant carries a bust of Tutankhamun, balancing it in a fashion that hardly inspires confidence.

Below: A moment to live for. Carter (kneeling) has opened four sets of shrine doors; now, through them, he can see the magnificent sarcophagus which holds a nest of coffins and the mummified body of Tutankhamun himself.

One large cache, discovered in 1882, had been hidden in the crevice of a cliff to the north-west, at Deir el-Bahri. Sixteen years later another group came to light in a tomb in the valley. Almost all the mummies of 18th and 19th dynasty rulers were now accounted for, and the prospect of finding an intact royal tomb in the valley receded with each new discovery.

By the time the British archaeologist Howard Carter (1874-1939) began excavating in the valley, many archaeologists believed that there was nothing more of significance to be found there. Like other pioneer Egyptologists, Carter did not have a conventional academic background. He had begun work in Egypt as a draughtsman, copying tomb paintings; during a stint with Flinders Petrie, Carter seemed so much the artist that Petrie remarked in humorous despair that 'It is of no use to me to work him up as an excavator!'

In 1899 Carter switched from art to administration, becoming Antiquities Inspector for Upper Egypt. But in 1903 he resigned following disputes with Theodore Davis, a wealthy American who was financing a programme of excavations. Carter's career seemed to be in the doldrums until he met Lord Carnarvon, a wealthy British aristocrat whose backing enabled him to work for some years at Thebes. Then in 1914, at Carter's urging, Carnarvon took over the concession to excavate in the Valley of the Kings, which Davis had just given up. The floor of the valley was covered with huge piles of debris left by previous expeditions, and Carter believed that some of the areas underneath them had never been properly excavated. Moreover a number of recent minor finds encouraged him to believe that he might yet locate an unknown tomb – that of an obscure pharaoh named Tutankhamun.

The outbreak of the First World War delayed the work, which only began in earnest in 1917. Carter went painstakingly over the most promising area, shifting debris and digging down to the bedrock. Year after year the results were sparse, and Carnarvon and Carter agreed that 1922-3 should be their last season in the valley. From this point onwards the story reads like fiction. Carter had had to put off investigating one area because operations there would have blocked visitors'

Howard Carter and a colleague, A.R. Callender, clear the Antechamber of Tutankhamun's tomb. One of the two guardian figures is wrapped and almost ready to go; the other still stands beside the doorway to the burial chamber.

access to the tomb of the 20th Dynasty pharaoh Ramesses VI. But in this final year he started before the tourist season, clearing away the workmen's huts in front of the tomb; these were themselves antiquities, probably used by the labourers who worked on Ramesses' tomb. Then Carter's men began to shift the soil beneath the huts.

The following morning, 4 November 1922, Carter arrived at the site, puzzled by the silence: work had stopped with the discovery, under the very first hut, of a step cut into the rock. By the end of the next day, sixteen steps down, the upper part of a sealed door had been uncovered. Since the workmen's huts had blocked the site for over 3,000 years, it could not have been broken into since the 20th dynasty – and perhaps not at all.

Carter stifled his impulse to go on, realizing that Carnarvon had a right to be present at the opening of the tomb. Refilling the stairway, Carter sent his patron a jubilant telegram, and a fortnight later the two men saw the entire door to the tomb revealed. On it was the seal of a pharaoh: Tutankhamun. The door was broken down and a rubble-filled passage cleared. Faced by the door to the tomb itself, Carter made a small breach in one corner. Only his own narrative can do justice to what followed:

'At first I could see nothing, the hot air escaping from the chamber causing the candle flame to flicker, but presently, as my eyes grew accustomed to the light, details of the room within emerged slowly from the mist, strange animals, statues, and gold – everywhere the glint of gold. For the moment – an eternity it must have seemed to the others standing by – I was struck dumb with amazement, and when Lord Carnarvon, unable to stand the suspense any longer, inquired anxiously, "Can you see anything?" it was all I could do to get out the words, "Yes, wonderful things."'

The gold mask of Tutankhamun, perhaps the most famous image of Egyptian artistic skill and pharaonic opulence. The mask was placed over the face of the dead king.

The 'glint of gold' came from the gilding on an amazing jumble of objects that lay in the room among rubble, pottery sherds and the withered remains of flowers. There were animal-form beds and other pieces of furniture, dismantled chariots, a small shrine, and dozens of chests crammed with valuables, sacred and profane, made of such materials as alabaster, bronze, ebony, gold, ivory, lapis-lazuli and turquoise. A splendid throne of gold and silver was decorated with a touching, poetic scene showing the young king with his wife, Ankhesenamun. A child-like painted plaster head of Tutankhamun, emerging from a lotus flower, was another of many images of the king in the tomb – including two life-size wooden sentries who stood against a wall, guarding another sealed entrance.

Carter named this first room the Antechamber, rightly anticipating even more awe-inspiring finds beyond. One reason for the unkempt appearance of the Antechamber was that the tomb had, after all, been robbed in antiquity. Valuable items had certainly been carried off, but the thieves had been interrupted before they could make a thorough job of it, and the valley guards had only superficially tidied the disturbed objects before re-sealing the tomb.

After weeks of hard work, cleaning and cataloguing everything in the Antechamber, Carter broke through the sealed door between the two sentry-figures, into the Burial Chamber. This was almost entirely filled with a huge shrine of gilded wood which left hardly any space for Carter and his colleagues to work in. When opened, the shrine was found to contain a second shrine. Carter noted exultantly that its clay seals were intact, which meant that no one had looked inside it – or looted it – since the actual interment of the pharaoh, and that Tutankhamun himself must lie in state within.

There were no fewer than four of these shrines-within-shrines; the fourth contained a large and splendid quartzite sarcophagus; and within the sarcophagus Carter found a nest of three coffins. The third, innermost coffin revealed just what it meant to be a god-king of Egypt: it was made of solid gold, weighing 110 kilograms. Finally, in the gold coffin, lay the earthly remains of Tutankhamun himself, his face covered with a wonderful gold portrait mask. Bandaged in with the mummy were hundreds of jewelled objects, many of them amulets intended to ensure the king's safe passage through the underworld and his happiness in the afterlife. Ironically, the mummy itself was in very bad condition as a result of the over-lavish use of unguents, which had burned instead of preserving it; unwrapping and examining it, even after three thousand years, proved to be a gruesome business.

Even now Carter's task was far from done. There were two smaller chambers in the tomb, both filled with 'wonderful things'. One chamber, which Carter called the Treasury, was guarded by the black, dog-like figure of the god Anubis. As well as a wealth of statuettes and other funerary and grave goods, it held a gilded shrine containing an alabaster chest; inside each of the hollowed-out compartments in the chest lay a miniature coffin containing the king's viscera. There were also two other touching little items: coffins containing the mummified foetuses of two baby girls a few months old, which are generally assumed to be Tutankhamun's stillborn children

Tutankhamun's sceptre, found by Carter in the Annexe of his tomb. It is made of wood covered with sheet gold; the designs have been skilfully hammered out from the back (repoussé technique).

Tutankhamun's sandals. An Egyptian king was buried with a wardrobe appropriate to his rank. This is in fact one of dozens of pairs of sandals found in the tomb.

When lying down, Egyptians used headrests as supports. This very elaborate ivory rest, found in Tutankhamun's tomb, carries the head of the god Bes, a rather comical but also powerfully protective deity.

by his young wife Ankhesenamun. The Methodical Carter left the smallest room, the Annexe, until last. He had already dealt with such quantities of material that work there did not begin until November 1927, five years after the discovery of the tomb. The room was in even wilder disorder than the Antechamber; it had evidently been ransacked by the thieves, and the guards, instead of putting it into some sort of order, had simply stacked the Antechamber furniture in such a way as to conceal the Annexe doorway. Although many of its contents were damaged, they too were exquisite and abundant.

Apart from the larger items in the four-chambered tomb, thousands of objects lay scattered or crammed into boxes or chests. There were too many to list in full here, but the following selection gives some idea of their variety: sandals, sceptres, bows and arrows, staffs, trumpets, fans, flails and fly-whisks, vases, tableware, rolls of linen, amulets and mirrors; a complete set of scribe's equipment; amazing numbers of dried fruits, statuettes and jewels; superb inlaid gaming boards; and models of ships, a granary and many human figures called *shabti*, intended to act as substitutes for the king if any labour services were required by the gods in the afterlife.

In Europe and America the discovery of the tomb was the sensation of sensations, making headlines in the newspapers for months and inspiring 'Egyptian' designs in contemporary costume and interiors. Tutankhamun became the best-known of all the pharaohs – ironically, since he had previously been one of the most obscure, dying when he was about seventeen, and could hardly have exercised much real power. He had been given a hasty, second-class burial, in a ready-made tomb, only one room of which was properly finished and decorated. In fact the tomb that Carter discovered had been intended for a less exalted person, Tutankhamun's chief minister, Ay; but although Ay was an old man, he outlived his young master, succeeded him on the throne, and eventually occupied the spacious chambers intended for his predecessor. In spite of the superb workmanship of many objects in the tomb, the broken lid of the sarcophagus and one or two other poorly fitting items also suggest that

Poster for the film *The Mummy's Curse* (1944), one of a series in which Lon Chaney played a vengeful mummy. This horror genre largely derived from the opening of Tutankhamun's tomb and the supposedly mysterious deaths

Tutankhamun's interment was a rushed affair, not up to the best pharaonic standards. His triumph has been posthumous – poetic justice of a kind to delight an ancient Egyptian, supremely concerned with the afterlife.

Lord Carnarvon lived to see the opening of the burial chamber, but he never looked upon the face of Tutankhamun. He died suddenly in March 1923, after a mosquito bite on his cheek became infected; blood poisoning, compounded by pneumonia, carried him off. The consequences were unexpected. During the 19th century, writers such as Edgar Allan Poe and Sir Arthur Conan Doyle had popularized stories in which mummies came alive and revenged themselves on those who had desecrated their tombs; Carnarvon's unlucky accident re-launched the idea, giving rise to spine-tingling tales of 'the Mummy's Curse' in newspapers, magazines, popular novels and movies. Each death among Carter's colleagues (however old they happened to be at the time) fuelled new speculations, even although the principal culprit, Carter himself, worked on the contents for years and survived the curse until 1939, when he died at the age of sixty-five.

The finding of Tutankhamun has inevitably been seen as a climax of Egyptological history. But in fact there was much that still had to be done, and was done brilliantly, by others. Important discoveries continued to be made, and the painstaking task of recording thousands of inscriptions went on from generation to generation. There is still no end in sight. Nevertheless, after Champollion, Petrie and Carter, three thousand years of Egyptian history had come very distinctly into focus.

2 THREE THOUSAND YEARS OF HISTORY

A DISTINCTIVELY EGYPTIAN WAY OF LIFE WAS ESTABLISHED REMARKABLY EARLY IN THE HISTORY OF THE LAND – REGULATED BY THE RISE AND FALL OF THE NILE, RULED OVER BY A SEMI-DIVINE KING, AND ORGANIZED BY LITERATE BUREAUCRATS. AFTER THE SPLENDID ISOLATION OF THE PYRAMID-BUILDING OLD AND MIDDLE KINGDOMS, THE NEW KINGDOM PHARAOHS MADE EGYPT ONE OF THE GREAT POWERS OF THE NEAR EAST. LATER, REVERSING CENTURIES OF DECLINE, THE GREEK DYNASTY OF THE PTOLEMIES GAVE EGYPT A FINAL PERIOD OF RATHER LURID GRANDEUR, UNTIL THE ALL-CONQUERING ROMANS PUT AN END TO THE AGE OF THE PHARAOHS.

EARLY EGYPT

Egyptian civilization is usually said to have begun in about 3100 BC, when the land was united by a king named Menes or Narmer, who founded the 1st Dynasty. But this event was, of course, the culmination of a long period of development. Stone Age hunters came and went for 150,000 years before climatic changes created the characteristic Saharan and Nilotic environment around 7000 BC. Then, some time before 5500 BC, the first settled farming communities were formed along the banks of the Nile.

The subsequent period from 5500 to 3100 BC is known as the Predynastic period. The very existence of a Predynastic culture was unrecognized until 1895-1900, when Flinders Petrie discovered burial pits in which the dead were interred with arms and legs tightly drawn up, in a fashion so 'un-Egyptian' that at first Petrie believed they belonged to a separate people! Many aspects of the Predynastic period are obscure, although it was undoubtedly a vital stage in the formation of Egyptian civilization – all the more so since that civilization was intensely conservative, clinging to ideas, images and techniques even when they might have come to be regarded as obsolete.

After centuries during which skills such as tool- and pottery-making developed, there was a sudden acceleration that began around 3600 BC. An early form of hieroglyphic writing appeared, and the rich and powerful began to bury their dead in imposing brick tombs known as mastabas. Well-crafted grave goods, in materials such as copper, ivory, gold, silver and turquoise, testified to the Egyptians' already strong belief in an afterlife. Despite the distances involved, influences from the Mesopotamian civilization of Sumer were almost certainly responsible for the development of writing and for the presence of some artefacts dating from the late Predynastic period, although these soon acquired distinctly Egyptian characteristics. Immigrants from outside Egypt may also have brought in new skills and speeded up developments.

The unification of Egypt is generally assumed to have been a gradual process of growth and merging. By the late Predynastic period there were two centres competing for supremacy, Hierakonpolis in Upper (southern) Egypt, and Buto in Lower Egypt (effectively the Delta). Around 3100 BC the kings of Upper Egypt finally extended their authority throughout the land; evidently their triumph had a wider basis than military strength, since modern research has revealed that the Upper Egyptian culture had already permeated the north. Nevertheless there were important differences of character and climate between 'the Two Lands', the marshy Delta contrasting with the valley-and-desert of Upper Egypt. Whenever the central government broke down in ancient Egypt, the country tended to fragment into these constituent parts.

Two different names, Menes and Narmer, are given for the first king of Upper and Lower Egypt; but they may well describe the same man. A strong tradition is associated with Menes, but evidence of his existence is tenuous; the word may

Opposite: A triumphant King Narmer smites a foreign captive; the scene is on the back of the 'Narmer Palette', often interpreted as celebrating the unification of Upper and Lower Egypt.

Above: Stone maceheads, intended to fit on to a wooden haft. These beautiful polished objects were made in the 4th millennium BC, before Egypt existed as a single state.

Left: Figure of a bearded man, carved from the tusk of an elephant. It was found in Middle Egypt and is dated to the Amratian or Naqada period, c.4000-3500 BC.

be a title rather than the name of a king. By contrast, Narmer was definitely a historical character, mentioned in a number of inscriptions. The most famous and informative is a striking piece of worked green slate, 'the Palette of Narmer'. The Egyptians ground down pigments on palettes in order to make face-paint, but grand ceremonial versions such as Narmer's were also used as votive offerings. On one side the king, a towering figure, is shown as poised to strike a helpless enemy whom he clutches by the hair – an image that became the received way of representing every Egyptian king with military pretensions, whether justified or otherwise. In this scene Narmer wears the white crown of Upper Egypt; but on the other side of the palette he is shown in the red crown of Lower Egypt. The palette is therefore the earliest representation of a king of all Egypt, and it has been plausibly interpreted as a celebration of his achievement in unifying the land. This seems confirmed from what we know of Narmer's shadowy predecessor, Scorpion, who appears on a macehead wearing only the crown of Upper Egypt.

According to tradition, the capital of the Upper Egyptian rulers was Thinis, a city said to have been close to the sacred site and burial place of Abydos. These Upper Egyptian bases became less convenient for royal use after the unification of the Two Lands, and a new capital was created by Narmer, or possibly by his successor Aha. Memphis, just above the Delta, stood on the geographical frontier between Upper and Lower Egypt. Access to both must have been important, for north-south tensions seem to have persisted all through the Archaic or Early Dynastic period – the four hundred years of the 1st and 2nd Dynasties – until the last 2nd Dynasty king, Khasekhemwy, who resolved them in some unknown fashion.

By this time many abiding features of Egyptian life were already in place. The king was

Wearing the white crown of Upper Egypt and carrying a crook and flail, Hatshepsut, the only female pharaoh, celebrates her heb-sed or jubilee. The ceremonial entailed running between markers which represented the frontiers of her domains.

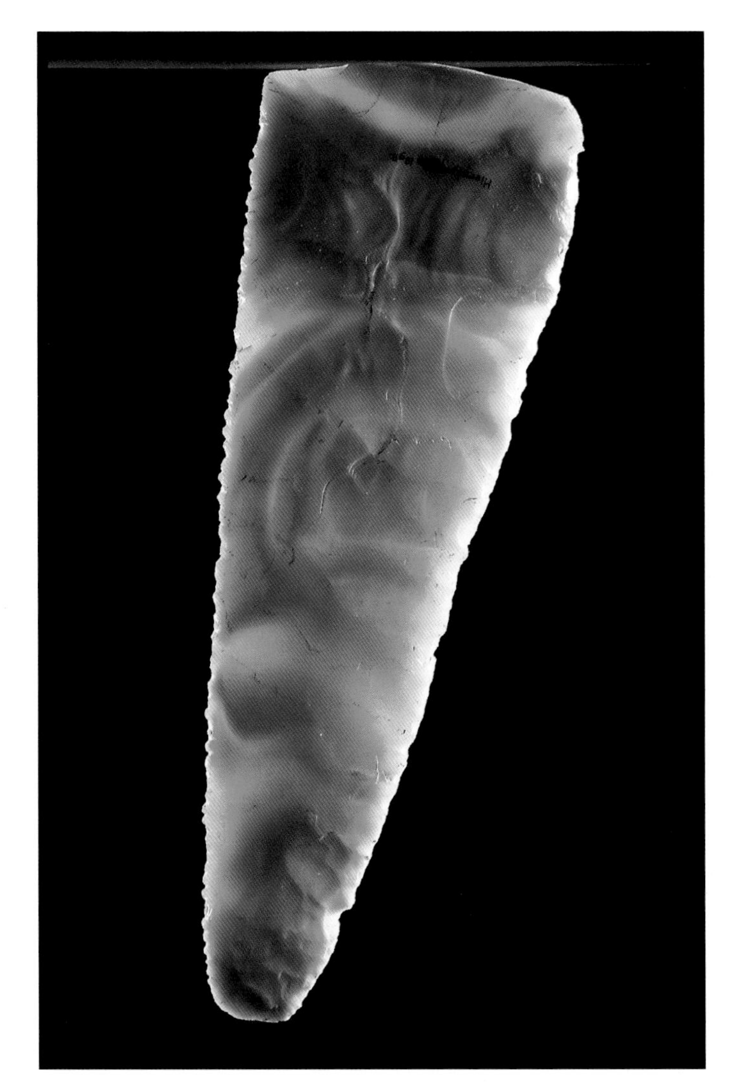

an absolute and semi-divine being, identified with the falcon god Horus and associated with the up-and-coming sun god Re. A vital kingship ritual, the *sed* festival, was well established. The king celebrated the thirtieth anniversary of his reign by receiving the homage of his subjects and running between markers representing the boundaries of Egypt, thereby asserting his right to rule. Tombs became increasingly imposing, especially at sacred Abydos and a later, rival necropolis at Saqqara, just outside Memphis. Finally, the outcome of now-obscure conflicts also took a form that would become familiar, when the names of some 1st Dynasty kings were erased from inscriptions by their successors; the reason, or at any rate the pretext, for ignoring or rewriting the past in this way was usually a ruler's deviation from convention or religious orthodoxy.

In one important respect, early tradition was modified. Royal tombs of the first two dynasties were surrounded by subsidiary tombs for individuals buried at the same time after being sacrificed so that the king should continue to be served in the afterlife; in some instances their numbers ran into hundreds. By the end of the 2nd Dynasty the practice had been discontinued, and models of servants took the place of human sacrifices.

The advances of the Early Dynastic period made possible the even more impressive achievements that followed during Egypt's first great age: the Old Kingdom.

THE OLD KINGDOM

The Old Kingdom (2686-2181 BC) was remarkable for the scale and quality of its monuments and the extraordinary stability of its political and social arrangements. Changes of dynasty seem to

Above left: A flint knife from the Predynastic period; it is another example of the high level of workmanship attained even before the emergence of a unified Egyptian civilization.

Above: Urn with a giraffe pattern. Curiously, pottery of the Predynastic period was decorated in a lively fashion, with human and animal figures, but these are not found on later Egyptian wares, which are mostly workaday objects.

The Stepped Pyramid of King Djoser at Saqqara. This was the first pyramid and the first large stone building in history. Like later pyramids, it was intended to serve as the king's tomb.

have been accomplished without violence, usually signifying nothing more than the failure of a direct male line; in most instances a relative married the daughter of the previous king and, as far as we can tell, things went on as smoothly as before. If there were conflicts and conspiracies in Egypt, they went unrecorded until late in the Old Kingdom. Armies were occasionally raised for border skirmishes or punitive expeditions against troublesome tribes, but there was no serious threat from the outside world; the most far-flung expeditions were mounted for trading purposes, to acquire cedar-wood from Lebanon or ivory and gold from Nubia.

During the Old Kingdom, the pharaoh's divine authority became even stronger, thanks in part to the increasingly powerful cult of the sun-god Re. In more practical terms, the government became an efficient, record-making, tax-collecting bureaucracy, controlled by a chief minister or vizier. Neither the royal authority nor the efficiency of the bureaucratic machine can seriously be doubted, since immense resources and a huge labour force had to be harnessed and directed for projects – above all pyramid-building – on an unprecedented scale.

The Old Kingdom began with the 3rd Dynasty pharaoh Sanakht, who ruled for nineteen years. He and his successor, Djoser (2667-2648), seem to have faced some opposition, but Djoser must have triumphed completely, for he was able to construct a large, enclosed funerary complex at Saqqara, far grander than anything that had ever been seen before. Its most remarkable feature was a new kind of tomb: the stepped pyramid, in effect a series of square platforms of decreasing size, placed one on top of the other.

Quite apart from its very imposing dimensions (it stands 60 metres high), Djoser's step pyramid was, in effect, the first large stone building in history; in Egypt, earlier tombs had been constructed with mud bricks, with at most a stone burial chamber in the centre. The architect of Djoser's pyramid was his chief minister, Imhotep, whose reputation as a kind of superman is reflected in a contemporary inscription recording that he served the king as treasurer, high priest, builder and sculptor. His name was remembered down the generations and his achievements may even have been magnified, for he eventually came to be worshipped in a surprising additional capacity, as the god of healing as well as of building.

The first true pyramid was begun for the last 3rd Dynasty king, Huni (2637-2613), and completed by his 4th Dynasty successor, Sneferu. At Meidum, south of Saqqara, a step pyramid was erected; then the steps were filled in with rubble and the sloping surfaces cased in limestone. The outcome demonstrated that even Egyptian builders had to learn by trial and error. At some point the casing collapsed and the Meidum pyramid reverted to its step form; later, having lost its upper four levels, it acquired its present-day, blockish, tower-like appearance, which is quite distinctive but completely accidental.

Sneferu was more successful in building on his own behalf, erecting two pyramids at Dahshur. The more northerly is known as the 'bent'

Imhotep, the architect of the first pyramid. Over the centuries his reputation grew, and he came to be worshipped as the god of healing; many votive figures of him have survived.

pyramid, because, about half way up, the sides abruptly change direction and rise to the apex at a less steep angle. The reason for this decision is unknown, but it seems likely that the disaster at Meidum occurred while the Dahshur pyramid was being raised, prompting the builders to play for safety by adopting a more stable design. However, Sneferu's other, southern pyramid, though cautiously low-angled, was the first true and soundly constructed example of the form.

Sneferu was an energetic ruler who sent military expeditions against the Nubians and Libyans, on occasion leading his troops into battle. Although the First Cataract at Aswan marked the southern boundary of Egypt, trade with Nubia had been important since Predynastic times. By the Old Kingdom period the Egyptians seem to have maintained some kind of military presence beyond their southern border, if only to protect their trading posts and gold and copper mines, and this no doubt necessitated occasional forays such as Sneferu's. According to Egyptian records he brought back prisoners and cattle, but there is no knowing whether this and similar Old Kingdom expeditions really achieved anything. Sneferu's successors, Khufu (or Cheops, 2589-2566) and Khafre (Chephren, 2558-2532), are remembered solely as pyramid builders on a megalomaniac scale. When people talk of 'the Pyramids', they mean the mighty group at Giza, a site chosen by Khufu, probably because it was close to Tura, where the fine white limestone used for the casing of pyramids was quarried. Khufu's handiwork is now always called the Great Pyramid: it was the first of the Seven Wonders of the Ancient World (and is the only one that still survives), and was the world's tallest man-made structure until little more than a century ago. The pyramid raised by Khufu's son, Khafre, was only slightly smaller but actually looks about the same size, since it was built on higher ground. Nearby stands the Great Sphinx, a huge human-headed, lion-bodied figure, carved from a natural outcrop of rock; its features are believed to be those of Khafre himself. The methods used to construct pyramids are still not known for certain. But however it was done, a huge labour force and enormous resources must have been invested in the pyramids of Khufu and Khafre. Legends portraying them

King Khafre, or Chephren, one of the mighty pyramid-builders; detail of a seated statue, c.2500 BC, one of the finest Old Kingdom works of art. The god Horus, in his falcon form, sits behind the king, protecting him.

'First time of striking the easterners' proclaims this ivory label for a pair of sandals belonging to King Den (reigned c.2950 BC), one of the early 1st Dynasty rulers. A group of these labels was found in Den's tomb at Abydos.

as tyrants may have been prompted by this consideration, but it is also possible that they embody a genuine folk memory. Significantly, the next king, Menkaure (also known as Mycerinus, 2532-2503), built a smaller pyramid and was remembered as a kindly ruler. One remarkable story portrays him as having flouted the gods' decision that Egypt should suffer for 150 years. As a result he was condemned to reign for only six years, but evaded the intention of the decree by burning candles and living through both night and day to double his 'real' span. If modern datings of his reign are correct, the gods must have responded to this witty ruse by changing their minds. Menkaure did in fact build the last of the royal pyramids at Giza, although on a much smaller scale than his predecessors.

After the death of Menkaure's short-lived successor, Egypt was ruled by the 5th Dynasty kings (2494-2345), and seems to have remained prosperous and traded more consistently with the outside world. During this period there were changes in the religious hierarchy, notably the establishment of Re as Egypt's supreme god and the construction of sun temples which may have diverted resources from pyramid-building. At any rate, although royal pyramids continued to be built, they were neither as large nor as durable as those at Giza. Battles and starving people appear on objects bearing the name of Unas, the last king of the 5th Dynasty, but the 6th Dynasty king Pepi I (2321-2287) seems to have been a successful warrior. His son, Pepi II (2278-2184), came to the throne when he was only six years old, and is said to have reigned for ninety-four years. Inscriptions on the tomb of an official named Harkhaf provide a rare glimpse of the king as simultaneously god and boy. They record that when Harkhaf reported that he had acquired a dancing pygmy or dwarf during a mission deep in Nubia, Pepi promised him a rich reward if he managed to bring his prize back alive. The king was so excited that he issued instructions to provincial governors in the south, ordering them to keep a twenty-four-hour watch on the pygmy to ensure that he reached the court intact. Decades later, Pepi's senility may have led to misgovernment; or provincial governors may have grown over-mighty; or Egypt may have become impoverished as a result of bad harvests. Whatever the reason, the Old Kingdom scarcely survived Pepi II, and the centralized government of the pharaohs collapsed into chaos.

King Menkaure, or Mycerinus, flanked by the goddess Hathor (left) and a figure symbolizing one of his provinces (nomes). This triad (three-figure) statue, dating from c.2500 BC, was found in Menkaure's valley temple at Giza.

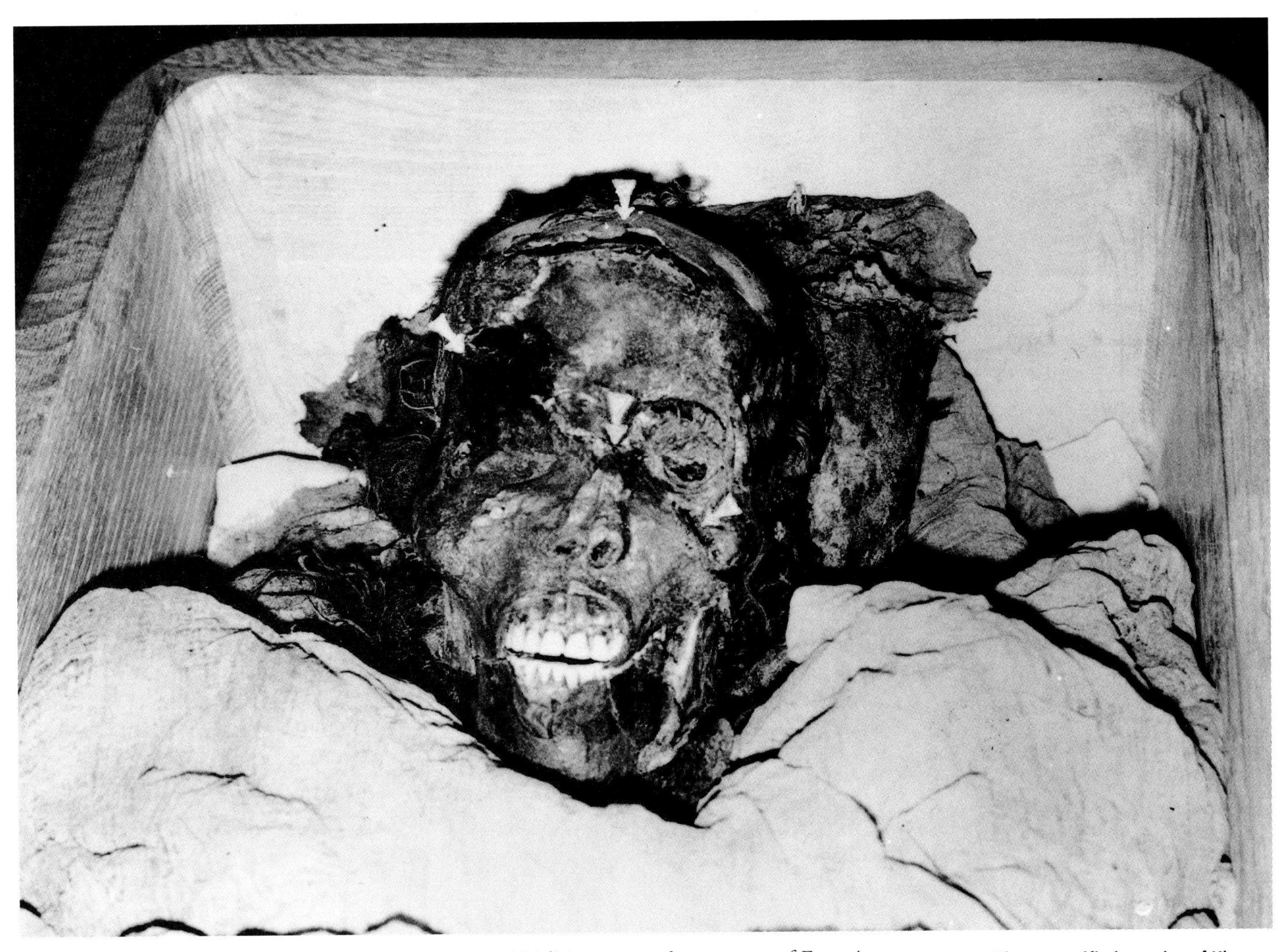

The mummified remains of King Seqenenre. His head displays the fatal wounds inflicted by an axe, probably while fighting the Hyksos, as well as earlier injuries which he survived.

THE MIDDLE KINGDOM

From the end of the Old Kingdom, Egyptian history followed a fall-rise-fall pattern in which periods of decline and fragmentation alternated with great ages of power and prosperity. This has also occurred in other civilizations, but Egypt was unique in the extent to which institutions and ideals persisted through one swing after another, changing – if at all – only slowly and subtly. After the collapse of the Old Kingdom there was no single political authority for over a century. This period of confusion is usually known as the First Intermediate Period, lasting from about 2181 to 2055 BC. It culminated in a south-north contest between dynasties based on the cities of Thebes and Herakleopolis. The victory of the 11th Dynasty Theban ruler Mentuhotep II (2055-2004) inaugurated a new age of Egyptian greatness and stability, the Middle Kingdom (2055-1795). For Thebes it also signalled the beginning of a steady rise that would in time make the city the most splendid in the land.

Mentuhotep and his successors quickly restored Egypt's prosperity, initiating large-scale public works and renewing long-distance trade. However, Mentuhotep IV was overthrown by his chief minister, who as Amenemhat I (1985-1955) founded the 12th Dynasty. Amenemhat seems to have been a self-made man, and by Egyptian standards he was a bold innovator. He founded a new, though short-lived, capital in Middle Egypt, Itjtawy (on a site that has never been located), and he introduced a new dynastic device, co-regency, that was also adopted by his successors. At some point the king co-opted his chosen heir as joint ruler, thereby minimizing the likelihood of plotting by impatient sons during his lifetime and disputed successions after his death. Co-regency quickly proved its worth when Amenemhat was murdered; his son Senusret, though absent on a mission when his father died, experienced no difficulty in assuming power.

A series of long reigns helped to make the Middle Kingdom a time of economic progress and literary and artistic achievement. The pharaohs authorized projects which included not only temple-building but the construction or renewal of canals. They also resumed the building of pyramids as their tombs, although on a relatively modest scale. If we are to believe the self-glorifications on his own inscribed monuments, the greatest Middle Kingdom king was Senusret III (1878-1855), who established a more centralized administrative system, built on a huge scale, and launched an onslaught that brought more of Nubia under Egyptian control than had ever been done before.

The female pharaoh Hatshepsut being embraced by the supreme god, Amun. Reliefs of this kind emphasized the pharaoh's relationship with the gods; for Hatshepsut they were also a way of claiming divine approval for her unusual exercise of power.

Senusret's successor, Amenemhat III (1855-1808), was wealthy enough to build pyramids on two different sites, although his motives for doing so can only be surmised. But then things began to go badly wrong for the dynasty, and within a few years it had disappeared.

The early years of the Second Intermediate Period (1795-1550 BC) are very obscure. It is difficult to know just how bad conditions were, although the very poverty of the records suggests that all was not well with the 13th Dynasty. The situation certainly deteriorated in the late 18th century BC, when a rival dynasty took power in part of the Delta and an outside people began to pose a serious threat.

The outsiders were the Hyksos ('foreign princes'), Levantines who were based at Avaris, on the eastern edge of the Delta. Subsequent accounts portrayed them as viciously determined to conquer and wipe out the Egyptian way of life, but modern scholars regard this picture as wildly exaggerated.

The Hyksos are now thought to have arrived in Egypt over a long period as immigrant workers, traders or even slaves, and to have spread peacefully, at least for a time. But when they did fight, they had the advantage of a new military technology – notably the horse-drawn chariot – which the Egyptians eventually copied.

The Hyksos spread west and south, capturing the ancient capital of Memphis. Further south, a new native dynasty had emerged, again based on Thebes. For a time it seems to have co-existed with the Hyksos, who were allowed to sail in peace past the First Cataract and trade with Nubia, while in return the Thebans had access to the Delta for grazing. War finally broke out when the Theban ruler Seqenenre (c.1560) claimed that he had been insulted by the Hyksos king Apophis, who had provoked him by complaining that his sleep was being disturbed by the snoring of Seqenenre's sacred hippopotami – several hundred kilometres upriver!

Akhenaten, his favourite queen, Nefertiti, and their children bask in the life-giving rays of the Aten, the disc of the sun which Akhenaten proclaimed as the sole deity.

This colossal figure of Akhenaten typifies the unusual facial and bodily features that have long puzzled historians. Did the pharaoh suffer from a rare disease, or are his strange features simply a matter of artistic convention?

The evidence of Seqenenre's violent death is visible on the head of his mummy, although we cannot be sure that he was killed in a conflict with the Hyksos. The fight was taken up by his son Khamose, but it was another of Seqenenre's sons, Ahmose, who finally drove the Hyksos out of Egypt and became the founder of the New Kingdom.

THE NEW KINGDOM

The reign of Ahmose I (1550-1525) ushered in a five-hundred-year age of Egyptian greatness. Far more is known about the New Kingdom (1550-1069 BC) than about earlier periods. One reason for this is that New Kingdom pharaohs destroyed earlier records by recycling or building over the monuments of their predecessors. But other evidence is available because New Kingdom Egypt played a much more active role on the international scene; in fact some of the most intriguing documents relating to Egyptian affairs were found far away, in the archives of rival states. As a consequence, several of the pharaohs emerge as distinct personalities – and, coincidentally, most of their mummies have survived, complementing their official images with presences of an eerie vitality. Ahmose I was the first king of one of Egypt's most colourful dynasties, the 18th. After a rapid consolidation, Ahmose's successors pursued a consistently expansionist policy. Tuthmosis I, a soldier who came to the throne in middle age, penetrated Nubia as far as the Fourth Cataract, and also seems to have reached the Euphrates in campaigns against the formidable empire of Mitanni. At any rate his inscriptions proclaim that he 'made Egypt greater than any other land'.

Tuthmosis was also probably the first pharaoh to be buried in a rock-cut tomb in the Valley of the Kings, on the west bank of the Nile opposite Thebes. The pyramids, all too visible and accessible, had fallen prey to tomb-robbers; the New Kingdom pharaohs doubtless hoped that a remote, guarded necropolis would give better results; but their hopes were doomed to disappointment.

Tuthmosis II (1492-1479) carried on his father's policies, but his career has been overshadowed by that of his half-sister and wife Hatshepsut. When the king died, his son Tuthmosis III was still a child, and Hatshepsut, his stepmother, ruled jointly with him. Within a very short time she felt strong enough to have herself declared pharaoh in her own right; images of the queen show her wearing the full regalia of this male office, including the false beard that had to be worn for ceremonial purposes. Hatshepsut was, as far as we know, the first female monarch in history. Her fifteen-year reign (1473-1458) seems to have been tranquil, so her right to rule must have been widely accepted. She took care to be generous towards the temples, and much of her own building had a propaganda aspect, carrying inscriptions that emphasized her royal blood as the daughter of Ahmose I and, in a familiar religious paradox, asserted her divinity as the daughter of the god Amun, who had disguised himself as Ahmose in order to impregnate his queen.

During Hatshepsut's reign there was some military activity beyond the borders. Interestingly, the reliefs on the walls of her great mortuary temple at Deir el-Bahri make far more of Egypt's peaceful relations with the outside world. As well as trade with the Near East, an expedition to the Land of Punt is vividly pictured. Particularly valued as a source of myrrh, Punt lay a considerable distance down the east coast of Africa, far enough away to seem exotic, perhaps even romantic, to the Egyptians. The reliefs capture characteristic details that must have been based on first-hand reports, including a lovingly rendered portrait of Punt's monstrously obese queen and a creature described as 'the donkey that had to carry the queen'.

Much of Hatshepsut's authority was delegated to a powerful chief minister, Senenmut, said to have been of humble birth; possibly, like other rulers of questionable legitimacy, Hatshepsut favoured able, rootless individuals who owed everything to her. Senenmut died at about the same time as Hatshepsut – perhaps coincidentally, or perhaps because they stood in the way of a now-adult Tuthmosis. He caused Hatshepsut's name to be erased from inscriptions, and it has usually been assumed that this represented his revenge for being kept in the shadows for so long.

However, recent research indicates that the blotting out was done late in Tuthmosis' reign, so there may be another explanation. The general Egyptian verdict on this remarkable woman must have been that her reign was an abnormality best forgotten, since she is omitted from later king lists.

When Tuthmosis III (1479-1425) did finally take power, he proved himself to be the mightiest of all Egyptian conqueror-kings. According to the inscriptions he raised at home and abroad, he waged war in the Levant year after year, seizing hundreds of cities. His culminating success was the capture of Kadesh, a Syrian city not far from present-day Homs. Later experience was to show that this took in about as much territory as the Egyptians could hope to control, even with the help of satellite rulers; the geographical factors that made Egypt hard to invade also set limits to her expansion into Asia.

The fruits of Tuthmosis' conquests were huge quantities of loot which enriched the court and the temples, especially the great complex at Karnak. But Egypt was prospering in any case, and Tuthmosis' reign marked the beginning of a century or more of abundance. Despite the king's victories, Egypt's Levantine and Nubian empire remained insecure, and each new pharaoh had to fight to keep it. Only Amenhotep III (1390-1352), benefiting from an extended truce with Mitanni, was able to enjoy a long, golden age of peace. It was followed by what was probably the most remarkable, and certainly the most uncharacteristic, episode in Egyptian history.

AKHENATEN, HERETIC PHARAOH

The reign of Amenhotep IV (1352-1336) was exceptional and abnormal in almost every respect. The king took a new name, founded a new capital,

The pharaoh Amenhotep IV renamed himself Akhenaten, signifying a change of allegiance from the god Amun to the solar disc Aten. The introspective quality of his head is very striking.

Above: Akhenaten making an offering. This charming blue-crowned statuette was discovered in the ruins of the sculptors' studio at Amarna. Interestingly, the king's physical peculiarities are less noticeable here.

Above right: Akhenaten kisses his daughter as she sits on his lap: an unfinished carving which gives us an intriguing glimpse of the Egyptian sculptor at work. The demonstrative family affection shown in works of the Amarna period is most unusual.

sponsored a new art and, above all, introduced a new religious cult designed to overthrow the old gods. After his death he became another of those aberrant figures – like the female pharaoh Hatshepsut – whom the Egyptians chose to erase from their records and forget.

Amenhotep may have ruled jointly with his father for a few years, but by the fifth year of his reign he had certainly assumed full sovereignty. He took the name Akhenaten, effectively proclaiming his allegiance to Aten and, implicitly, his rejection of all-powerful Amun.

Previously the Aten, pictured as a solar disc, had been the subject of a minor cult, representing a single aspect of the sun's divine power. Under Akhenaten it became, in effect, the godhead, demanding an exclusive devotion; rival cults were abolished, the temples of Amun were closed, and their enormous wealth was confiscated.

Akhenaten's policy can be interpreted in political terms, as an attack on an overweening priesthood. But the king's response was so radical that his own religious enthusiasm can hardly be questioned. Breaking with the past, he built a new capital, Akhetaten, and moved there with his court. The new cult was ardently honoured, and Akhenaten himself is said to have composed a famous 'Hymn to Aten' which has survived on inscriptions.

The real significance of the Aten cult remains debatable, like almost everything connected with Akhenaten. Many Egyptologists, influenced by the Judeo-Christian tradition, have praised the pharaoh as the first monotheist in history. But he can equally well be seen as an intolerant fanatic, determined to force his own idiosyncratic beliefs on everybody else; and this interpretation is strengthened by the fact that every Aten text also glorifies the pharaoh as the only channel through which the divinity could be known. In anyone but a pharaoh – already ranked as a god-king – this could only be described as megalomania.

Akhenaten's appearance, as recorded in statuary and on monuments, has also puzzled posterity. His full, epicene features, long head and bloated feminine body are so pronounced that they have been attributed to a serious glandular disorder. If so, Akhenaten did not attempt to hide them in his official portraits; instead, the pharaoh's courtiers and servants were pictured in the same way, so that Akhenaten's abnormalities became the artistic conventions of his period. An alternative view is that the entire 'Akhenaten look' was no more than an artistic fashion, and that the pharaoh, like his subjects, looked no different from his predecessors.

Akhenaten had six daughters by his chief queen, Nefertiti, who held a remarkably prominent place in the reliefs and other picture records of the reign. Interestingly, she was also largely exempt from the ruling artistic convention; perhaps she was too beautiful to show in such a distorting light. At any rate the celebrated head of the queen (now in Berlin) is generally regarded as the loveliest female image to have survived from all antiquity. Like other pharaohs Akhenaten had a number of wives, including two of his own daughters; Nefertiti herself seems to have died or lost favour towards the end of the reign.

Akhenaten's capital, Akhetaten, became known in later times as Tell el-Amarna. Anachronistically, Akhenaten's reign is sometimes referred to as the Amarna period, and some fascinating diplomatic documents unearthed at Akhetaten are generally known as the Amarna Letters. Written on clay tablets in the cuneiform (wedge-shaped) script of Mesopotamia, the letters are mainly from client rulers in the Levant; under increasing pressure from the Hittites, they were appealing for help to their Egyptian overlords, apparently without getting much satisfaction. It has often been assumed that Akhenaten was too remote from political realities to take decisive action, but this impression may be misleading. The letters are unique – unfortunately, since that means there are no other reliable foreign policy documents with which they can be compared.

After Akhenaten's death the Egyptians quickly reverted to traditional ways, probably under the guidance of two dominant personalities: the veteran chief minister Ay, who may have been Nefertiti's father, and a rising military man, Horemheb. Akhenaten was succeeded by Smenkhare, a shadowy figure whose reign probably lasted for only a few months. The next pharaoh was Tutankhaten, a seven- or eight-year-old who was quickly renamed Tutankhamun (1336-1327); the change, substituting -amun for -aten, signalled a return to religious orthodoxy. The temples were re-opened, Akhetaten was abandoned, and the court moved back to Memphis.

Destined for posthumous greatness, Tutankhamun died after a brief, unmemorable

Pharaoh in his chariot, putting his enemies to flight. This copy of a wall painting shows Ramesses II in action at the battle of Kadesh, fought against the Hittites in about 1274 BC.

reign. He left a widow, Ankhesenamun, who was probably his half-sister as well as the daughter/wife of Akhenaten. Representing the royal blood line, she became the key to the succession – and she was evidently confronted with unpalatable alternatives at home, since she took the extraordinary step of writing to the Hittite king, Suppiluliamas I, asking him to send her one of his sons as a husband; the letter she sent was discovered in the Hittite royal archives at Hattusas (Turkey). Suppiluliamas complied, but his son was murdered en route. Ankhesenamun was married to the aged Ay, who became king in time to officiate at Tutankhamun's funeral – which meant that the entire drama following the pharaoh's death must have unfolded and reached its climax within the seventy-day limit prescribed for embalming and pre-burial rituals.

Ramesses II wearing the blue war crown. Ramesses (1279-1213 BC) filled Egypt with warlike or domineering images of himself, although his military achievements were not quite as brilliant as he claimed. This wall painting is a relatively restrained effort.

Ay ruled for four years, dying without producing an heir. His successor was the general Horemheb (1323-1295), whose inscriptions claim that he restored order and justice after a period of gross neglect and corruption. Horemheb made a determined attempt to wipe out the immediate past, dismantling temples to the Aten and erasing every visible reference to Akhenaten, Smenkhare, Tutankhamun and Ay. He even back-dated his own accession to the end of Amenhotep III's reign so that there would be no question-raising gap in future king lists. In view of Tutankhamun's return to orthodoxy it is difficult to account for Horemheb's victimization of the boy king and his successor Ay; perhaps, during their reigns, the Aten cult had not been vigorously suppressed, and they were posthumously punished for being 'soft' on heresy.

Horemheb too died without an heir. He left his throne to a companion-in-arms who, as Ramesses I, became the first of a line of kings whose origins lay in the Delta rather than Upper Egypt.

THE RAMESSIDE PHARAOHS

Ramesses I (1295-1294) can never have realized that he was founding a new dynasty, the Ramessides, whose towering reputation would cause weaker, unrelated rulers to associate themselves with its glories by taking the same name.

The first Ramesses died after ruling Egypt for less than two years, but his son and grandson established an unshakable authority and were among the mightiest of all the pharaohs. Seti I (1294-1279) reasserted Egyptian authority in the Levant, capturing Kadesh and matching the Hittite empire at the height of its power. Perhaps conscious that his family's claim to the throne had no strong historical basis, Seti took pains to present himself as a traditional figure, at one with the most venerated pharaohs of the past who had

A Nubian slave or captive (these amounted to more or less the same thing), vividly portrayed in a fragment of a relief. Egypt's relations with Nubia began in very early times, gradually moving from economic penetration to conquest.

restored the monuments and the greatness of Egypt. Inscriptions and reliefs emphasize his active piety and associate his line with earlier dynasties. In the temple of Seti at Abydos, a large relief on one wall shows the king and his son Ramesses contemplating two long rows of cartouches, representing all the kings of the Two Lands right back to the 1st Dynasty; Hatshepsut, Akhenaten and other dubious figures from periods of weakness and confusion are conveniently omitted in a celebration of age-old Egyptian values culminating in repeated cartouches enclosing the name of Seti himself.

As if intending to rival the pyramid-builders of old, Seti was buried in an enormous tomb, cut some ninety metres deep into the living rock of the Valley of Kings. But in death the great pharaoh had no more power than his feeblest predecessor to prevent his resting place from being ransacked by thieves and stripped of its valuables. However, Seti's mummy was one of those rescued by priests and hidden at Deir el-Bahri until its recovery in 1882. In remarkable condition after three thousand years, its hawk-like features suggest an impressive personality and, incidentally, bear a strong family resemblance to those of his immediate successors.

Seti was a mighty builder, but in this respect his son Ramesses II (1279-1213) outdid him and every other pharaoh in history. Ramesses completed the awe-inspiring Hypostyle Hall at Karnak begun by Seti, constructed an entirely new capital in the Delta, Piramesse ('Domain of Ramesses'), and built a huge mortuary temple, the Ramesseum; it was from here, on the west bank of the Nile at Thebes, that the 19th-century strongman-archaeologist Belzoni hauled away a colossal stone head of the king, destined for London. The most famous of all Ramesses' works, the rock-cut temples at Abu Simbel, are far to the south in Nubia, by this time regarded as permanently subject to Egypt.

Ramesses' grandiose inscriptions are found in many other places, on his own works and also on those of earlier rulers. Such takeovers were common, but the scale of Ramesses' operations was unprecedented, and it is hard not to regard him as a monster of boundless egoism. This impression is reinforced by the four colossal portraits of the king that guard the Great Temple at Abu Simbel, and by the association of Ramesses with Shelley's famous sonnet 'Ozymandias'. Ozymandias is a Greek version of the pharaoh's name. The poem portrays a tyrant whose self-glorification is mocked by the shattered fragments that are all that remain in the desert to commemorate him; the boasting line on his pedestal, 'Look on my works, ye mighty, and despair!' is shown to be utterly empty.

Such poetic justice was not done to the real Ramesses, for his works have fared better than those of Shelley's fictionalized Ozymandias. And

One of the letters from the diplomatic archive at Amarna, despatched c.1350 BC. Tushratta, king of Mitanni, complains that his envoys have been detained in Egypt, and that Akhenaten has not sent the expected messages and presents.

it must be admitted that Ramesses *was* a colossus after his fashion, reigning for sixty-seven years, living into his nineties, fathering well over a hundred children, and apparently succeeding in everything he undertook.

Only Ramesses' military career, although respectable enough, was less record-breaking than he cared to admit. Early in his reign war broke out with the Hittites, and in 1274 the pharaoh advanced into Syria with a large army. Once more the area around Kadesh proved crucial. Misled by false intelligence, Ramesses was taken by surprise, with his army divided, and disaster was only narrowly avoided. The result seems to have been a draw; but on Ramesses' monuments the battle of Kadesh became the mightiest of victories, won by the pharaoh's brilliant decisions and personal valour. His version of events prevailed in Egypt, but not at Hattusas, where the Hittite king's inscription was equally emphatic in claiming the battle as a great victory. Ramesses' later campaigns in Syria were equally indecisive, and both the Egyptians and the Hittites came to recognize that they could expand no further. In 1259 the two powers agreed on a non-aggression pact, and over the next few years their relations were consolidated into a positive alliance which maintained the Near Eastern status quo.

So far as we know, Ramesses died of natural causes in advanced old age. His mummy has been found, so he was not engulfed by the Red Sea while pursuing the Israelites as they fled from bondage; nevertheless most historians believe that he must have been the pharaoh mentioned in the Bible who refused to let the Israelites go until Moses had caused Egypt to be smitten by a series of terrible disasters. However, the Israelites are not even mentioned in the surviving records of Ramesses' reign. The only possible conclusion is that their exodus, if it did occur during Ramesses' reign, was momentous in their eyes but an insignificant episode as far as their Egyptian masters were concerned. One of the alternatives, of course, is that the story belongs to a different, perhaps earlier period, when the enslaved foreigners may have been known by a different name.

In Egyptian records the first unambiguous reference to the Israelites comes from the reign of Mereneptah (1213-1203), who was about sixty years old when he succeeded his long-lived father Ramesses II. Soon after Mereneptah's accession Egypt's Levantine satellites rose in revolt. They were vanquished, and the pharaoh's 'Victory Stele' lists the defeated peoples and gloatingly records the retribution visited upon them. The statement that 'Israel is laid waste, her seed is no more' is patently exaggerated, but it does confirm that the Israelites had left Egypt by Mereneptah's time and established themselves in or near the Promised Land.

In 1207 the pharaoh was faced with a danger closer to home when Libyan tribes threatened to invade the Delta from the west. Having consulted the famous oracle of Amun, Mereneptah dreamed that the god Ptah appeared to him, commanding an urgent military response. Meeting the Libyans on the western frontier, Mereneptah won a crushing victory, in which over 6,000 of the enemy are said to have been slain, before marching south to suppress a revolt in Nubia. Ominously, the Libyans had been reinforced by some tribes belonging to the 'Sea Peoples', a loose confederation of peoples on the move whose activities had begun to destabilize the entire eastern Mediterranean and Near East.

After Mereneptah's death the 19th Dynasty came to a rapid end; the circumstances (a disputed succession, a minority and the reign of a woman, Queen Twosret) suggest that the decline of royal authority was the result of a series of political accidents rather than long-term weakness.

At any rate the first 20th Dynasty king, Sethnakhte (1186-1184), was later reputed to have restored the empire during his short reign. Although he was almost certainly not related to the 19th Dynasty pharaohs, his son bore the talismanic name Ramesses. As Ramesses III (1184-1153) he became the last really outstanding native ruler of Egypt, recording his achievements on his mortuary temple at Medinet Habu. Ramesses defeated another Libyan invasion, only to be faced in the eighth year of his reign by a renewed threat from the Sea Peoples. They had cut a swathe through the eastern Mediterranean, causing a series of upheavals and bringing down the Hittite empire. The origins and history of this great folk movement are still obscure, but it is certain that the Sea Peoples were not merely soldiers or raiders; they brought their families and possessions with them in ox-carts and presumably intended to settle in Egypt's fertile land. Nor were they simply a horde: as they marched down through Syria they were accompanied by a large fleet, menacing Egypt on two fronts.

In the ensuing crisis Ramesses' garrisons beyond the eastern frontier held up the invaders while he mobilized his forces and brought them up. Some of the Sea Peoples were bought off and fought on the Egyptian side, helping Ramesses to drive off the main force. At the same time the Egyptians defeated the enemy fleet at an engagement fought in one of the mouths of the Delta. The Sea Peoples were not destroyed, but they moved on westwards and the threat to Egypt passed. After Ramesses had suppressed a second Libyan incursion, Egypt was at last free from outside pressures.

Ramesses III ruled Egypt for a further twenty-odd years, but his reign was marred towards its end by serious internal problems. The workmen employed to construct and decorate the royal tombs went on strike, complaining that their allocations of food were not arriving; their work had such high priority that the failure to keep them supplied suggests that the central administration had run into serious difficulties.

Even more sensational was the detection of a plot to murder the king. Its central figure was one of Ramesses' minor wives, Tiy, who aimed to secure the succession for her son Pentewere. A striking feature of the affair was the number of important officials who were implicated. Ramesses was dead by the time the accused were brought to book, so it is possible that the proceedings were really show-trials, designed by the ruling group to eliminate a rival faction. Such a fraught political situation would explain the final hearing, in which the defendants included some of the judges who had been appointed to try the conspirators; accused of improper relations with the defendants, they had perhaps been contemplating a change of sides. In the event, over forty individuals were found guilty. The higher-ranking prisoners were allowed to commit suicide; the rest were executed.

The next eight pharaohs were all named Ramesses. But evoking earlier glories proved powerless to halt the steady decline that now set in. Within twenty years of Ramesses III's death

Painted limestone bust of Nefertiti, the favourite queen of the heretic pharaoh Akhenaten. This famous work was discovered by a German archaeologist, Ludwig Borchardt, and is now in the Berlin Museum.

there had been a civil war and Egyptian influence beyond the eastern frontiers had disappeared. A story preserved on papyrus, *The Tale of Wenamun*, conveys the Egyptians' sense of dismay at this state of affairs: Wenamun, an official sent to obtain cedarwood from Lebanon, is robbed of his funds and receives scant courtesy from the prince of Byblos, once an Egyptian client state.

As so often happened in times of weakness, Egypt broke up into its constituent Two Lands. The immense wealth of the temples strengthened this tendency, enabling Herihor, the high priest of the temple of Amun at Thebes, to adopt many trappings of royalty and negotiate on equal terms, as ruler of Upper Egypt, with the last 20th Dynasty pharaoh, Ramesses XI (1099-1069), whose authority had effectively become confined to the Delta.

With the passing of the 20th Dynasty in 1069, the last vestiges of New Kingdom glory disappeared and another 'Intermediate' age began.

THE FINAL PHASE

Three hundred years of confusion and fragmentation followed the end of the New Kingdom. During this, the Third Intermediate Period (1069-747 BC), it is not certain that any Egyptian king controlled the entire country, and dynasties probably overlapped, reigning simultaneously in different capitals for at least part of the time. The founder of the 21st Dynasty, Smendes I (1069-1043), established his capital at the Delta city of Tanis. The subsequent history of the dynasty is obscure, partly because the Delta climate was a less effective preservative of documents, objects and mummies than the extreme dryness of Upper Egypt. But however obscure they may now seem, the Tanite kings were not insignificant. In 1939 excavations by the French archaeologist Pierre Montet uncovered six royal tombs of the 21st and 22nd Dynasties; they yielded treasures (including a silver coffin and gold face masks) that are comparable with Tutankhamun's in richness if not in artistic quality.

A precarious reunion of Egypt may have been effected by Shoshenk (945-924), ruler of Bubastis, who founded the 22nd Dynasty. A military man, he came to the throne in orthodox fashion as his predecessor's son-in-law. However, Shoshenk was descended from Libyans who had settled in Egypt, and still ranked as their chief; his line is known as the Libyan or Bubastite dynasty.

At Thebes, Shoshenk's son became High Priest of Amun and the king's exploits were celebrated on a new gateway at Karnak, the Bubastite Portal; so it looks as though the king did manage to regain control of Upper Egypt. The most notable of the exploits referred to on the portal was an expedition under-

Father and son: Seti I and Prince Ramesses (later Ramesses II) contemplate a list of their royal predecessors. The list is selective, leaving out rulers such as Akhenaten and Hatshepsut, who did not fit in well with Egyptian tradition. Painted relief from the Temple of Seti at Abydos.

taken in 925, when Shoshenk led his troops deep into Palestine; most scholars believe that he appears in the Bible as a king named Shishak, said to have humbled both Judah and Israel.

The king and queen of the Land of Punt; relief from the Temple of Hatshepsut at Deir el-Bahri. The expedition sent to Punt is celebrated on the temple reliefs with an enthusiasm usually reserved for great military victories.

Other Libyan kings were less fortunate. A rival, 24th, Dynasty emerged at Leontopolis, and the situation steadily deteriorated. By the late 8th century the country had broken up into a number of petty kingdoms without even a façade of unity.

Salvation came from an unexpected quarter. After centuries of military and commercial penetration, Nubia had been subdued and thoroughly Egyptianized during the New Kingdom period. The weakness of the later Ramessides allowed a native dynasty to assume power at Napata, far to the south, but by then Nubia was Egyptian in culture and religion. The Napatans used hieroglyphs, worshipped Amun and practised Egyptian burial rites; their kings adopted the regalia and titles of the pharaohs and were buried in the old fashion in pyramids. Consequently the Napatan intervention in Egyptian affairs may have seemed more like a restoration than a foreign invasion. In about 747 the Nubian king Piankhi overran the south and then compelled the rival kings in the north to submit to him. Piankhi (747-716) is usually regarded as the first pharaoh of the 25th (Nubian or Kushite) Dynasty, and his reign marks the beginning of the Late Period (747-332) of Egyptian history. However, after asserting his authority Piankhi rather surprisingly returned to Napata, and it was left to Shabaka (716-702) and Taharka (690-664) to become true kings rather than overlords of Egypt.

The Nubian pharaohs restored order, helped by religious adjustments which allowed the king's daughter to take the key position of God's Wife of Amun. But the new stability was soon under threat from outside, as the hyperaggressive Assyrian military machine, more powerful than anything seen before, ground relentlessly across the Near East. Having conquered Egypt, the Assyrians had to reconquer it several times, finding the country impossible to hold down as soon as their army was withdrawn. After many ups and downs, the Assyrians sacked Thebes with terrible efficiency in 664 and the last Nubian king, Tanutamun, fled south to the safety of Napata. Nubia's Egyptianized culture flourished for several hundred years more, but her direct role in Egyptian history came to an end.

Egypt remained nominally under Assyrian rule until 653, but real power rested with the princes of Sais, another of the Delta cities. Originally a 'collaborator' with the Assyrians, Psammetichus I (664-610) gradually reunited Egypt, becoming the first king of the 26th (Saite) Dynasty. He strengthened his army by taking on Greek mercenaries and encouraged foreign settlers who brought in new craft and commercial skills. This modernizing, commerce-conscious trend continued under Necho (610-595), who

Amenemhet III (1855-1808 BC), the last great ruler of the Middle Kingdom. The rather forbidding appearance of this bust is typical, despite the fact that Amenemhet's reign was one of general prosperity in which important public works were undertaken.

formed the first proper Egyptian navy and began to cut a canal from the Nile to the Red Sea. Possibly in reaction against these cosmopolitan influences, Egypt experienced something of a 'national' revival in religion and art, involving the re-use of half-forgotten rituals and styles. In 570 anti-foreign feeling helped to bring about the violent overthrow of the pharaoh Apries, and soon afterwards the Greek community was segregated by being resettled in the Delta city of Naucratis. But it was no longer possible to keep out the rest of the world. In 525 new empire-builders, the Persians, invaded Egypt and overthrew the last Saite king, Psammetichus III. Egypt was reduced to a province, ruled by a satrap (Persian governor), but the Persian kings were shrewd enough to take over the trappings of pharaonic power in an attempt to conciliate the country. Darius I (522-486) completed Necho's canal, but later kings neglected or exploited Egypt. There were frequent revolts until dynastic infighting in Persia allowed the Egyptians to regain their independence at the end of the 5th century. After two short-lived dynasties had come and gone, Nectanebo I (380-362) founded the 30th Dynasty. But the Persian threat was soon renewed, and in 343 a new invasion ended with the defeat and death of Nectanebo II. Nectanebo was to be the last Egyptian king of Egypt. The second period of Persian rule lasted for little more than a decade (343-332), when it was overthrown by the most famous of all world-conquerors: Alexander the Great.

GRECO-ROMAN EGYPT

In 336 BC Philip II of Macedon was assassinated. His son Alexander inherited his father's throne, along with Macedonian hegemony over the Greek city-states, a powerful army, and Philip's plans to attack the huge but increasingly vulnerable Persian empire. Crossing the Bosphorus into Asia Minor, Alexander inflicted devastating defeats on the Persians in 334-332, driving them out of Asia Minor and conquering the east Mediterranean seaboard. When he pushed on into Egypt in the autumn of 332, the resident satrap (governor) prudently surrendered without any attempt at resistance, and the populace welcomed Alexander as a liberator.

Though pharaoh by force of arms, Alexander took pains to establish his legitimacy. He travelled to the celebrated oracle of Amun at the oasis of Siwa in the Libyan desert, where the god recognized him as his son, and consequently as the true king of Egypt. This may have been no more than political play-acting on both sides, but it is possible that the incident convinced Alexander that he was indeed divine. He was crowned at Memphis, put in hand repairs to the temples damaged during the Persian onslaught of 343, and founded a new twin-harboured capital, Alexandria, that remained one of the great centres of Mediterranean commerce for the next thousand years.

Alexander left Egypt after six months. He hunted down the Persian king Darius III and marched on as far as India before turning back. In 323 he died at Babylon, not yet thirty-three years old; his body is said to have been preserved in honey, in a golden coffin, at Alexandria, where admirers visited his tomb until it disappeared in the 4th century AD. Since his early demise prevented his policies from maturing, historians are still disputing whether Alexander possessed a genuine multi-national vision, or whether his adoption of Persian costume and divine attributes were simply expressions of megalomania. The results of his conquest of Egypt are less doubtful: the land of the pharaohs became integrated into the largely Greek culture of the eastern Mediterranean and Near East, now in its post-classical 'Hellenistic' phase.

For a few years the empire created by Alexander remained nominally intact, although real power was held by leading generals, each of whom dominated a particular region. Eventually those who survived some fierce infighting became kings in their own right. In Egypt the general in charge was Ptolemy, who ruled the land from 323 but only ascended the throne eighteen years later as Ptolemy I Soter ('Saviour'; 305-285). He founded a dynasty that encouraged immigration and fostered the emergence of a new Greek-speaking aristocracy. Under the pharaoh and his son Ptolemy II (285-246), Alexandria became a thriving capital on the Greek model, the famous Library was created, and the first lighthouse, built on the island of Pharos, became the second of Egypt's Wonders of the World. In time more cities grew up with agoras (market places), gymnasia and other features that marked them out – and their populations too – as Hellenistic rather than Egyptian in character.

However, the Ptolemies also made significant concessions to Egyptian tradition. They ruled, and were portrayed, as pharaohs, and they quickly took up the custom of brother-sister marriage. Their city plans may have been Greek, but they also built or rebuilt temples to the native gods, including still-celebrated examples such as Dendera, Edfu and Philae. There was also a tendency for Greek and Egyptian ideas to merge, notably in a new hybrid god, Serapis.

The long-term effect of these developments was to weaken the native culture. The countryside was probably little affected by Greek influences, but the priests were the only remaining members of the elite who could read Egyptian and wished to preserve the old traditions. The Hellenistic world was essentially urban, irreverent and subject to outbursts of mob violence; and this was the world to which the Ptolemies really belonged. They did not behave like a family of god-kings: from the time of Ptolemy IV (221-205), tales of lurid sexual relationships, violence and betrayal give their dynastic history the air of sensational fiction. Some of these latter-day pharaohs were

Ptolemy I was one of Alexander the Great's generals. He was appointed governor of Egypt and made himself king after Alexander's death. His dynasty ruled Egypt for almost three centuries, from 305 to 30 BC.

overthrown and lynched by Alexandrian mobs; others were faced with rebellions in Upper Egypt by what seem to have been 'nationalist' groups striving to restore the old order.

Meanwhile the balance of power in the Mediterranean was changing. The early Ptolemaic kings had substantial possessions in the Aegean, Asia Minor and the Levant, but by 200 BC they had been lost. And while Ptolemies, Cleopatras and Berenices married and murdered one another, Rome's power grew. When the inept Ptolemy XII (80-51), derisively known as Auletes, 'the flute-player', was driven out by popular wrath, he recovered his throne with the help of a Roman army, procured by bribing leading Romans.

Ptolemy XII's daughter played an equally dangerous game. As 'Cleopatra' she is probably the most famous of all ancient Egyptians. She in fact reigned as Cleopatra VII (51-30 BC), coming to the throne and marrying her younger brother, Ptolemy XIII, when she was seventeen. They were soon at war, and the situation was unresolved when two rival Roman generals, first Pompey and then Julius Caesar, arrived in 48 BC. Pompey was in flight, having lost the battle of Pharsalia; when he reached Egypt he was beheaded by order of Ptolemy's ministers. Despite this helpful gesture, Caesar sided with Cleopatra in the dynastic quarrel, and Ptolemy was drowned during the ensuing struggle. Cleopatra had a son, Caesarion, whom she claimed was Caesar's, but in 47 BC Caesar, presumably unimpressed, returned to Rome.

Caesar was assassinated in 44 BC, and over the next few years two men emerged as masters of the Roman world. Caesar's nephew, Octavian, ruled in the west, and Mark Antony in the east. Despite his marriage to Octavian's sister, Antony became deeply involved with Cleopatra. By 36 BC they were openly living together in royal state, and in 34 Antony distributed Roman provinces among her children. Whether the relationship between Antony and Cleopatra was a passionate love affair or a calculated political alliance remains an unanswered question. Antony's free-handed ways with Roman territory made it easy for Octavian to mobilize opinion against him, and war broke out.

The decisive battle was fought at sea in September 31. At Actium, the flight of Cleopatra in mid-battle, followed by that of Antony himself, gave Octavian an overwhelming victory. In August of the following year a triumphant Octavian entered Alexandria, and Antony and Cleopatra committed suicide; according to legend, Cleopatra, finding Octavian insensible to her charms, died from the bite of a tiny snake, the asp, rather than grace his triumph.

In 27 BC Octavian took the title by which he is best remembered, Augustus, and became in effect the first Roman emperor. However, Egypt did not become part of the Roman empire but remained his personal property, bequeathed as such to his successors. For centuries its agricultural wealth made it the granary of the empire, vital in keeping the Romans well-fed enough to minimize popular discontent. The Roman emperors continued to present themselves as pharaohs, but the dominant culture remained Greek. Though Egypt prospered, and versions of her religious cults became popular among the Romans of the late imperial period, the civilization of ancient Egypt had probably foundered even before the triumph of Christianity inaugurated a radical new era.

Alexander the Great: a typically heroic image on a gold coin from Sicyon, c.323 BC. In the course of his assault on the Persian empire, Alexander marched into Egypt, where he was hailed as the new pharaoh. During his brief stay he founded the city of Alexandria.

Cleopatra (left) was the last Egyptian ruler of the Ptolemaic line. Although Greek by origin and culture, she is shown here in traditional fashion as the goddess Isis, wearing a solar disc between cow horns.

3 EVERYDAY LIFE

BECAUSE OF THEIR ELABORATE PREPARATIONS FOR THE WORLD TO COME, THE EGYPTIANS WERE ONCE THOUGHT OF AS A GLOOMILY DEATH-OBSESSED PEOPLE. PARADOXICALLY, MUCH OF OUR INFORMATION ABOUT THEIR DAILY ROUND COMES FROM PAINTINGS, RELIEFS AND MODELS IN TOMBS, WHICH RE-CREATED SCENES THEY EXPECTED TO SEE AND ENJOY AGAIN IN A SECOND LIFE THAT WAS JUST LIKE THE ONE THEY HAD LEFT BEHIND. THESE WORKS SHOW THE EGYPTIANS LEADING FULL LIVES, FARMING, HUNTING AND FISHING, MAKING AND DOING, BRINGING UP FAMILIES, FEASTING, FIGHTING AND WORRYING ABOUT THEIR HEALTH – PRETTY MUCH LIKE MOST PEOPLE IN MOST TIMES AND PLACES.

THE FARMER'S YEAR

Like all ancient civilizations, Egypt was an essentially agricultural society. The overwhelming majority of the people lived and worked on the land, and their labour underpinned the achievements of kings and courts, armies, cities and arts. In fact the exceptional fertility of Egypt was to a great extent responsible for the long-lived, self-renewing character of her way of life. Yet fertile Egypt consisted of little more than a narrow strip of land on either side of the Nile. To its inhabitants this *was* Egypt, the bountiful Black Land, Kemet; the Red Land all round it (Deshret – the desert) was disliked and distrusted, although the Egyptians were prepared on occasion to exploit such resources as it offered.

The Black Land was so called because of the deep, rich appearance of its soil, thrown up by the Nile in flood. All settled life in Egypt was dependent on the more or less predictable action of the river, and Herodotus' comment that 'Egypt is the gift of the Nile' has been quoted so often that it has become a cliché. Nevertheless it still neatly sums up the explanation that follows. Every summer, heavy rains swelled the Blue Nile as it passed through Ethiopia. When the waters reached the Nile Valley they surged over the banks of the river, flooding the surrounding area. In October the water receded, leaving behind a mineral-rich silt that was ideal for growing crops.

As a consequence Egyptian farmers received an annual gift of fresh, fertile land that never needed to recover from years of relentless use. The farmers learned to build their settlements on high ground, above the expected level of the inundation; while it lasted they lived as islanders, keeping in touch with their neighbours by paddling to and fro in papyrus boats. The level reached by the flood was vitally important to the community and politically sensitive enough for the authorities to set up Nilometers to monitor the situation. If the level rose too high, settlements would be swept away and fields ravaged; if it was too low, the crops would fail and people would go hungry. In either case there would be disruption and, if the fail-safe system of state granaries broke down, starvation, discontent and perhaps a rebellion capable of bringing down the dynasty.

A complex system of dykes and canals was developed to deploy Nile water more efficiently, extending the area that could be cultivated and making it possible to compensate for any aberrations of the river or the climate. This has generally been seen as a very early achievement of Egyptian civilization, although some scholars believe that artificial irrigation was in fact introduced much later, towards the end of the Old Kingdom period, when rainfall in Upper Egypt declined dramatically. In most other respects technology remained primitive, or at any rate labour-intensive. When the soil threatened to dry up, the farmer brought water from the river or a canal in two buckets suspended from a pole carried across his shoulders. The first labour-saving device, the shaduf, was not introduced until the New Kingdom period. It was essentially a long wooden

Opposite: Ploughing and reaping. Ancient Egypt was a fertile land, but in this tomb painting the owners, Sennedjem and his wife Iynfert, are blessed with fields of impossibly high wheat and flax.

More visions of plenty: a scene at the butcher's, in the top register, is succeeded by two lines of servants bearing a variety of edible offerings.

pole with a container at one end and a counterweight at the other; placed on a pivot, it could be dipped in the water to fill the container and then swung round so that the water could be poured into a ditch leading into the fields. A further improvement, the sakkia, a cattle-drawn waterwheel, only appeared in the Ptolemaic period. Peasant life on the Nile changed so little over thousands of years that both of these ancient devices were being used by fellaheen (peasants) until a very few years ago, when they were finally replaced by motor-driven pumps.

The heavy hand of government. In this wall painting, scribes are recording the year's grain yield, of which the greater part is destined for the pharaoh's storehouses; from the tomb of Menna, a land agent under Tuthmosis IV.

The Egyptian farmer's tools were simple but, thanks to the climate and soil, perfectly adequate. Shovels, hoes and other basic implements were made of wood; where two or more units were involved, they were bound together by cords made from plant fibre. Axes were equipped with stone heads, sickles with blades of flint or, later, bronze. Ploughs, drawn by cattle, had blade-like wooden ploughshares that cut into the soil without turning it over. When a field had been ploughed and sown, groups of domesticated animals were driven into it to trample down the seed, saving it from the attentions of birds.

Apart from weeding and making sure that their fields did not dry out, Egyptian peasants had little to do until the crops were ripe in March or April. Then the harvest was brought in by a collective effort involving all the able-bodied villagers. In the cornfields the men advanced in a line, cutting the stalks with their sickles and casting each handful to the side, where the women and children bundled them up. The sheaves were carried to a threshing floor, where animals were again made use of; this time their trampling separated the ears of corn from the straw and chaff. The village girls completed the operation by winnowing – flinging the grain in the air so that the chaff was blown away, while the heavier wheat fell back on to the ground. Then the grain was poured into sacks and transported to the granaries.

To the Greek historian Herodotus, the Egyptian peasant seemed like a privileged being, at leisure during the flood months and not overburdened between sowing in November and reaping in the following spring.

By comparison with the farmer toiling to cultivate the hard soil of Greece, the Egyptian certainly was privileged. But Herodotus failed to realize just how closely the authorities monitored and directed the lives of ordinary Egyptians. At leisure, the peasant

Servants dressing geese. The row of hanging fowls and the tall jars of oil or wine emphasize the abundant resources of the household – in this instance the 'eternal house' (tomb) of Nakht, a scribal contemporary of Menna (opposite).

was liable to be conscripted to work on local construction projects; and whether he was sowing or reaping or storing grain, he was under constant supervision. Scribes, the watchful agents of the authorities, were on the spot at every stage, estimating the potential yield, noting the actual amounts harvested, and finally recording the number of sacks delivered to the official granaries. Neither the land nor its products belonged to the peasant: they were the property of the king, or of the nobles or temples who in theory held them from the king. In other words the Egyptian peasant had a status not unlike that of the medieval serf. He was obliged to part with most of his produce in 'taxes' (the term is not really accurate, but useful) and could be punished if the scribes discovered any discrepancies in their accounting; paintings on tomb walls, showing peasants being beaten, suggest that this was one of the many Egyptian customs that were expected to continue unchanged in the afterlife. Unlike the serf, the peasant did receive something tangible in return, since the state granaries issued seeds for sowing every year, and their accumulated stores enabled the population to survive in lean years, much as it did in the Biblical narrative of Joseph, the Israelite who became pharaoh's chief minister.

Wheat and barley provided Egyptians with their staple food and drink, bread and beer. They also grew flax, from which they made linen, and crops such as clover and veitch for cattle feed. The period between the cereal harvest and the July inundation was long enough to allow the cultivation of a second crop, consisting of beans, peas, onions, garlic, cabbages and a variety of other vegetables. Dates, figs and grapes were grown. Egyptian paintings of vineyard scenes and men treading grapes are appropriately lively, though the end product was mainly consumed by the wealthier members of society.

Animals on parade. The Egyptians were no different from us in their enjoyment of stories and drawings in which animals behave like humans. This detail comes from a series on a long papyrus scroll, showing, among other things, animals playing a board game.

In the villages, human beings and domesticated animals lived at close quarters with one another, and on occasion cattle were stalled in one of the rooms in the family home. Well-observed and apparently affectionate paintings of cats, geese and other beasts suggest that Egyptians developed a certain fellow-feeling with animals, which also manifested itself in their religious cults. But on the farm every creature had a useful function. Dogs hunted, cats kept down the rodent population, and cattle pulled ploughs and trampled seed and ears of corn, as well as providing meat and milk. Sheep, goats, pigs and poultry were also food sources.

But some animals were notable by their absence. The horse, believed to have been introduced by the Hyksos, remained an upper-class monopoly, while the camel was not domesticated until a remarkably late date. As the principal beast of burden and means of transport, it was the humble donkey who served as the indispensable ally of the Egyptian farmer.

HUNTING AND FISHING

Egypt's fertile soil made it relatively easy to feed her people, but hunting, trapping and fishing added variety to the national diet and were enjoyed for their own sake.

Hunting has been a prime royal sport in many cultures, lending itself to displays of skill and valour. Egyptian kings showed their mettle by venturing out into the Red Land – the desert – with their retinues and packs of dogs in order to kill or capture lions, hyenas, antelopes, ostriches and a host of other creatures. The decorations on royal tombs most often show hunts in which the king of Egypt masters the king of beasts – sometimes several beasts at a time. Tomb scenes are not entirely reliable, in that they show the ideal life their owner will lead in eternity rather than the life he actually led; so not every king may have been able to match Amenhotep III's boast that he had slain two hundred lions. However, Amenhotep's martial predecessor, Tuthmosis III, despatched large numbers of ostriches and took advantage of his conquest-travels to hunt elephants in Nubia.

These great formal hunts must have looked even more impressive during the New Kingdom period, when the pharaohs began to use chariots. But it seems unlikely that many of them took the form of extended pursuits across the desert. As tomb paintings show, some hunts were set up by sealing each end of a steep-sided valley with nets, leaving enough free space at one end for animals to enter, lured by food and water left as bait. When there was enough game in the valley, the hunters moved in and slaughtered or captured them. It is also possible that hunts were staged in enclosures, using captive animals. Apart from expeditions into the desert by royal and high-ranking personages, most hunting took place in the marshy areas of the Nile Valley. These were most extensive in the Delta, where dense reeds, water-lilies and thickets of papyrus plants sheltered abundant wildlife. One

One of 'the Meidum Geese', a famous set of paintings on plaster from a 4th Dynasty tomb; it is a superb example of observation and naturalistic technique, attained at a remarkably early date.

popular pastime was bird-hunting with throwing sticks, shown in a celebrated fragment of wall painting from the tomb of Nebamun, an 18th-Dynasty noble. In a scene alive with movement and colour, he stands in his papyrus boat, holding three herons by the legs and poised to fling his snake-shaped throwing-stick at a flock of birds. His wife and daughter are with him on the boat, a decoy goose stands in the prow, and Nebamun's cat performs a feat of delightful, impossible dexterity by taking three birds simultaneously. (Cats were actually used to alarm birds, driving them out of their safe places in the thickets of papyrus.)

Fowling and fishing in the marshes seem to have been widely pursued as pastimes. Skill with the throwing-stick was cultivated and spears were wielded as harpoons, but there were also quieter-minded anglers who trailed single lines in the water. By contrast, professional fowlers and fishermen needed to catch larger numbers on a regular basis. These fishermen-by-trade set traps in the form of bottle-shaped reed boxes which their prey could swim into but could not find their way out of. Larger catches were available to groups who worked as teams, dragging large nets, weighted on one side with stones, through the water and on to the riverbank.

Bird-catchers also used nets, ingeniously arranged to fall on to a tree or over a pool to which the birds had been lured. Wild ducks and geese might well be needed to replenish depleted stocks of the domesticated fowl, but quail, plovers, herons and cranes were all taken for the table. However great their fellow-feeling for animals, the Egyptians were cruelly practical, often breaking the wings of captive birds.

Hunting waterfowl; painting from the tomb of the 18th Dynasty scribe Nakht. He wields his throwing stick while his family look on; like many Egyptian designs, this one is near-symmetrical, with the scribe and his family appearing in similar poses on each side of the picture.

Netting fish. Like other representations of working people, this tomb relief has a greater sense of movement and variety of poses than scenes in the hieratic style generally used to portray the upper classes.

Provided the hunter was not careless in the vicinity of crocodiles, only one type of activity in the marshes was dangerous: pursuing a hippopotamus. This was done by groups of men in boats and bore a certain resemblance to whaling in later times. The hunters flung harpoons which snapped on impact, leaving the heads embedded as practised in the animal's body. The harpoons were attached to ropes, so the hippopotamus (like the hunted whale) carried its attackers along with it if it attempted to flee. When it turned to fight it was a dangerous antagonist, capable of overturning boats and killing men; but pitted against intrepid professionals it can have stood no real chance of getting away.

THE SOCIAL ORDER

The apparently unchanging character of Egyptian civilization owed a great deal to the fixed nature of the social order. From birth to death, all Egyptians knew their places and hoped to prosper in them, but they never normally expected to alter their lives in any radical fashion. Increasingly hallowed by time, the social order was accepted as natural and eternal, and, as far as we can tell, Egyptians at the bottom of the hierarchy accepted the privileges of their superiors as part of the scheme of things. Any exceptions to the rule of fixture that did occur were too rare to affect society and could be put down to the will of the gods.

The basis of Egyptian society was inheritance – not just of rank and social standing, but also of occupations. Artists and barbers, nobles and scribes, all followed in their fathers' footsteps and expected their own sons to do the same. Movements between occupations were rare, perhaps occurring most often when disgrace brought demotion or the hereditary principle pressed square pegs into round holes – when, for example, the son of a scribe was patently a dunce or a craftsman's boy failed to master his father's skills. A system of fixed hereditary occupations has been the rule in other societies, but has proved difficult to maintain for more than a few generations. In Egypt it remained the norm throughout the Dynastic period, partly because the Egyptians were conservative-minded, but also because the main agents of disruption – factors such as a money economy, technological change, military emergencies – were either absent or of relatively limited importance.

At the apex of the social hierarchy, alone and unchallenged, stood the pharaoh. He was both an earthly ruler and a semi-divine being whose presence linked Egypt with the realm of the gods. He performed the rituals that safeguarded the material well-being of Egypt as well as the social order. His authority was so absolute that an exceptional being such as Akhenaten was obeyed even when his commands overthrew the pieties which he was supposed to embody. Significantly, palace coups and conspiracies directed against the king – the very stuff of most dynastic histories – are virtually unheard of in Egypt until late in the New Kingdom period; at the very least, this means that if any dark deeds were perpetrated at court, the facts were withheld as being too sacriligious for publication.

The pharaoh's position was unique, but the royal family and the nobility, though earthly beings, were also raised far above all other mortals. The nobles were usually closely related to the king, and they filled most of the leading positions at court, in central and local government and in the army. Technically they held their large estates at the king's pleasure, like feudal barons during the Middle Ages, but (also like feudal barons) they soon came to be regarded as the outright owners of their lands, and during the Intermediate Periods when royal authority was weak they often operated as effectively independent rulers.

The middle ranks of society were made up of administrators – the host of literate functionaries whom the Egyptians themselves called scribes. These in fact ranged from first-class civil servants to relatively lowly clerks. In a large, organized society without a monetary system, record-keeping and accountancy were indispensable if the royal administration – or private estate owners – hoped to keep track of existing resources, commodities stored or in transit, and taxes that had been paid or were still outstanding.

Literacy was the great social divide – not least in the eyes of the scribes, who of course wrote the school texts which provide most of our ideas on the subject. If these are to be believed, a lower place on the social ladder was occupied by craft workers, builders and other specialists, most of them at best semi-literate (that is, unable to read properly but familiar enough with hieroglyphs to carve them accurately).

Any would-be-static social order has to cope with the fact that parents are not neatly replaced, one-to-one, by their children. In particular, younger sons create problems, especially where the inheritance – for example a peasant's plot – is too small to divide between all the surviving males. The younger sons must go out into the world without resources or a defined role – a highly undesirable state of affairs in a conservative social order. And in fact new jobs were created, although not necessarily as a matter of conscious policy. Over long periods, the expansion of the state and royal and noble display created a demand for police, guards, attendants and

The garden of a country estate, with an ornamental fish pond. The birds and fish are realistically painted, though with a touch of humour, but the scene is laid out schematically rather than as it would appear to the eye.

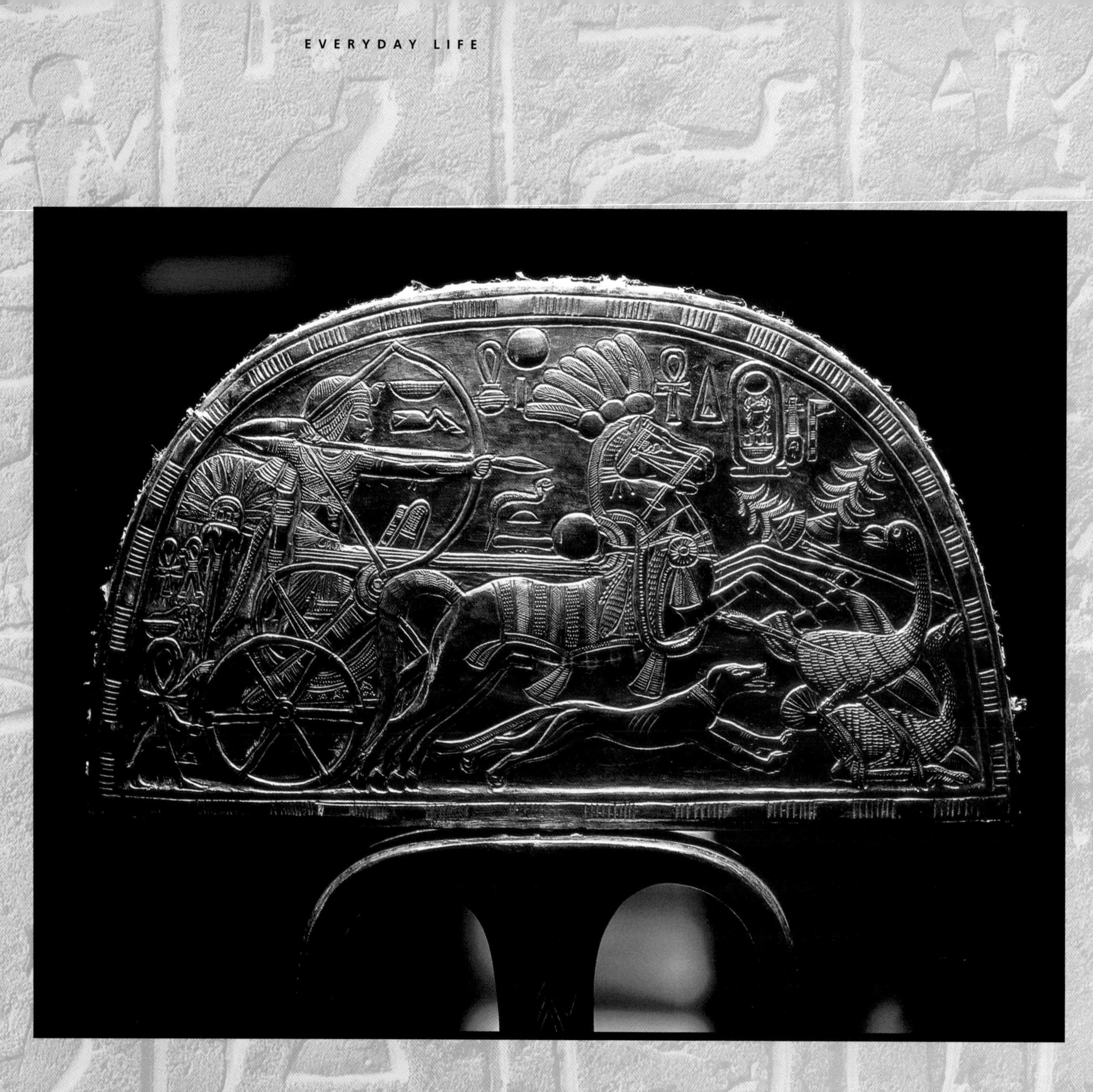

Tutankhamun hunting from his chariot; part of the king's ostrich-feather fan, made from beaten gold. No less than six complete, though dismantled, chariots were found in Tutankhamun's tomb.

Left: A servant girl carrying a large jar and a bag; her nakedness conveys her low status, rather contradicted by her wig and large, elaborate collar. The object is actually a wooden cosmetic spoon.

similar functionaries. From the Middle Kingdom onwards the development of a regular army absorbed some surplus manpower, although surviving descriptions of severe discipline and harsh punishment suggest that for ordinary recruits it must have been the career choice of the last resort.

A steadily expanding priesthood may also have absorbed some outsiders, although priests were allowed to marry and were most often the sons of priests. The priesthood stood apart, forming a separate hierarchy and visibly different from other men in both physical appearance and dress. Their powers and responsibilities are more fully described in Chapter Seven

The lowest social class of any size was the peasantry, living in semi-serfdom at the mercy of scribal tax-collectors. On occasion the peasant had to take orders from members of a less easily placed group, the servants who worked for nobles and administrators. The peasant who paid his taxes probably avoided the beatings that seem to have been the lot of many servants; but service also had its advantages. As in more recent times, everything depended on whether you were an unskilled servant-of-all-work or a dignified Jeeves-like figure such as a cup-bearer, trusted to behave discreetly at private parties and in some instances privy to the family secrets.

The Egyptians also kept slaves, although not in large numbers. Most of them were probably prisoners of war, captured during the expansionist phase of the New Kingdom. Servants seem to have been free to take service with a different master, whereas slaves were definitely property which could be lent, hired out or sold. But in practice most servants would probably have found it difficult to leave a master or mistress without permission, and in many documents it is not easy to distinguish between slaves and servants.

HOUSE AND HOME

Most Egyptian families lived in modest plastered and whitewashed dwellings, sharing four to six rooms with their pets and, on occasion, domesticated animals that needed special attention or protection. The wealthy owned far larger, multi-roomed houses, but these were nevertheless made of the same basic material: mud brick. In fact, all secular buildings in Egypt – even Pharaoh's palaces – were normally built with bricks that had been made from rich Nile mud, shaped in moulds, and dried out in the sun. Only temples and the tombs of the dead, destined to last through eternity, were fashioned from stone.

This does not mean that mud brick was a kind of second best, reserved for a despised earthly existence. Bricks had important advantages. They were inexpensive and accessible, being made from readily available local materials. Brick houses could be raised quickly and were more comfortable to live in than stone structures. (Wood was not a practical alternative, since Egypt had little timber.) Mud-brick walls had to be thick, inside and out, to carry the roof, but the result was a well-insulated house that stayed cool in the summer and retained any internal warmth in the winter. Unless they were soaked by heavy and protracted rains – which are notably absent from the Egyptian climate – mud-brick structures needed little maintenance and endured for surprisingly long periods. A few features, such as the door and the door- and window-frames, might be made of wood, and native palm trunks served well enough as timbers for the roof of an ordinary house. Sealed with reeds and clay and smoothed over, the roof was flat enough to sit out on; for some reason a number of families even seem to have done the cooking there.

Though houses were often overcrowded, some attempts were made to ensure privacy from outsiders. Windows were small and high up (which may also have helped to catch the breeze), with stone or wooden grilles; lacking panes of glass, they must have been blocked or covered with a sheet during the weeks when Egypt's notoriously fierce, hot wind – the khamsin – blew from the west. Generally speaking, workrooms and reception rooms were close to the courtyard or entrance, where large water jars and corn bins stood. The more private rooms were further in, with the women's quarters furthest back or even on the floor above.

An ordinary Egyptian house; like other tomb models, this one is a valuable source of information about everyday life. Notice the steps leading to the upper floor and the roof, often the coolest place after sunset.

In peasants' houses the kitchen was probably the only room with a single main function; since there was hardly any furniture, the other rooms could be adapted at need to social activities or sleeping. Most people were used to sitting on the ground, so a mat was sufficient to make them comfortable. Basic built-in facilities for sitting, table use and sleeping were provided by low brick platforms down the sides of some walls. Meals were taken from wooden or pottery bowls spread out on the floor or possibly from a low table. During winter the family huddled round the simple brick-surround hearth where a dung-fire burned, filling the room with smoke. In summer the interior provided a more pleasantly cool refuge from the intense heat, and later in the day, if there was a cool breeze, the family could mount a set of steps and go up on to the roof to enjoy it.

The upper and middle classes had more in the way of furniture, although their houses would still look bare to modern eyes. Beds, chairs, stools, chests and, less often, tables were the main items. Inevitably the best-known pieces extant come from noble or royal tombs. For severe, gilded elegance, there is nothing to match the furniture that was discovered in a hidden chamber close to the Great Pyramid. It belonged to Queen Hetepheres, the mother of the Old Kingdom pyramid-builder Khufu, and is all the more remarkable in that Hetepheres lived some twelve hundred years before other tomb owners – including Tutankhamun – whose furniture has survived. Apart

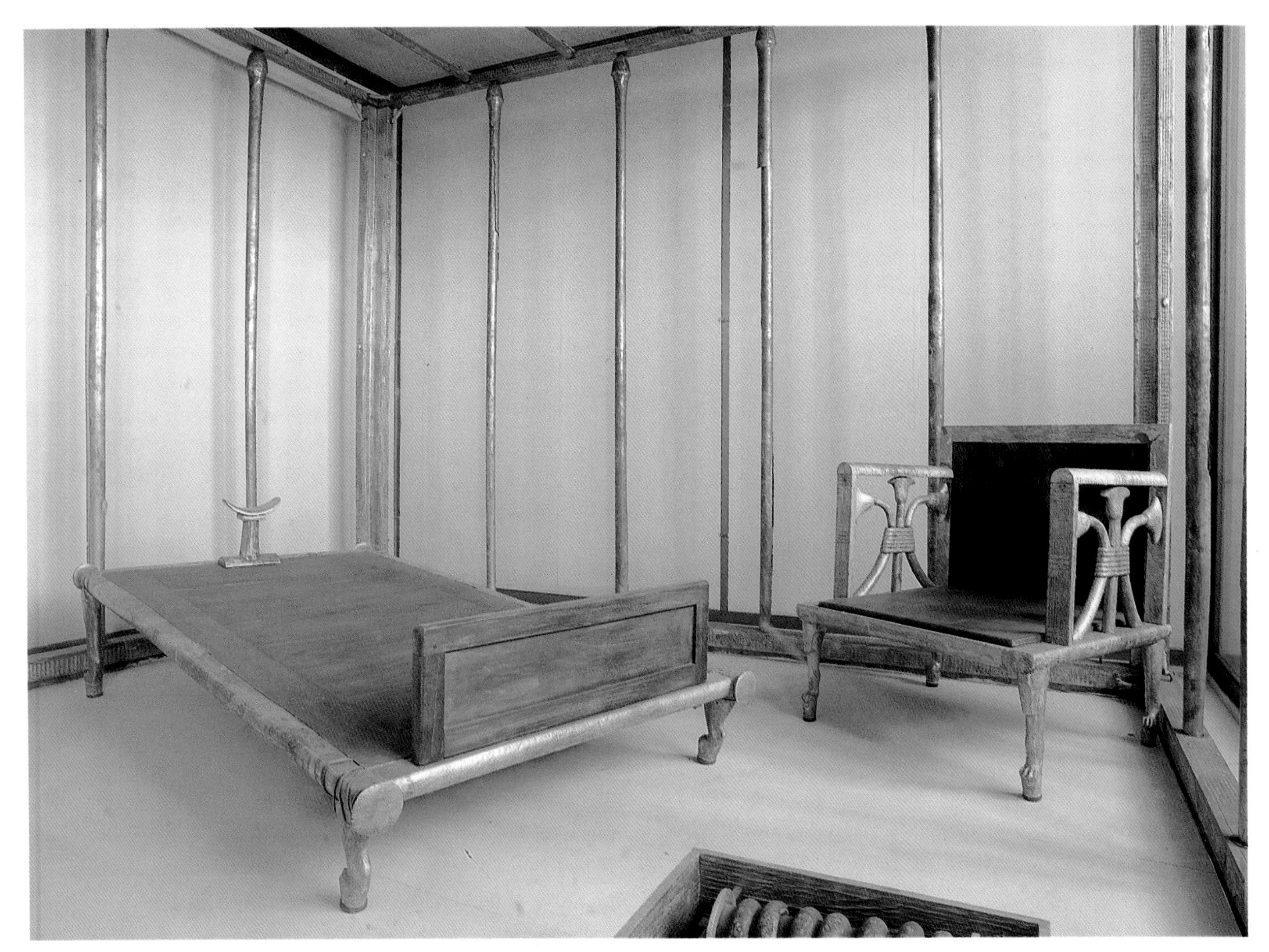

Furniture from the tomb of Queen Hetepheres, the wife of the 4th Dynasty king Sneferu. The canopy, bed and chair, found in her tomb at Giza, are unique examples of Old Kingdom furniture.

from a bed and a chair, the contents of the chamber included a carrying chair which, like a sedan chair, could be lifted on poles and taken from place to place with its owner in it. There was also a very large framework of wooden rods, evidently intended to be draped with curtains or netting; this canopy may have been designed for use while travelling, to keep out the dust, or, like a curtained four-poster bed, to ensure privacy.

Of the beds that have survived, some are relatively simple wood and wickerwork objects, but most are elaborate items made by highly skilled craftsmen, carefully jointed and with legs terminating in claw feet. Tutankhamun's collection included examples with gilded relief panels, a travelling bed that folded up, and three superb animal-form ritual couches, of a type otherwise known only from fragments and tomb paintings. Instead of a pillow, the sleeper lay on a curious head-rest consisting of an upturned curving piece with a central support underneath it; the height of the support indicates that Egyptians must invariably have slept on their sides, presumably making their necks more comfortable by using some kind of lining or padding. Headrests were usually made of wood, but among the eight examples found in Tutankhamun's tomb were beautifully carved rests in ivory, glass and faience.

Kings and nobles sat in throne-like armchairs, inlaid or gilded and beaten in relief. Low armless chairs – some of them remarkably low – also existed, but most people used stools or the floor. The other main type of furniture was the chest, a multi-purpose item which could serve at need as cupboard, table or seat. Tables were low and small since, even at a feast, there were never more than two people at the same board. Fine lamps graced some houses, but poor families made do with one or more bowls of oil which fed the home-made wicks that floated in them. In any case, rising

The great Temple of Amun at Karnak, with the Sacred Lake, beside which stood the enclosure of sacred fowl. The temple was so enormous that it included temples and chapels dedicated to other gods.

early to do as much work as possible before it became intolerably hot, the ordinary Egyptian was tired by the time darkness fell, and ready for sleep rather than a long and leisurely evening.

TOWNS AND CITIES

Egypt's fertile soil enabled the land to support many thousands of retainers and servants, officials, priests, soldiers and craftsmen – along with a surprisingly large number of towns and cities. Some of these grew up in direct response to economic conditions, as market centres or stopovers on trade routes. A typical example was the island town of Elephantine, close to Aswan, on Egypt's southern frontier: demand for gold, ivory and other African products ensured its steady expansion right down to the Greco-Roman period. Other towns developed around cult centres or became provincial capitals devoted to housing and servicing Egypts administrators and tax collectors. In most places growth was piecemeal and unplanned; people altered, rebuilt or expanded their dwellings over generations, creating a jumble of twisting thoroughfares and cul de sacs. In direct contrast, a good many other cities were founded on the orders of the pharaoh, and were models of town planning, with the streets laid out in a New-York-style grid. Among these were settlements established to house and serve the officials and priests who celebrated the mortuary cult of a pharaoh or queen; the best-preserved example is Kahun, built close to the pyramid and mortuary temple of Senruset II. On a larger scale, Akhenaten built a new capital, Akhetaten ('Horizon of the Aten'), on the Nile, no doubt to make a clean break with the old Amun cult that he intended to replace; its three broad highways, and remains of palaces, temples, mansions and houses, represent an ideal though unfinished city, set up on a spacious new site and with no apparent thought of cost-cutting.

Kahun was inhabited for less than a century, Aketaten for about twenty years; then they were simply abandoned. That is why they are relatively (though only relatively) well preserved, and their layout can be identified. Cities that once rivalled or surpassed Akhetaten in splendour – Memphis, Heliopolis, Thebes, Piramesse – have yielded only limited information. The most famous city of all, known to the Greeks as 'hundred-gated Thebes', lies buried under the modern town of Luxor, although the great temple-complex at nearby Karnak survives as a wondrous ruin. Another major reason for the paucity of evidence is that mud-brick buildings, though admirable for their purpose, were not made to last for centuries; consequently houses and palaces decayed, leaving only the temples behind. Moreover, what did survive was plundered. Generations of peasants collected ancient mud brick, which makes excellent fertilizer. Even stone was not safe, for the pharaohs themselves showed a surprising lack of respect for their predecessors, economizing by plundering their monuments and using the stone for their own glorification. As a result, ancient Egyptian towns, where visible at all, might easily be dismissed as heaps of rubble and pottery sherds, and do in truth offer very little information except to the trained eye of the archaeologist.

It is thanks to the archaeologist that we can create some sort of picture of the towns. They were enclosed by brick walls, usually at least 12 metres thick and 30 metres high, shutting out the sight of everything inside except the tops of the very tallest buildings. The contrast between rich and poor was extreme. Zoning was enforced at Kahun, where a wall ran through the town, separating the working-class back-to-backs in the west of the town from the mansions of the opulent east. There may have been less obvious segregation elsewhere, although temples and other important buildings were often separately walled in. An analysis of housing at Akhetaten has suggested a breakdown of the population into manual workers (54-57 per cent), a comfortable middle class of officials, priests and workshop masters (34-37 per cent) and a royal, noble and ministerial elite (7-9 per cent) occupying mansions and palaces with stables and gardens attached and a large staff of sevants and officials on hand. Apart from describing the wonders of Pharaoh's palaces, Egyptian literature gives no very clear picture of urban life. Markets in towns must have been at least as lively as those shown in tomb paintings, where drink, stress and petty theft are much in evidence. The independent craftsmen-traders we hear about – bakers, barbers, laundrymen – were probably town based. And there were certainly taverns where men and women fraternized, as well as red-light districts. Warnings issued to students by teacher-scribes suggest that the pleasures and temptations of city life had already assumed a familiar form.

EGYPTIAN WOMEN

Like females in most pre-modern societies, Egyptian women were the subordinate sex, less important in their own right than as the daughters, wives and mothers of men. We know of a few outstanding female personalities, notably queens such as Hatshepsut and Nefertiti, but their eminence depended on their relationships with men. Perhaps only Hatshepsut can be said to have shaped her own destiny, forcefully converting her initial role as widow-regent into a full-blown pharaonic kingship. Significantly, her success was achieved by assuming a male persona rather than by replacing it with a female equivalent.

However, Egyptian women did enjoy a num-

Hatshepsut appears as pharaoh of Egypt in this relief. But to retain power she was forced to act out male roles – as here, where she wears the false beard adopted by pharaohs on ceremonial occasions.

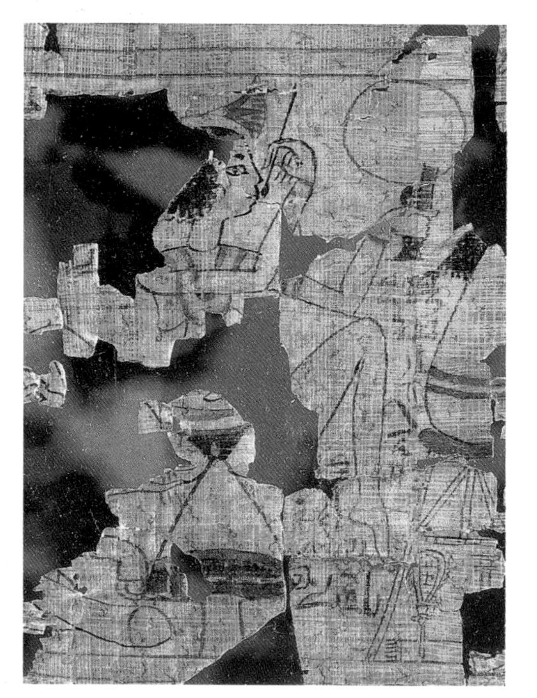

A girl makes up her face between sessions of lovemaking; the detail comes from the Turin Papyrus, a uniquely candid picture-record of encounters between prostitutes and clients in a brothel.

ber of rights that were unusual in the ancient world. On this, as on so many subjects, the Greek historian Herodotus is informative. The freedom allowed to women was one of the reasons why he thought of Egypt as a topsy-turvy land whose customs were the reverse of those prevailing in every other civilized society. In Greece women were segregated in the household and emphatically subject to their husbands. Egyptian wives could inherit, control or dispose of property in their own names, could sign contracts, and could go to law. Examples of all these are on record, including the case of a woman who lent her own husband a sum in silver at interest of thirty per cent per annum, requiring him to pledge all his property as surety for the loan. Of course a few anecdotes – some of them obviously describing exceptional situations – prove very little, and we cannot be sure that women's rights were always enforceable in practice.

There was certainly nothing like equality in the workaday world. The list of possible occupations for a woman would remain familiar for millennia: servant, weaver, laundrywoman, shop manager, mourner, singer, dancer, musician, prostitute. In addition, women could carry out secondary priestly functions in the temples, as well as singing in choirs and taking part in other religious performances; unlike secular female entertainers, these singers and dancers were highly respectable married women.

Marriage, for the overwhelming majority of women, was a career in itself and the only one they were equipped to follow. Even the daughter of a scribe was not normally taught to read and write; depending on her status, she would learn in the parental home either to keep house or to manage a household in which others did the manual work. The peasant's wife may well have had a harder life than her husband, since there was no suspension of housework when the waters rose. Mud-brick houses with little furniture may not have required much cleaning, but there was always corn to grind, beer to brew, bread to bake, cooking to do and cloth to weave. Moreover, to judge from tomb paintings, a wife might help her husband in the fields, walking behind him sowing as he ploughed, or joining in the harvesting.

Marriage itself was a curiously ill-defined institution, apparently subject to no legal or religious constraints. In a society where so many practices were minutely regulated, the basic family unit came about through a private agreement to cohabit, although such arrangements must have been shaped by custom and local standards. Even the 'wedding' may have consisted of nothing more than a feast, followed by the bride moving into her husband's dwelling. From the New Kingdom period, and possibly much earlier, a contract was often drawn up between the husband and the bride's father, ensuring the property rights of the wife and children; by the Third Intermediate Period the contract tended to be between husband and wife, although there is no evidence that any wider emancipation of women had occurred. How the contracts came into being is not very clear, since they were finalized after the marriage rather than before it, yet they included punitive clauses such as provision for the payment of alimony if the husband insisted on a divorce. However ill-defined Egyptian marriages seem to us, the Egyptians themselves had no great difficulty in identifying wives and distinguishing them from concubines.

Most girls married very young, usually when they were between twelve and fourteen. Husbands tended to be older: scribal texts advise young men to make a place for themselves in the world first, which in an Egyptian context meant waiting until about the age of twenty. Where there were good dynastic or economic reasons the gap might be much greater. Matches between relatives were common, since they kept resources within the family. First cousins and uncles and nieces often married; with very rare exceptions, brother-sister and father-daughter alliances were only entered into by the pharaohs, whose religious and dynastic practices were atypical.

Most marriages were probably arranged for prudential reasons, but we have no way of know-

Egyptian mother and child: bronze and gold group showing the goddess Isis, identified by her large headdress of cow horns enclosing a solar disc, suckling the child Horus.

Affectionate couples and families often figure in Egyptian art. This painted limestone group shows the dwarf Seneb, a wardrobe master, with his wife and children, who are shown according to Egyptian convention, with their fingers in their mouths; c.2400 BC.

ing how often – or even whether – fathers forced their children to marry against their inclinations. Songs of love and loss have come down to us from the New Kingdom; however, since a cult of romantic love has coexisted with hard-headed matchmaking in other societies, the songs tell us about aspirations rather than realities.

Since the surviving records were all written by men, there is not much to be said with any certainty about the married state. Sculptures and paintings project an image of connubial happiness, often showing the wife with her arm on her husband's shoulder or round his waist. Scribal literature advises young men to cherish their wives (though often adding that they shouldn't put up with any nonsense from them), and one convincing piece of evidence survives in the form of a prayer addressed by a husband to his dead wife, whose ghost had been troubling him. Seeking release, he reminds her that he had always been a good husband to her: 'I took you as my wife when I was a young man, and you were still my wife when I made a successful career. I did not divorce you and I did not make your heart ache. . . Everything I acquired was laid at your feet. . . I never made you suffer. . . You never found me deceiving you. . . and I had many garments made for you.'

Stories and legal records make it clear that Egyptians were not exempt from marital difficulties. Adultery occurred, although it was roundly condemned; but infidelity in a wife was far more severely judged than in a husband. This double standard is neatly illustrated by the solemn declarations of innocence made on oath in temples: all the examples so far discovered are by women.

The 'other woman' was unlikely to be an additional wife. For a long time the multiple marriages of the pharaohs misled historians into believing that polygamy was commonly practiced. It is now believed to have been rare, if only because few men could afford to support two wives and two families.

The greatest threat to a wife's position was infertility: bearing children, especially male children, was the most important of all her tasks. Wives undoubtedly accepted this valuation, which had a basis that was both political and religious: children were expected to become the supports of a couple's old age (especially male children, who, unlike daughters, did not leave the parental family and join a stranger's); and it was the first-born son's privilege and duty to bury his father, care for his tomb, and keep the dead man's name alive. A woman who failed to give her husband a son (and the failure was seen as hers) might be divorced. But an alternative was for the man to take a concubine and have children by her; in time, the wife could formally adopt the offspring of this union as her own children.

Such hard-headed arrangements suggest that marriage was an institution based firmly on mutual interest and not lightly terminated. However, divorces did occur and, like marriages, were privately arranged; generally speaking the wife departed with her property, unless some further stipulations in the contract came into force. More often a couple lived together until separated by death – which, given low life-expectancy, often came all too soon. Significantly, when listing the most vulnerable members of society, Egyptian texts name widows, divorced women and orphans. Not surprisingly, widows and widowers often married for a second or third time.

SEX AND LOVE

Despite the wealth of information we possess about the ancient Egyptians, their attitudes towards sex and love cannot be very clearly defined. As in other societies, official morality, literary conventions and actual behaviour may have diverged more or less widely; and at this distance in time it is hard to identify the unstated assumptions – the things 'everybody knows' that distinguish acceptable from atrocious actions of a type that may look near-identical to outsiders.

Some superficial forms of candour are probably

Above: Ithyphallic figure (that is, with erect penis) from the Temple of Amun at Karnak. The connotations of such figures had more to do with the fertility of the land and the people than with eroticism.

Left: Polished stone phallus from the Predynastic period. Many ancient cultures made ritual use of phallus-form objects, directly associating them with life, strength and fertility.

misleading. Representations of the god Min, with his giant phallus, or of female genitalia on charms, had more to do with fertility than sex as an activity divorced from childbearing. Many 'dolls' can be interpreted as toys, or sex objects, or fertility symbols. The same kind of doubts hang over nakedness, which was certainly common in a number of contexts: fishermen might work completely naked, women might go topless in the fields – as a modern western girl may on the beach. Whether that means that nakedness never carried an erotic charge for the Egyptians is another matter: it is arguable that in a different context, for example at a party, revealing clothes (or their absence) had much the same effect under the 18th Dynasty as they do now. One entertaining piece of evidence is a story about the Old Kingdom pharaoh Sneferu. His mood of boredom dissolved when a courtier suggested that he should go boating on the lake in his park. The delighted king ordered twenty gold-plated oars to be brought, along with 'twenty women with the shapeliest bodies, breasts and braids, and who have not yet given birth' – and twenty nets, which the women were to wear instead of their clothes. Rowed up and down by the women, the king was happy. The good mood produced by this erotic titillation survived even when one of the women lost a jewel in the lake and obstinately refused Sneferu's offer to replace it; he good-humouredly sent for a magician who obligingly lifted up the water so that the jewel could be recovered from the bed of the lake! Apart from occasional sketches on ostraca (pottery sherds or limestone fragments), unmistakably secular sexual episodes are known from only one damaged papyrus, now

A family group; wall painting from the 18th Dynasty tomb of Inherkha. The children are shown as naked, with the long 'sidelock of youth' hanging from their partly shaven heads.

in Turin. Arranged like a series of comic-book drawings, it shows a small, balding, rather seedy-looking but supernaturally well-endowed man having sex in a variety of positions with a singing-girl. She is dressed in, or rather decorated with, a necklace, bracelet and waistband, and between sessions appears to be making up her face; the captions consist of her encouraging exclamations, designed to keep her partner up to the mark. The setting is usually taken to be a brothel, in which case the man is a customer, eventually carried out – drunk? exhausted? – by the girl and two helpers. These erotic scenes occur opposite animal satires of a familiar Egyptian type, so their intention was probably comic; it is possible that the man represents a 'funny foreigner'.

As we saw earlier, marriage customs permitted polygamy and concubinage, although in practice neither was anything like as common as was once believed. But the different standards applied to males and females were certainly matched by the different opportunities available to rich men and poor men. In all societies, slaves have been sexually available to their masters, and servants too have rarely been in a position to resist sexual harassment. However, Egyptian records are silent about the legal position, if any. Homosexuality is also rarely mentioned, although King Pepi II is said to have had an affair with one of his generals; it seems to have been regarded as a vice, but not a matter for legal action. Egyptian scribal writings are rather hostile to women, who are commonly portrayed as fickle and feather-headed. 'Do not open your heart to your wife, for what you say to her in private will be repeated in the street.' But the scribes are also intensely aware of the sexual allure of women and its potentially disturbing effects on earnest students and respectable married men. As ever, novelty is an aphrodisiac: 'Beware of a strange woman who comes from some unknown city. When she approaches, do not look at her or make her acquaintance. She is as the eddy in deep waters, the depths of which are unfathomed.' By contrast, during the New Kingdom a great deal of poetry was written in which both men and women feel love and desire, are strengthened by their feelings, vow to overcome every obstacle, meet at secret spots and consummate their union with joy. A lover wades across the river, reckless of crocodiles in the shallows; a girl imagines bathing in front of her sweetheart's eyes; another maiden contemplates the flowers in her garden, associating each kind with the beloved and declaring that 'in it is a pool that your hand has made', and that when she walks with him 'my body is satisfied and my mind glad'. It is still a moot point whether all this represents a literary convention – the fantasy of male poets – or reflects the common experience.

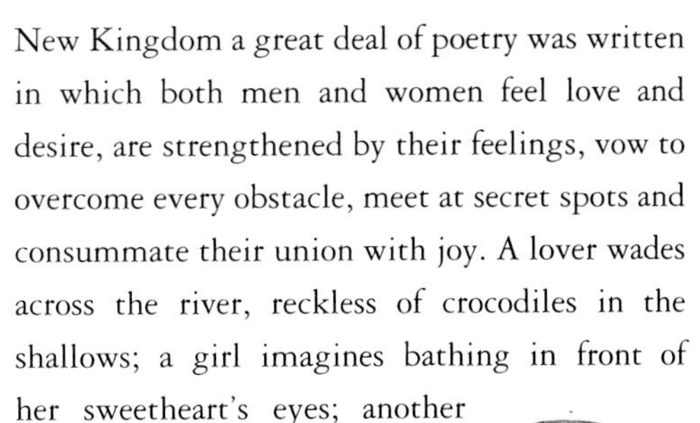

Above: A wheeled toy horse, made of wood. It is a pull-along toy with a hole in the muzzle through which a string could be inserted; c.AD 200.

Left: Egyptian toys. The fierce cat-like creature is remarkably sophisticated, with a hinged moveable jaw, inlaid eyes and bronze teeth. The toys perhaps date to around 1400 BC.

Tools of the trade. A scribe's palette or writing case, complete with reed brushes and 'inkwell' for a block of pigment. These were such indispensable pieces of eqipment that hieroglyphic picture versions were used for the words 'scribe' and 'writing'.

CHILDHOOD

In a typically sententious piece of Egyptian 'wisdom literature', the scribe Any pictured the bond of obligation between parent and child: 'Repay your mother for all her care. Give her as much bread as she needs, and carry her as she carried you, for you were a heavy burden. When in due time you were born she still carried you on her neck, and for three years she suckled you; nor was she repelled by your excrement.'

The emotions connected with this extended suckling were strengthened by religious associations, for one way of picturing the semi-divinity of the pharaoh was by images in which he suckled at the breast of his goddess-mother Isis. In practice, queens and other high-ranking women were less high-minded, generally employing a substitute in the form of a wet-nurse. The subsequent relationship between child and nurse also became very close – so much so that Amenhotep II continued to visit his old wet-nurse after he had become pharaoh, climbing on her knee to signify his continuing devotion. Many children died in infancy, but the high birthrate ensured that most couples had large families. Egyptian art normally presents an ideal, and therefore partial, view of things, but the consistently tender images of family groups do suggest that children were deeply cherished. In the admittedly untypical art of the Amarna period, Akhenaten and Nefertiti are repeatedly shown as indulgent parents who allow their children to climb all over them while the whole family bathes in the life-giving light of the Aten. As they grew, children took part in a variety of games including races, wrestling, mock-fights and dances of the 'ring-a-roses' type. They also enjoyed ball games and played with a variety of toys. Some of these were quite sophisticated pull-along animals with moveable limbs, but simple home-made tops or rattles were more common. At worst, the children themselves could make models of human and animal figures from the rich mud of the Nile; these not only dried out and were used, but have survived for millennia. Many dolls have also been found, but it is rarely possible to be sure whether they were used as toys or as ritual objects.

In Egyptian art, children are usually shown as naked; this may have been an artistic convention, but given the climate they probably did dispense with clothes for much of the time. A more distinctive identification was the 'sidelock of youth' sported by both sexes – a long tress, worn over one ear, and all the more obvious because the rest of the head was shaved or closely cropped. The sidelock continued to be worn until a child was ten or so. It is possible that, for boys, the cutting of the sidelock coincided with circumcision, although it has usually been supposed that the operation took place at about the age of fourteen. This aspect of Egyptian life remains obscure, since not all males seem to have been circumcised; yet we hear of 120 boys having the operation at one time, which makes it sound very much like a rite of passage into manhood. Although Herodotus believed that the motive was hygienic, the operation was performed by a priest who used an old-fashioned flint knife. A relief showing a circumcision, with the boy standing and bracing himself, also suggests that the occasion was intended as an initiation and a test. No indisputable evidence exists for female circumcision.

For most boys and girls, the free, irresponsible period of childhood was very short. The children of the poor probably performed simple tasks on the farm – bird-scaring or fetching and carrying – at a very early age. Going out into the fields, accompanying the herds or looking, learning and lending a hand in the workshop, boys entered the adult world; if, as was usually the case, this was effected inside the family, it probably happened without any consciousness that an apprenticeship was being served. Similarly, girls learned domestic skills in the house and the yard; and by thirteen or fourteen they were preparing themselves to marry.

AT SCHOOL

Education in the formal sense was restricted to a tiny minority. Probably fewer than one per cent of the population was able to read and write, yet this was the key to power, privilege and ease. Even in Egypt there were self-made men – mainly, perhaps, military men – who rose in the world without knowing their letters, but they were rare indeed. Those who had learned to wield a pen were graduates of schools for scribes, but becoming a scribe might be only the first step in a man's career as a minister, civil servant, magistrate, manager, agent or priest.

'Scribe' remained a useful all-purpose word for such occupations, and the mere act of writing conferred dignity; high-ranking ministers and officials liked to have themselves portrayed sitting in the characteristic scribal position, with their knees up and forming a flattish surface on which to rest their papyrus scroll.

The royal children – perhaps including the princesses – were taught in the palace, alongside the children of selected nobles. Elsewhere, only males went to school. A few surviving notes and letters from the building workers' village at Deir el-Medina suggest that some ordinary women may have been literate or semi-literate, presumably thanks to their association with skilled men whose numbers included draughtsmen and architects. School classes were held at administrative and other centres which could be expected to recruit high-flying scholars; as the wealth and influence of the temples increased, a particularly important role was assumed by temple schools set up in a building known as the House of Life. Most pupils were local boys, but a few were sent away by parents who could afford it, in order to study at a particularly suitable school. Boys set out from home each day with a packed lunch of bread and beer. Lateness, like other shortcomings, was punished with a beating, but boys were late, or rowdy, or lazy, nonetheless. Although scribal literature exhorted pupils to exert themselves, the fundamental belief was that 'A boy's ear is on his back: he listens when he is beaten.'

The nature of school work explains the need for beatings to concentrate the mind. Learning con-

Even superhumans were young once. In this fine relief, Ramesses II, the most vainglorious of all pharaohs, appears as an uncharacteristically boyish and immature figure.

For well-born Egyptians (men as well as women), cosmetics were indispensable personal aids. These painted cosmetic pots are made of core (moulded) glass; they date from the 18th Dynasty (1550 BC onwards).

sisted almost exclusively of repetitive copying or laborious memorization. Initially, while developing their writing skills, boys used ostraca, only progressing to valuable papyri when they had attained a considerable proficiency. They first mastered the more fluent and practical hieratic script before going on to the decorative, ceremonial hieroglyphs, which were drawn rather than written. Their equipment was that of the professional scribe – a neat palette-box containing reed pens and black and red ink blocks which were, in effect, watercolours, needing to be moistened before use.

The voices and values of scribes monopolized the texts that schoolboys were required to memorize, chant and copy. These scribal 'instructions' are often set out as though the author is a wise father giving good advice to his son. They include moral reflections, exhortations to work hard and, most interestingly, heavy-handed propaganda extolling the benefits of the scribe's way of life. Much of the propaganda took a negative form, describing the drawbacks and privations suffered by non-scribal groups, and thereby giving us a detailed, if jaundiced, account of, for example, the peasant's daily round.

In the Houses of Life, and probably in other schools, pupils were also taught elementary mathematics, and acquired some knowledge of geography and astronomy from the texts they were required to memorize. No evidence has been found for the teaching of foreign languages, on the face of it a striking indication of the inward-looking nature of Egyptian society; if this were really so, foreign correspondence of the kind found in the Amarna Letters must have been conducted by bilingual outsiders. On the other hand, there may have been advanced courses or on-the-job learning opportunities that we know nothing about, for officials at some levels certainly needed expertise of a kind that was not available in schools. When the scribe Hori wanted to show up the inadequacies of one of his colleagues, he asked him a series of questions ranging from the geography of Syria to the number of men needed to transport an obelisk. No doubt the qualified scribe had a well-trained memory, but the impression remains that, if Hori's colleague could reasonably be expected to answer such questions, his studies must have been of a kind that extended well beyond his teens.

Found in the tomb of an Egyptian lady: a splendidly designed hand mirror, pots for ointments and khol (eye makeup), a jewellery box and less glamorous items such as bowls and a knife for preparing food.

LOOKING GOOD

Egyptians cared a great deal about how they looked. Over the millennia their society became highly sophisticated, and they increasingly turned into followers of fashion, changing their styles so often that figures in New Kingdom art can be dated by their hair and clothing. As with all pre-modern societies, statements of this kind apply to the leisured, affluent classes rather than the mass of peasants and workers; however, even they did what they could to imitate current modes, for example buying ceramic and coloured glass jewellery that resembled the more valuable items owned by the wealthy.

In Egypt's climate, being clean and being cool and presentable all went together. Body hair was often shaved off to make these desirable states easier to achieve and maintain. Some homes had stone-lined shower-rooms in which the master or mistress stood while a servant acted as a human faucet, tipping water in over the side. Since soap was unknown, washing was done with the aid of natron, a natural salt of which Egypt had abundant supplies; it was also used, dissolved in water, as a mouthwash – and, packed into cadavers, as part of the embalming process, soaking up the body fluids. The skin-drying tendency of natron was counteracted by the lavish application of moisturizers in the form of animal fats, oils or, for the very wealthy, more exotic and aromatic substances specially imported from Asia or the Land of Punt.

The wealthy and leisured washed several times a day and changed their clothes as often, employing the services of professional laundrymen. Clothing was light and simple, even for the well-off. At work the peasant wore a loincloth, or just a belt with a penis-sheath attached. On more formal occasions he wore a kilt, consisting of a single length of cloth wrapped round the lower body and tucked into a belt; this can in fact be regarded as the basic garment for all men, although variations in length, cut and pleating made it easy to distinguish the fashionable from the functional.

The equivalent for women, a single long shift, underwent more dramatic modifications. During

A cosmetic dish made of wood, subtly shaped in the form of a duck. Its handle takes the form of a girl who is swimming, or perhaps simply presenting the dish to its owner.

Amulet in the form of a pendant of gilded wood; from the tomb of Tutankhamun. On it, the 'great-of-magic' serpent goddess suckles the small figure of the king. The pendant is strung with beads made from a variety of materials.

the Old Kingdom it is portrayed as a 'tube' dress held up by broad shoulder straps; in most instances it is so close-fitting that it is hard to imagine the wearer being able to move.

By the New Kingdom, clothes were more elaborate and often more revealing, with diaphanous areas, plunging necklines and single-strap arrangements that showed glimpses – or more than glimpses – of one breast. Two-piece dresses had a vogue, and styles were generally looser and more flowing, displaying the pleating, folds and fringes that were the principal signs of haute couture.

Shirts and shawls were put on in cooler conditions, and as time went on a variety of overgarments were introduced. The most popular material was linen, with wool far behind; cotton was not used until the Greco-Roman period. Our main source of information – tomb paintings – may exaggerate the Egyptians' preference for stately whiteness, since it only occasionally shows dyed and embroidered fabrics. But generally speaking men and women preferred to add colour and glitter to their clothing by attaching beading or jewellery to it; one striking item of women's costume was a large net of beads worn round the middle.

Only a few people wore anything in the nature of a uniform. The chief minister, or vizier, is sometimes shown in a long, dress-like costume that presumably denotes his rank; and holders of some priestly offices sported leopardskins. Nakedness may also have been a kind of uniform, labelling servant girls, dancers and singers as belonging to the lower class and, possibly, as sexually available.

A few dozen examples of ancient Egyptian clothing have been discovered and preserved, including loincloths, shirts and tunics. Sandals and slippers have also survived. The sandals were made on the 'flip-flop' principle, of leather or fibre. People went barefoot in the house and a great deal of the time outside, but feet doubtless needed protection on some surfaces. Whether the young pharaoh Tutankhamun needed all the footwear he owned – at least ninety-three items – is another question.

Coiffures, cosmetics and jewellery added to the attractiveness of both men and women. Well-styled hair was important, although it might not be the wearer's own. Men, often exposed to the heat of the Egyptian sun, almost always wore their natural hair short; they were usually clean-shaven, although some Old Kingdom nobles grew moustaches and some men sported chin-tufts. Women adopted a severe style during the

A fine lady at her toilet. The 11th Dynasty Queen Kawit holds her mirror in one hand while she sips a drink and a maid carefully fixes her wig.

The crown and wig ornaments of the 12th Dynasty princess Sit-Hathor-Yunet; the wig itself is a modern but accurate version of the wigs always worn by ladies on formal occasions.

Old Kingdom, but later wore their hair shoulder-length and, as with clothing, favoured a more flowing look. Wealthy women employed hairdressers or trained maids; men arranged for a barber to visit or, if they could not afford private attention, had their hair cut in an open-air 'shop'.

Hair was washed and perfumed, but on formal occasions or at banquets and festivities, wigs were worn. These were objects of adornment, not intended to deceive the eye, and they can often be identified in pictures and statues.

Wig-making was a specialized occupation, and remains of a workshop have been found at Deir el-Bahri, including a model head with attachment-points marked. Good quality wigs were made from human hair, but cheaper, fibre-made models also existed. Like natural hair, wigs were perfumed and decorated with circlets of flowers or jewels. Fashion ruled here, too: in the longest-lived style the hair was divided into three parts, two of which hung down the sides of the face, but there were other styles, some of them remarkably large and full.

Even during the Predynastic period, men and women were using cosmetics to improve and dramatize their looks. The most essential equipment, which went with them into the tomb, consisted of a palette and a block of pigment for eye-painting. The palette was a carved flat stone on which the pigment was ground; even when it was clearly an elaborate ceremonial piece like the Palette of Narmer (page 26), its design included the relatively small functional part, the sunken oval on which the actual grinding was done.

The powdered paint, known as kohl, was mixed with water and applied with the fingers or a brush. During the Old Kingdom the pigment was a green malachite substance, but this was increasingly replaced by the galena-based black form of kohl. The paint was used to outline the eyes, making them appear larger. The general effect was enhanced by extending the painted line horizontally from the corner of each eye across the side of the face.

The other main type of make-up was a reddish ochre employed as rouge and possibly sometimes as lipstick. (The only real evidence for this is the papyrus showing a prostitute who appears to be painting her lips.) Oils and perfumes sweetened and softened the body, and wealthy Egyptians treated themselves to manicures and pedicures. Henna might be used to dye the hair, the nails, the palms of the hands and the soles of the feet. Bronze and silver mirrors, tweezers, nail-sticks and a variety of cosmetic boxes, pots and jars – some meant to hold anti-wrinkle creams – accompanied the upper-class woman through life and into the tomb.

Tattooing was practised from early times, but those who wore tattoos were mostly engaged in dubious employments, as dancers, singers and prostitutes. The presence of the jovial god Bes, tattooed high up on a girl's thigh, may well have been a clear erotic signal. If tattooing was rather disreputable, this may account for the absence of other body-piercing practices for most of Egyptian history; only in the New Kingdom did it become acceptable for men and women to have their ears pierced so that they could wear earrings.

Other types of jewellery for personal adornment were being worn some two thousand years earlier. Initially made of shells, stone, bone or ceramic wares, body ornaments for royalty took often spectacular forms during the early dynasties. There were no precious stones, but craftsmen fashioned beautiful things from gold, silver and semi-precious materials such as amethyst, carnelian, jasper, lapis-lazuli and turquoise. However, cheaper materials were also widely used, and coloured glass and bright, smooth faience were popular with all classes for the beads that made up necklaces, the broad pendants known as pectorals, and the even broader, multi-row collars that became badges of royal or noble rank. These, along with bracelets and anklets, belts and rings, bangles on the upper arm and diadems in the hair, must have created a dazzling effect when they were set against the white of elegantly plain linen.

FOOD AND DRINK

Egypt had abundant natural resources, envied by less favoured peoples such as the Greeks. In normal times there was more than enough to eat for all, even if its distribution was markedly unequal. When the annual inundation failed to occur, famine threatened, and a series of such failures is believed to have played a part in bringing down the Old Kingdom.

The establishment of state granaries, filled with stockpiles of cereals, lessened the impact of bad years and served a political as well as a humanitarian purpose: discontent was headed off, and Egypt remained free of social unrest for impressively long periods of time.

Bread was the staple for both rich and poor in a land where potatoes and other carbohydrate-rich foods were unknown. It was used to symbolize all nourishment (the term 'the staff of life' has direct Egyptian equivalents), and the walls of tombs regularly feature baking scenes and pictures of the deceased sitting at a food-piled table on which bread is specially prominent. Bread-making may well have been the housewife's most onerous task. Day after day she had to kneel in front of a saddle quern (essentially a flat stone with a shallow central depression), working backwards and forwards with a roller to grind the corn into flour; even after it had been sieved it was relatively gritty in consistency, making a major contribution to Egyptian dental problems. Then she added yeast and water, kneaded the mixture to make dough, added salt and spices, packed it into a mould, and baked it in an oven. Many types of bread were produced, in a great variety of shapes; some human- and animal-shaped loaves probably had a festive or religious significance. Adding fats and eggs, with dates and a sweetener, transformed bread into cake. Barley and wheat were also used to make beer, the staple drink of the poor. Relatively low in alcohol, it was a rich, soupy mixture, best imbibed through a straw to minimize the intake of floating particles.

Professional bakeries appeared during the New Kingdom, but their existence made no difference to the ordinary housewife. Much of her cooking was probably done outside the house, if only to avoid the risk of setting fire to it; in terms of comfort it may have been marginally preferable to work out in the hot sun rather than in a small room without a chimney, heated by a dung fire

Bakers busy at work, producing Egypt's staple food. These are wooden models of the 19th century BC, placed in the tomb to ensure that the owner would never lack the essentials of life.

A kneeling figure presents an attractive array of edibles; from the Temple of Ramesses II. Pictured offerings, whether to gods, men or mummies, emphasized the status of the recipient and magically ensured continued bounty.

and a brick oven. Most vegetables and pulses were boiled over the fire; meat, when available, was usually boiled or roasted. Dairy products and fruit varied the menu, and when the Nile was low it was easy to catch fish by simply scooping them up; since only a limited number could be eaten fresh, most of them would be salted and dried for future consumption. An upper-class family employed several cooks – and, interestingly, these 'chefs' were normally men. Not a single recipe has survived, so it is impossible to know whether these specialists prepared and served dishes in a particularly sophisticated fashion, but festive scenes in tomb paintings suggest that quality and abundance were what mattered. Meat-eating was a sure sign of high status: the poor might occasionally sacrifice a domestic animal or rejoice over a trapped hare or wildfowl, but the rich and powerful ate beef. Only they had estates large enough to support herds of cattle, and herds large enough to provide constant supplies of meat without becoming seriously depleted.

The cattle slaughtering scenes that appear on tomb walls demonstrate the owner's status while also magically ensuring that there will be no shortage of supplies in the eternal future. The rich monopolized two other expensive items, wine and honey; the masses had to be content with drinking beer and using dates as sweeteners.

Mealtimes may have varied according to status. Peasants, faced with a day's work in the fields, probably ate a heartier breakfast than their betters. Those who could afford it spent the hours of intense heat, as many people in the Mediterranean still do, indoors, taking their time over a meal and perhaps sleeping for an hour or two. Towards the end of the day the alternatives were to sup lightly, or to be the host or a guest at one of the banquets so beloved of Egyptians.

A perfume container. The more elaborate objects of this kind are often designed so that they include burden-bearing or humbly prostrate servant figures. This suggests that upper-class women were very much conscious of (and enjoyed) their social superiority.

ENTERTAINING, MUSIC AND DANCE

To judge from the vivid paintings on the walls of Egyptian tombs, throwing a party or banquet was one of the highlights of social life. The paintings are obviously intended to display the owner's generosity and to ensure that the same kind of good time is available in the life to come, but their lively atmosphere and telling details are convincing arguments for their accuracy.

By contrast, little written evidence of banqueting exists apart from moralistic scribal warnings against gluttony and drunkenness. These do not prove that either vice was widespread, although a fair number of male paunches are visible on statues and (vestigially) on mummies. On the wall of the tomb of Paheri, a painted lady calls out to a

A banqueting scene in which the seated guests are being attended to by servants. Clothing, or lack of it, makes class differences immediately obvious, although even some of the servant girls have been provided with cooling incense cones for their heads.

servant, 'Bring me eighteen cups of wine: I want to get drunk. My throat is as dry as chaff!' Other paintings show people being sick, presumably after taking eighteen cups or so; most of them are women, perhaps because the breach of decorum was felt to be more amusing when committed by a lady.

Apart from a few such details, parties are shown as decorous affairs. Guests, often garlanded with flowers, are seated according to their rank, the lowliest squatting on mats; the sexes are sometimes, but by no means always, segregated. The ladies carry lotus blossoms, which serve as pomanders, and politely hold them under their neighbours' noses.

The guests' wigs are crowned with incense cones, believed to be incense-impregnated solids of wax or fat which melted in the course of the festivities, bathing the head in a refreshing aromatic liquid. An alternative view is that such cones would be hopelessly unstable and unpleasantly messy; in which case they appear in paintings simply as visual signals that the wigs are perfumed. On the other hand, the clothes of some guests do seem to be spattered with something that may be wax or fat, so at present the question remains open.

As we might expect, there is an abundance of food, piled high on the tables. Servant girls go round with the drinks, which are red or, if the

host is a connoisseur, white wines. Entertainment is laid on. There may have been non-visual activities such as storytelling or recitations of poetry, but what we see are dancers, acrobats and musicians. The dancers and acrobats perform nearly naked, usually wearing ornamental girdles that set off rather than conceal their charms. Egyptian painting, despite its formalities, vividly conveys the sinuous motions of the dancers and the agility of the acrobats.

The musicians play a variety of instruments, including flutes, lutes, oboes, tambourines, harps and lyres; others, such as trumpets, drums and sistrums (metal rattles), were presumably thought more suitable for grand public or religious occasions.

Music was obviously important in Egyptian life – we hear of work songs, marching music, temple music – but since no system of notation existed to preserve it, any statement about its character can be no more than intelligent guesswork.

The musicians in party scenes look as though they are performing lively numbers, but these are said to have in fact been mournful (like the blues?), lamenting the brevity of life and enjoyment.

At the end of the party, the message was reinforced, if Herodotus is to be believed, when a small model of a mummy was put on show, accompanied by appropriate doom-laden sentiments. It is certainly true that variations on 'Gather ye rosebuds while ye may', an essentially pessimistic philosophy, occur surprisingly often in Egyptian literature. For all their confidence in an eternal afterlife, inscriptions and papyri often echo the sentiments expressed by the Instruction of Ptahhotep: 'Be merry all through your life, and do no more work than is necessary.'

The feasts and celebrations of ordinary Egyptians are less well documented. They worked long and hard, but there were a reasonable number of festive days – for example at New Year, after the harvest and during local religious festivals. Peasants had little to do during the inundation, whereas building workers, employed for nine days out of a ten-day 'week', had more regular time off.

Apart from wedding feasts, formal entertainments were probably rare by comparison with spontaneous outdoor celebrations such as singing, dancing, clapping to time. And, like their superiors, the common people enjoyed a variety of sports, games and other pastimes.

PASTIMES

Ordinary Egyptians indulged in a range of simple, inexpensive physical sports such as running, jumping, boxing, wrestling, swimming and fencing with sticks. Among the lighter moments during their working day were mock-fights between fishermen who stood up in their boats and swung at each other with long poles until one or the other was knocked into the water. On occasion there even seem to have been organized competitions in sports such as athletics and weight-lifting. As we have seen, hunting was primarily a

Music at home. In this tomb painting, a harpist plays for Anhour and his wife; the intimacy of the scene suggests that musical appreciation could be quite sophisticated, going beyond a crowd or group's enjoyment of lively or solemn rhythms.

recreation for the upper classes. Apart from rowing, their sports were warlike. Archery was particularly prestigious, which is no doubt why pharaohs excelled – or were said to excel – at it. Amenhotep II, like Homer's hero Odysseus, was reputed to have been 'so mighty of arm that none can bend his bow'. The introduction of the chariot added an exciting new diversion, racing and shooting from a moving vehicle, to the sporting repertoire.

The Egyptians were an outdoor people who generally rose with the sun and retired soon after dusk. Even the rich, who could afford to leave their oil lamps burning longer, did not keep late hours. So it is surprising to discover that Egyptians were addicted to board games.

Four ivory-and-wood boards and many pieces were recovered from Tutankhamun's tomb, and similar finds have been made among other upper-class grave goods. Even more striking is the fact that traces of grid patterns have been found at archaeological sites, indicating that ordinary people played the same kind of games outdoors, marking out a 'board' on the ground and creating their own makeshift pieces.

Easily the most popular game was Senet ('Passing'), which was played on a long thirty-square (10 x 3) board. Each side had a number of uniform pieces, pawn-shapes for one and disc-shapes for the other. Games of Senet are often illustrated in tomb paintings, where they take on a symbolic significance, evidently picturing the dead person's struggle to defeat malignant powers and attain eternal life.

Women are often shown playing Senet with their husbands, sometimes with other members of the family looking on; but the surest sign of the game's popularity is the existence of a caricatured contest between a lion and an antelope, who sit at the board in a distressingly frivolous mood, both apparently trying to move at the same time.

Another popular game, 'Twenty Squares', was laid out as a central line of twelve squares, with four squares down each long side at one end. The rules of Senet and Twenty Squares are not known, but both were probably 'racing for home' games resembling Ludo, with bonus and forfeit squares and moves determined by 'dice' in the form of marked casting-sticks and knucklebones.

An older 'Snake Game', featuring a coiled snake with its head in the centre of the board, was probably based on the same principle; perhaps less ingeniously designed than the others, it seems to have disappeared by the end of the Old Kingdom.

Storytelling has been popular in most societies, and many narratives in the written literature of Egypt almost certainly derive from oral traditions. A picture of storytelling at court is found in a papyrus (the Papyrus Westcar) which, rather like *The Thousand and One Nights*, contains a series of tales about magicians within a framing story. The tales are supposedly being told by his sons to Khufu, the pyramid-building Old Kingdom monarch, and they prove highly effective in alleviating his boredom. Of course *Khufu and the Magician* is a written story – about people tellling stories – and as such belongs to the extensive literature of Ancient Egypt.

A female acrobat performs a back bend, her long curly hair trailing on the ground. This snapshot – a painting on a fragment of limestone – suggests how little tastes in entertainment have changed over the millennia.

Female musicians display their charms while performing on the double oboe, lute and harp. This is one of a number of well-preserved wall paintings from the tomb of Nakht, several of which are reproduced in this book.

STORIES, SONGS AND SERMONS

A wealth of Egyptian writing has survived on stone, papyri, clay tablets, and the ostraca and wooden boards used for school exercises. Though primarily a record, writing also served to assert status, to express feelings and even to work magic. We have king-lists, proclamations, ritual and funerary texts, tomb-wall autobiographies, medical, mathematical and magical treatises, business records, diplomatic and private letters, and much else. Only a small proportion of these are literature in the qualitative sense, but its bulk is larger than generally realized.

The principal genres are fiction, poetry and 'wisdom literature'. The works of fiction might be better described as romances, since fantasy, magic and trickery play a large part in the narrative. However, many of the romances are given a specific historical setting and even involve royal personages in the action. *Khufu and the Magicians* is set at the court of the king, and the stories of magic told by his sons (in effect stories-within-the-story) take place in the reign of his predecessors. The tale moves into the present when one of Khufu's sons produces a 110-year-old magician named Dedi into the king's presence, claiming that he can restore a decapitated head to its body. Khufu offers to have a prisoner beheaded, but Dedi refuses to use a human subject in this way, and demonstrates his skill instead on a goose and

Nefertari, Ramesses II's favourite queen, sits at a board playing the game of Senet. Thanks to the formulaic texts on the wall around her, she will know the 'moves' needed to pass into the afterlife.

an ox. The king's indifference to human life provides another interesting piece of evidence that the builder of the Great Pyramid was remembered, justly or otherwise, as a tyrant.

An ebony game-box from the tomb of Tutankhamun; it is set on a sled-like stand with animal-form legs. The box has two game surfaces (one on its base) and space for a drawer to hold the pieces.

The Egyptians enjoyed travel stories, which fed their craving for adventure while confirming some of their worst suspicions about foreigners. *The Shipwrecked Sailor* begins realistically, with one member of a failed expedition trying to console the leader by recounting his own experiences as the sole survivor of a voyage south. He is cast up on an island which seems like paradise until he encounters a gigantic serpent with a long beard, a gold body and lapis-lazuli-inlaid eyebrows. From this point, fantasy reigns. The serpent proves to be benevolent (and, incidentally, the ruler of never-never-land Punt) and the adventurer is able to return home laden with exotic gifts. Comments scattered through the narrative take the Shakespearian view of travel, that 'when I was at home I was in a better place'. In spite of which, the number of surviving copies and excerpts suggests that a more sober traveller's tale, *The Story of Sinuhe*, was the most popular of all Egyptian romances. It begins in Middle Kingdom times with the death of Amenemes I while Sinuhe is returning from a military expedition with the crown prince. Something he overhears alarms him so much that he seeks safety in flight. He eventually reaches Palestine, where he takes service with one of the local rulers and, after various adventures, achieves wealth and high rank. But as an elderly man he is drawn back to Egypt, although he is evidently uncertain of his welcome; but Pharaoh proves generous and Sinuhe's future – including an appropriate burial – is assured.

Some tales have a moral content, teaching that truth and justice will triumph in the end. *Truth and Falsehood* is a near-allegory in which Falsehood manages to have his brother Truth convicted of theft, blinded, and forced to serve as Falsehood's doorkeeper. Later Truth escapes Falsehood's plot to kill him, and has a son who turns the tables. *The Two Brothers* is, among other things, a variation on the Biblical story of Joseph and Potiphar's wife: Bata, who works for his older brother Anpu, rejects the advances of Anpu's wife, who takes her revenge by accusing him of assaulting her. The cheat is soon discovered and the wife killed and fed to the dogs, but Bata in his turn undergoes a more elaborate and magical version of wifely betrayal, metamorphizing several times before emerging at last as his faithless wife's child and the heir to the Egyptian throne!

Finally, *Khaemwese and Tabubu* is a macabre tale worthy of Edgar Allan Poe. Khaemwese was the son of Ramesses II; thanks to his father's longevity he never became king, but his doings as high priest of Ptah seem to have made an impression on the folk memory, causing him to become the hero of a number of stories. In this one his fascination with the occult leads him to purloin a magic book from a tomb. Shortly afterwards he becomes so sexually obsessed with a woman named Tabubu that to possess her he agrees to

In ancient Egypt tradition was venerated, but records of the past selective. On a typical king list like the one here, deviant figures such as the women Hatshepsut and the heretic Akhenaten were discreetly omitted.

will her his property and allows his children to be murdered; as he sits with her, horrified but besotted, he can hear the dogs eating their flesh. He has still not achieved his desires when he wakes and finds himself alone. His children are still alive, and Khaemwese, realizing that he is being hounded from beyond the tomb, humbly returns the magic book.

Egyptologists owe a debt to long-dead schoolboys, and to the masters who forced them to learn a scribe's skills by copying passages from classic texts: as a consequence, manuscripts were multiplied, greatly improving the text's chances of surviving. This is especially true of 'wisdom literature', a group of writings that generally reflect scribal values. The Egyptians sensibly called them 'instructions', since they consist of aphoristic statements about the right way to live, combining prudence with morality. Some, such as the *Instruction of Amenemhat I*, were purportedly written by monarchs or viziers. Scribal values are right in the forefront of *The Satire of the Trades*, which gleefully lists the drawbacks of other callings – the barber trudging the streets and touting for custom, the fisherman living in dread of crocodiles, the weaver working in virtual confinement, beaten if he takes a day off. The conclusion: 'there is no work that is not done under direction except the scribe's: he does the directing'. Another text, in oddly modern vein, declares that writing lasts for ever, providing a better guarantee of immortality than building a pyramid or begetting children. However, some wisdom literature is less elitist. *The Eloquent Peasant* for example uses a tale of injustice rectified to show a humble man's worth. And the *Instruction of Ptahotep*, said to have been written by an Old Kingdom vizier, advises the would-be minister not to be too proud of his knowledge and to 'take counsel with the ignorant man as with the learned'.

Some Egyptian writings resemble Biblical 'wisdom literature' such as Ecclesiastes, lamenting the brevity of human life. Similar sentiments are touchingly expressed in *The Song of the Harper*, where praise of hedonism is undermined by an awareness of the imminence of death. Any serious appreciation of ancient Egyptian poetry is severely restricted by the absence of written vowel-signs in any of the scripts, our consequent ignorance of pronunciation, and the absence of the music which often accompanied it. In writing verse, the Egyptians seem not to have used rhyme or metre, but imposed a pattern on the text by devices such as parallelism and repetition, giving a chant-like effect. Paeans to the glory of individual pharaohs are formally much the same as hymns to the gods. The *Hymn to the Aten*, composed by Akhenaten, is often said to be the first example in history of a monotheist composition, although the emphasis on the king as the Son of God gives it an unexpected turn.

Even in translation, Egyptian love-poetry, described earlier, is attractive in its expressions of sorrow, longing, fulfilment and delight in nature.

'THE WORDS OF THE GOD'

Writing, perhaps the single most important element in Egyptian culture, seems to have been introduced in about 3200 BC, not long before the unification of the Two Lands. The basic concepts of the Egyptian system were not invented independently, but were almost certainly borrowed from the Mesopotamian civilization of Sumer. Though employed at first for humble purposes – mainly the listing of commodities – writing soon assumed its crucial role. It distinguished the elite from the masses, making the mere use of a pen an indication of high status. It also acquired the magical properties believed to be present in names or symbols. So strong was this power that pharaohs habitually took over older monuments and replaced their predecessors' names with their own. Even a royal portrait could be appropriated in this fashion, since the written word evidently mattered more than any question of likeness: if it named the subject as Ramesses, he *was* Ramesses. The same kind of magical thinking led prudent Egyptians to mar or leave incomplete any dangerous picture-sign (such as a snake) on a tomb inscription, thereby robbing it of its potency.

We use the Greek term 'hieroglyphs' to describe the components of the Egyptian script; its meaning – sacred carvings – highlights the extent to which it is identified with formal inscriptions on stone buildings and tombs. The Egyptians were even more emphatic: these were *medu netcher*, the god's words. This high conception was reflected in the great beauty of the script, which no doubt explains why it endured for thousands of years despite its practical shortcomings.

Hieroglyphs are neatly simplified pictures or diagrams. Many are instantly legible as, for example, an arm, a snake or an owl. Most others, although more stylized, have a recognizable affinity with the object they represent: the top half of a circle indicates a (mound-shaped) loaf, while a wavy line stands for water. Had hieroglyphs been no more than pictures, Champollion's task would have been relatively simple – and the Egyptians would not have been able to communicate a great deal. But as well as representing its picture meaning, each sign could be used to convey its sound. The sound-value of, mouth, was *r*, which could be combined with other sounds to represent words that had nothing to do with the original picture-meanings; a rough equivalent in English would be to put together little pictures of a car and a small dog in order to write 'carpet'. There were also hieroglyphs which represented groups of two or three consonants such as *mw* and *sdm*, enabling words to be written more economically. All the examples cited have been consonants because there were no hieroglyphic signs for vowels. Consequently, although scholars know the meanings of most Egyptian words, the number and placing of the vowels, and pronunciation in general, are still a matter of guesswork, helped out a little by referring to related Coptic words. Hence the variations from book to book in the English versions of Re or Ra, Amun (Amon), Sneferu (Snofru), wedjat (wadjit,

Hacked out of history. Egyptians 'corrected' the past by defacing monuments and stelae, as has been done here: the names of undesirables have simply been obliterated from the records.

uajet) and other names. There was a real possibility of the Egyptian reader misunderstanding parts of a text, which the scribe tried to minimize by repeating some elements, and by adding an extra hieroglyph (known as a determinative or sense-sign) to clarify the meaning of a word by indicating the general category to which it belonged – as if car-pet were to be followed by a helpful 'house' sign. Hieroglyphic inscriptions were usually designed to fill the available space in a boldly effective fashion. The text unrolls without punctuation or breaks between words or sentences, the only special mark being the cartouche surrounding the name of a king. It might read from right to left, from left to right, or from the top downwards; however, it is easy to tell whether the direction is leftward or rightward, since the human and animal figures are always turned towards the beginning of the passage. Other, handier scripts developed from hieroglyphs. Busy scribes, equipped with reed pens, produced increasingly simplified versions of the original signs, and by about 2500 BC one of these was effectively a separate script, now known as hieratic. Increasingly cursive (joined up) and written from right to left, hieratic itself split into separate scripts during the New Kingdom, one of which has a neat 'copper plate' for literary manuscripts, whereas the other was a rapid business hand. Later scripts were developed that made it possible to write even more rapidly. Demotic ('popular'), which appeared around the mid-7th century BC, became an all-purpose script, used on both documents and monuments; it was one of the three scripts on the Rosetta Stone whose discovery led to the decipherment of Egyptian writing.

A detail, showing Northern Constellations, from the ceiling of the burial chamber in the tomb of Seti I. The vast vault of the ceiling is, in effect, a star map, enabling the king to tell the time and date.

LEARNING AND THE SCIENCES

To the Greeks, Egypt was the fountainhead of knowledge, and Greek philosophers of genius such as Pythagoras and Plato were widely believed to have studied and acquired secret doctrines there. What actually impressed the Greeks was the antiquity of Egypt, for in reality the Egyptian mind had little of the Greek passion for seeking out the laws and principles behind phenomena.

The Egyptians made important discoveries and put them to practical use, but they were remarkably uninterested in generalizing from them. Moreover, at an early date their veneration for tradition and the written word led them to enquire less and rely on authority and precedent for the answer to problems. In the final analysis, mathematics (for example) was only an aspect of a magical universe dominated by the gods; if there was a proper study for mankind, it was not mathematics but theology, a science that the Egyptians pursued with ardour.

Even their own past aroused little curiosity in the Egyptians. As far as we know, pharaonic Egypt produced only a few lists of kings or events before the Greco-Roman era. Only then, under Ptolemy II, did the priest named Manetho compose a history of Egypt; the cultural ambience in which he moved is revealed by the fact that he wrote in Greek, although his calling makes it certain that in pursuing his researches he was able to read ancient inscriptions and papyri. Although known only in excerpted fragments and sometimes badly mistaken, Manetho's work has provided a basis for all subsequent historical investigation.

Egyptian geography was similarly list-oriented, apparently never going beyond the naming of provinces, towns, temples, local gods and products. The sciences in which the Egyptians did the most interesting work were mathematics, astronomy and medicine. In mathematics they used decimals, devising signs for 1, 10, 100, 1,000, 100,000 and 1,000,000 (the same sign also meaning 'countless'). They could add and subtract efficiently, but multiplication was done by breaking sums down into simpler sums, the products of which could be found by doubling, and finally added up:

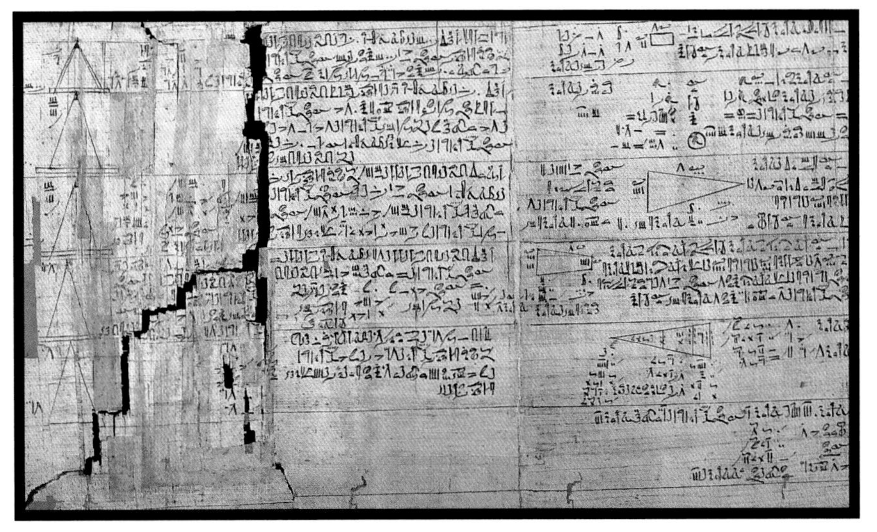

The Rhind Mathematical Papyrus shows the ancient Egyptians at their number-work; the papyrus is actually a copy, made c.1600 BC by the priest Ahmose, of an older treatise. The problems here concern triangles and land areas.

$$
\begin{aligned}
7 \times 7 = \quad 1 \times 7 &= 7 \\
2 \times 7 &= 14 \\
4 \times 7 &= \underline{28} \\
& \underline{49}
\end{aligned}
$$

The procedure was followed in reverse for division. Fractions were also reduced, ⅚ being treated as ½ plus ⅓. In spite of such clumsy methods, measurement of length, area, volume and angles was efficient enough to use in building pyramids. The principal measure of distance was the Bible-familiar cubit, which represented seven hands' breadths. The surviving mathematical texts consist of problems and solutions, without statements of principles or rules.

Similarly, the astronomical observations made by the Egyptians were never used as the basis for theorizing. They found the night sky of intense interest, if only because the king, and perhaps others, could hope to become 'imperishable stars', and the map of the heavens was directly related to the Egyptian calendar. Sirius, the bright 'dog star', rose above the horizon on about 19 July, beginning the new year and, more or less simultaneously, the inundation.

As well as identifying five of the planets, or 'ever-restless stars', the Egyptians constructed star maps, felt to be so significant that they might be painted on the ceiling of a tomb; the most famous example is Seti I's. The maps, or clocks, consisted of 36 groups of stars, or decans, each decan rising at dawn for ten days of the year.

Slightly adjusted by the addition of five divine 'birthdays', this gave a 365-day year, which the Egyptians divided into twelve 30-day months, each with three 10-day weeks; the days were divided into twenty-four hours, counted if necessary by water-clocks. The 365-day year was, of course, six hours short of the true year, eventually leading to serious discrepancies between civic and seasonal time.

The temples are likely to have been the main places of learning, which perhaps centred on the schools-cum-scriptoria known as 'Houses of Life'. These may also have housed Egypt's libraries, although small niches in the temple walls seem to have served a similar purpose. Distinguishing between a library and a record office is difficult until the Ptolemaic period, when the great library at Alexandria became renowned as one of the glories of antiquity, only to perish by fire in the late 3rd century AD.

HEALTH AND HEALING

Egyptian medical expertise was famous throughout the ancient world. In the 6th century BC the kings of Persia made a point of having Egyptians as their personal physicians; but the Persians were late-comers compared with the Hittite monarch Hattusilis III, who sent a message to Ramesses II (1279-1213 BC) asking for a doctor able to treat his sister's infertility. (Ramesses saved himself the trouble by providing a common-sense diagnosis: at sixty, his ally's sister was unlikely to benefit from even the most skilful treatment.) The Greeks were equally impressed, so much so that Herodotus put forward the dubious claim that most Egyptian physicians were specialists, concerned only with the ailments affecting a particular organ.

This reputation was at least partly based on the antiquity of Egyptian records. Doctors were able to consult a number of manuals, of which the oldest copy now surviving, the Kahun Medical Papyrus, dates from about 2000 BC; however, it is more than likely that this manual and similar compilations originated even earlier, during the Old Kingdom period. They contain long lists of ailments, notes on probable developments, and details of the appropriate remedies. From a present-day point of view the contents are an extraordinary mixture, ranging from common-sense prescriptions to concoctions reminiscent of witches' brews, featuring ingredients such as mice droppings and snake fat; wisely, doctors stirred their medications into milk, honey or beer to make them more palatable.

To judge from the manuals, Egyptian medicine was most effective in the treatment of external afflictions such as wounds, swellings and fractures. Doctors set splints, lanced swellings and pulled together the lips of wounds with bandages; it is possible that stitches were used for more serious cases. We know a good deal about the Egyptians' teeth, but rather less about dentistry; it is not even clear whether a separate dental profession existed. Yet examination of skulls

A boy being circumcised; he places his hand on the priest's head to steady himself. Detail from a relief in the tomb of Ankhmahor at Saqqara; c.2200 BC.

and mummies has shown that tooth problems were endemic and must have caused considerable suffering. Modern sweet-related decay scarcely existed, but teeth worn down – often right down to the pulp – were universal, mainly because of the gritty elements in stone-ground bread and the presence of the fine desert sand that crept into everything including food. Even pharaohs were not exempt, and suffered from the consequent infections, abcesses and loosening of the teeth. Attempts seem to have been made to support loose teeth with a type of packing, and a form of bridgework was devised in which lost teeth were held in place by being tied to their neighbours with gold or silver thread.

The Egyptians' concern for their appearance is confirmed by the number of 'cosmetic' items in the medical papyri. These included cures for baldness (a revolting combination of large-animal fats) and treatments for greying hair, offensive body odours and bad breath. Curiously enough, there are no diets for the overweight.

The treatment of internal ailments was the least impressive aspect of Egyptian medicine. Physicians had some knowledge of anatomy, although far less than their mastery of embalming techniques might suggest. Since embalming was a religious ritual, medical men would not have been present when it was carried out, and the subject was probably not one that could be discussed with outsiders. The Egyptians had identified pulse points, but they thought of the heart not as a pump but as the centre of consciousness and personality. Moreover it was linked to other parts of the body by a system of channels, through which not only blood but air, semen and excrement circulated. In so far as they possessed a general theory of medicine, they believed that good health was ensured by keeping the channels open and free from malign influences. The 'theory' may well be based on an analogy between the functioning of the body and Egypt's life-giving river/irrigation system.

Inevitably, Egyptian physicians were unable to identify a range of ailments that are now known from the scientific examination of mummies. They range from tuberculosis and cancer to parasitic infestations – including bilharzia, then as now an unwanted gift of the Nile. Many illnesses have been diagnosed on the basis of pictures and statuary, including the Frohlich's disease, a glandular disorder, believed to account for the otherwise extraordinary appearance of the heretic pharaoh Akhenaten.

Despite their doctors' great reputations, Egyptians do not seem to have been healthier than most other peoples in antiquity: examination of skeletons and mummies suggests that ordinary working people had a life expectancy of about twenty-five, by contrast with an upper-class figure of around forty. Most of the evidence about workers is limited because it comes from their skeletons (mummification was for the better-off), but it does reveal that many of them engaged in labour heavy enough to cause significant bone damage.

Many apparently bizarre prescriptions in medical manuals represent a magical rather than a scientific attempt at a cure. This is in fact a modern distinction that no Egyptian would have recognized: since evil spirits, or the gods themselves, inflicted illness, any effective remedy was part of the spiritual dimension. The wearing of amulets – protective charms – was essential, in life and after-life, as a form of preventive medicine. Prayers at the shrines of gods such as Bes or Imhotep were part of a healing process that might culminate in residence at a cult centre, in the hope of experiencing a dream cure – or, to put it another way, the patient hoped to recover through rest and psychic self-help.

An example of ancient dentistry. These teeth were bound together with gold wire so that the sound tooth would support a neighbour that was loose or had fallen out; the modern equivalent of this advanced technique is bridgework.

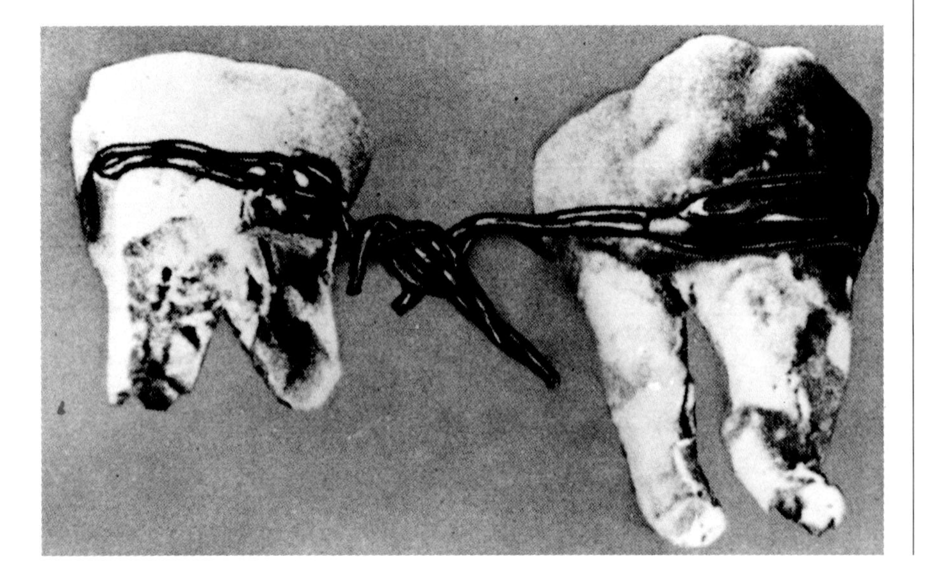

The Temple of Isis on the island of Philae, here shown on its original site, standing directly above the Nile just south of Aswan. Though ancient, the temple was extensively rebuilt during the Ptolemaic and Roman periods: hence its wonderful condition.

TRAVEL AND TRADE

Most Egyptians never went further from their homes than the nearest provincial town, but an active minority did travel from place to place. Nobles shuttled between their estates and their town houses. Officials went up and down the Nile with stone for building projects or grain for the king's stores. Merchants carried wares for sale, while pilgrims sought divine favour by journeys to Abydos and other sacred centres.

Travelling, even for long distances, was most commonly done on foot. Donkeys were used as pack animals but were not normally ridden, and camels were probably not domesticated until several hundred years after the introduction of the horse by the Hyksos. Papyrus boats were useful for hunting or crossing short stretches of water, using a paddle or pole, and the light Egyptian chariot was suited to brief, spectacular forays into the desert or on the battlefield. But the most comfortable and reliable form of long-distance travel was by one of the many vessels plying up and down Egypt's greatest highway, the Nile.

From the Nile, a traveller could easily reach every corner of settled, civilized Egypt. As if arranged by providence, the river flowed north and the main winds blew south, so that travel in either direction, assisted by oars and sails, provided no serious problems. A great deal is known about Egyptian ships, not only from tomb paintings and models, but also from ship burials. No fewer than five of these existed around the Great Pyramid, and one actual ship, the 'solar bark' of King Khufu, was found disassembled but intact, in 1954; it has since been reconstructed, and is displayed in the Bark Museum at Giza. Apart from a mast and sail, its basic design – upturned prow and stern, central cabin, banks of oars for rowing and one or more steering oars – changed in only a few details over a millennium or more, although a wider range of types developed during

The solar bark of King Khufu, found in a pit close to the Great Pyramid in 1954. It is a miraculously preserved example of the shipping that piled up and down the Nile 4,500 years ago.

the New Kingdom. With pilgrim and pleasure-boats afloat, barges carrying building stone and fishermen pursuing their trade, the river must have presented the liveliest of spectacles.

Egyptians were much less enthusiastic about venturing beyond the Nile Valley. When they did, they preferred to travel as part of a large, military-style expedition, and their reports of a successful venture read like splendid victories won against formidable odds. The surrounding desert was as hostile as most foreign lands, but it held precious materials, and mines and quarries were worked under military guard; Wadi Hammamat in the eastern desert provided gold and building stone, but stone was quarried at other sites, some of them very remote. Some of the oldest maps in the world were made to identify these places.

There was no coinage in Egypt (or in the rest of the ancient world) until the 6th century BC. Consequently all trade was based on barter. In Egypt most commodities did have a generally accepted value, based on the amounts of each that could be exchanged for a given weight of metal. But even when the value of an object for sale was known, the would-be buyer still had to assemble objects of equivalent value that the seller was prepared to accept in exchange. The difficulties were formidable (a man selling a bed may not be willing to be paid entirely in geese), and it is not surprising that we hear very little about the activities of merchants, although they certainly did exist. Most transactions took place between ordinary people at local markets, where surplus produce or craftsmen-made objects might be exchanged.

The largest transactions of all were state-controlled. Taxes were assessed and collected in kind, as were salaries and wages. Large-scale trade with foreign lands was also state-sponsored, and was often conducted in the guise of a friendly ambassadorial trip. From the early Dynastic period to the end of the New Kingdom, the city-state of Byblos, close to modern Beirut, was Egypt's main trading-point with Asia, supplying the cedars and other timber products that the pharaohs lacked. It became an outpost of Egyptian culture and, while the Egyptian empire was at its height, effectively a client state. But when an Egyptian fleet arrived to trade, its goods, including ivory, alabaster and gold, were presented to the king as Pharaoh's gifts, and the Egyptian ships were filled up with 'gifts' of the kind they had come for. The absence of these ceremonious goings-on undoubtedly added to the difficulties of Wenamun, the hero of the story described earlier (page 46); instead of arriving as an open-handed ambassador, he had turned up in a borrowed ship with a hard-luck story that only emphasized the decline of Egyptian prestige under the last Ramessides.

Their familiar relationship with Byblos suited the conservative temperament of the Egyptians. But they were ready to travel much further afield for products that they wanted badly enough. One of these was lapis-lazuli, which came from distant Bactria, on the borders of India. To buy it Egyptian agents went to Tefer, a Mesopotamian city on the trade route to Bactria; and for a time the pharaohs thought it worth contracting an alliance with this land beyond the Persian Gulf.

As we have seen, the Egyptians penetrated Nubia, or Kush, from early times, valuing it as a source of gold, ivory, ebony and slaves. Like Byblos, Nubia was heavily influenced by Egyptian culture and at times owed allegiance to the pharaoh. This was not the case with Punt, a kingdom so distant that storytellers sometimes would use it as a never-never-land setting for their tales. It offered a range of exotic African products, but what drew the Egyptians above all was incense, which was needed in huge quantities for the service of the gods. Although expedition reports include the complimentary speeches supposedly made on both sides, relief scenes from Hatshepsut's temple suggest that in fact 'silent trading' took place, with each party laying out a range of goods, increasing or subtracting from the piles until both were content to make an exchange.

Living in troubled times, Ramesses III attached corps of archers to his fleet and caravans. Later pharaohs wielded power less effectively, but contacts with Crete, Greece and Cyprus nevertheless multiplied, eventually drawing Egypt into the classical Mediterranean world.

Workmen carrying an incense tree, transported from the Land of Punt in order to establish it in Egyptian soil; painted relief from the Temple of Hatshepsut, the female pharaoh who sent out the expedition to Punt.

4 RULERS AND WARRIORS

THE KING OF EGYPT WAS A GOD ON EARTH, AND EXERCISED A GOD-LIKE AUTHORITY. MINISTERS AND BUREAUCRATS CARRIED OUT THE ROYAL WILL, COLLECTING TAXES, ORGANIZING PROGRAMMES OF PUBLIC WORKS, AND RECRUITING FOR THE ARMED FORCES. ON THEIR MONUMENTS THE PHARAOHS WERE SHOWN AS MIGHTY WARRIORS, BUT ACCIDENTS OF GEOGRAPHY ENSURED THAT THE EGYPTIANS WERE NOT A WARLIKE PEOPLE FOR MOST OF THEIR LONG HISTORY. HOWEVER, DURING THE NEW KINGDOM THEY BECAME ACTIVE EMPIRE-BUILDERS, CLASHING WITH RIVALS IN FIERCELY CONTESTED BATTLES AND ALWAYS (AT LEAST ON THEIR MONUMENTS) EMERGING VICTORIOUS.

THE GOD-KING

The king played a central role in the Egyptian scheme of things. He combined the human and the divine in his own person, and consequently acted as an intermediary between the everyday world and the realms of the spirit. A god incarnate, he owned the land and ruled it absolutely; his word was – truly – law. This conception of a god-king appears to date back to the beginning of Egyptian history, and even the earliest records imply an identity between the king and the falcon-god Horus, son of the supreme, life-giving sun-god Re.

The king's responsibility was to maintain or restore the cosmic order, known as Maat. This was visualized as a harmonious state of affairs that ought to prevail at every level, including the spiritual, political and social. Without Maat there could be no peace, prosperity or justice in the

Ramesses III offers incense to the god Ptah. The god appears in his funerary aspect, in effect as an incarnation of the god of the dead, Osiris.

land, and among the indispensable conditions for its establishment were a legitimate, literally god-given king and the existence of appropriate relations between Egypt and its gods.

'Appropriate relations' included not only devotions but abundant, valuable offerings and the building and rebuilding of temples. Monarchs who labelled themselves as 'beloved of Maat' gave grandiloquent accounts of their activities and even claimed extra credit by implying that their ancestors had let things slide. 'Nothing like it had ever been seen before my time,' boasted Tuthmosis III of his work on the temple of Ptah in Thebes. 'I made it greater than it had been before.'

The enrichment of the temples from generation to generation was potentially dangerous, and when the power of the Ramesside pharaohs declined in the early 11th century BC, control of Upper Egypt passed to Herihor, the high priest of Amun, and his successors. In less troubled times the pharoah could rely on his divinity to control the priesthood. In a sense he was the true high priest, since he was supposed to conduct every significant ceremony in the temples, although for practical reasons this was done by priest-substitutes. When the pharaoh did happen to be present, he took over, for example, 'visiting his father' Amun at Thebes. On temple walls it is always the pharaoh who stands face to face with the god, making offerings.

Despite the priest-substitutes, ritual performances took up much of a monarch's time. Every year he carried out the ceremonies required to make the Nile rise and flood the land; later, when it was about to fall, he inaugurated the 'Opening of the Dykes'; and later still he sailed through the dykes in his barge to celebrate another successful taming of the waters. Reaping a handful of wheat in honour of the god Min, or making carefully timed appearances on the balcony of a palace, the king performed magical acts whose remote descendants survive in the cutting of ribbons and smashing of bottles against ships' hulls.

In order to carry out his duties the pharaoh wore a variety of crowns and regalia. Depending

Opposite: Ramesses II holds an offering table. In theory, only the pharaoh could have direct contact with the gods, since he was himself a god in human form; in practice, high priests acted as surrogates for most of the time.

on the occasion, he put on the long, balloon-like white crown of Upper Egypt or the wide red crown of the north, with its flat top, high curving tail and curious, coiled ribbon projecting at the front. The double crown, known as 'Two Mighty Ones', neatly fused the two and symbolized the union of Upper and Lower Egypt. The addition of plumes on either side of the white crown turned it into the *atef*, worn during certain religious ceremonies; it was particularly associated with Osiris, the god of death and resurrection. During the New Kingdom period the helmet-like blue crown was introduced; Ay, Tutankhamun's successor, is wearing it on the wall painting of the young king's funeral.

A pharaoh is sometimes shown wearing a wig, but in portrayals with no specific ritual connotations his head is more often covered by a *nemes* headcloth. This red-striped fabric was arranged so that it lay close across the brow, with a large flap hanging down each side of the head; to judge from the many surviving images of the *nemes*, it created a simple but elegant effect. The pharaoh's brow was commonly adorned with the *uraeus* (a rearing cobra) for his protection. The cobra was a southern symbol, often twinned with its Lower Egyptian counterpart, the vulture. The pharaoh also wore an artificial false beard on ceremonial occasions and, with arms crossed and held tightly to the chest, carried a crook and flail.

One ritual of obvious importance, the *sed* festival, remains something of a puzzle. The *heb-sed*, or royal jubilee, was celebrated when a king had reigned for thirty years. During its course the enthroned king received the homage of his subjects and asserted his sovereignty by running between sets of markers that represented the boundaries of Egypt. As so often, the origins of

Foreigners bringing tribute, including a giraffe, to their Egyptian overlord; from the tomb of Amenhotep Huyi, an official of the 14th century BC whose life was one of the great success stories of antiquity: he was eventually deified.

the custom go back to the beginning of Egyptian history. Narmer, the first king of the Two Lands, is shown on a mace-head celebrating his *heb-sed*, and there are many later images of kings enthroned or running. (And not just kings: Hatshepsut too runs, wearing a crown and false beard, on a relief at Karnak.)

The point of the festival was evidently to demonstrate, or perhaps to renew, the vigour of the monarch and his mastery over Egypt. The puzzle is that many kings are recorded as celebrating the festival, although relatively few of them enjoyed a thirty-year reign. One possibility is that in such cases the celebration is a pictorial fiction, anticipating an event that failed to materialize. A more convincing explanation is that some excuse was found to bring the festival forward in time. It was a public holiday, so such a decision would not have been unpopular among the people; and one advantage of holding the festival early must have been that the king was more likely to be fit enough to run. If, as seems possible, the *heb-sed* was originally a test of the king's physical fitness to go on ruling, evasive action on the part of later monarchs would be quite understandable.

Despite his vital religious functions, the pharaoh never became the kind of sacred king whose ritualized existence made it impossible for him to take an unceremonious step. He remained an active earthly ruler, expected to look after his subjects and lead them to war. Ministers and generals might in practice take many decisions, and no doubt there were very young, very old or merely incapable individuals who were never more than figureheads; but in normal times the pharaohs seem to have remained the masters of Egypt's government and army. The consciousness of being a god must have made it easier to command others; indeed, every royal idea appears to have been greeted with rapture, and we can only speculate on the oblique means by which advisers must have worked to change the king's mind or convince him that their own proposals were better.

The king moved around a good deal, on tours of inspection, and everywhere he and his court found a palace ready to be occupied. In fact the palace was the most visible symbol of royalty, the *per-aa* or 'Great House'. From the New Kingdom onwards the term was applied to the king himself: he became the *per-aa* or, turned into English via Greek, pharaoh. Interestingly, we still speak of royal dynasties as houses.

Egyptian archers. They appear on a large relief, celebrating the hunting exploits of Ramesses III, on the pylon of his temple at Medinet Habu. Rather oddly, the archers and other soldiers carrying shields are shown marching in formation as if to war.

In view of all this, unquestioned royal authority and an unchallenged succession were clearly vital to the health of the state. Consequently reliefs and statues proclaimed the pharaoh's legitimacy by showing his divine birth, his suckling by various gods, and their bestowal of the monarchy upon him; no doubt this religious sanction was all the more energetically deployed when some shadow in fact hung over its subject. One way in which a new ruler could establish himself was by his filial conduct towards his predecessor, whatever their actual relationship: he proved himself a true son by performing the appropriate rites at the funeral (as, for example, Ay did for Tutankhamun) and subsequently made sure that the tomb and mortuary monuments of the dead man were completed.

The political records of ancient Egypt rarely let us behind the scenes, but it is difficult to believe that there were no intrigues and factions at the court of the god-king. In particular, the fact that the pharaohs co-opted their heirs suggests that the succession could be a dangerous issue, bringing into play the ambitions of courtiers and the rivalries of queens.

EGYPT'S QUEENS

On royal monuments an Egyptian queen is usually shown as standing dutifully by the side of her king, or watching admiringly while he performs great deeds. As his wife she enjoyed the reflected glory of his semi-divinity, and her own prestige was assured if she bore him a male heir; but her role in affairs of state was largely confined to ceremonial and religious duties. As in other cultures, queens probably influenced their husbands in private, and a few exceptional women were able to make a visible public impact on events.

An Egyptian king had a number of wives and concubines, but there was normally a single Great Wife who was regarded as his official consort. It was she who would appear with him in public and, if sufficiently fertile, provide the heir to the throne. Some Great Wives obviously inspired deep affection in their husbands. Nefertiti, the heretic Akhenaten's queen, is given unprecedented prominence on monuments of the period: unusually, she is sometimes portrayed on her own, and in one scene she is even shown smiting her enemies in approved kingly fashion. Less predictably, the ultra-polygamous Ramesses II honoured his Great Wife, Nefertari, in spectacular fashion, in effect making her a goddess by dedicating one of his Abu Simbel temples to her.

The backbone of government. The scribe sits in classic position, upright and cross-legged, ready to write on the partly unrolled papyrus on his lap. His reed brush, originally held in his right hand, has gone missing.

In many cases the Great Wife was a close blood relative of the pharaoh. For a long time, the frequency of royal brother-sister unions led scholars to believe that the succession passed through the female, so that a male candidate could only make good his claim by marrying the king's daughter. The theory was partly prompted by a puritanical belief that these 'unnatural' relationships could only have been formed for imperative political reasons. It has been discredited by the evidence that royal marriages also took place between unrelated couples, and that queens of non-royal blood might be highly honoured. However, where there was no male heir, marriage with the previous pharaoh's daughter did become important in giving the man who took over (for example a military man like Horemheb) a more legitimate claim than his rivals, and several new dynasties were founded in this way.

When a pharaoh married a close relative he was only doing what his grandest relatives – deities such as Osiris and Isis – had done long before. The mating of semi-divinities cannot have seemed unnatural, and it did incidentally prevent a possibly dangerous outsider from entering the royal family. Marriage outside the sacred line may well have been repugnant to its female members, and it is noteworthy that the pharaohs refused to send their daughters abroad as the brides of allied monarchs, even though they happily added foreign princesses to the ranks of their own wives.

Equally honoured with the Great Wife was 'the Mother of the King' – usually the widowed queen whose son had ascended the throne; some queens, notably Tiy, Amenhotep III's wife and Akhenaten's mother, were visibly successful in both roles. On occasion an able queen mother could exercise real political power by acting as the regent for her still-small child. (Ironically the

This touching scene shows two obviously young people, Tutankhamun and his queen, Ankhesenamun, in a garden setting; the object is a painted ivory panel on a wooden chest buried with the king.

super-successful Hatshepsut used her position as a stepmother to make herself 'king'.) The most striking examples come from the early New Kingdom period, during or after the expulsion of the Hyksos. Ahmose, the founder of the 18th Dynasty, put up a stele in the temple of Amun at Karnak, praising his mother Ahhotep as the 'mistress of the land', who had looked after the army, rounded up fugitives and deserters, and driven out rebels – just when, or in what circumstances, we do not know. Ahmose seems to have appreciated women's qualities, for he consulted his sister-wife, Ahmose-Nefertari, before making decisions. She may have been regent during the early reign of her son Amenhotep I, and after her death a cult grew up around her.

Unlike the Great Wives, the many secondary queens led obscure lives. Even the imported daughters of foreign kings, after a grand ceremonial welcome, were consigned to the harem, along with other wives, concubines, children, nurses and servants. During the New Kingdom the harem seems to have become a large, influential institution, of some economic importance, but the nature of its operations is still unclear.

GOVERNING THE LAND

Social and political stability, desirable in themselves, were also part of the cosmic order that it was the duty of the pharaohs to uphold. More prosaically, a sophisticated system of government and administration had to be developed to support the royal and religious establishment and organize monumental works on a scale not seen elsewhere until the 19th century AD.

The kingdom of Egypt was a bureaucratic state, dependent on the written assessments and records made by a host of scribes; they were, in effect, Egypt's civil servants, although their paymasters included nobles, great estate owners and temples as well as the royal administration. Whatever the peasants may have thought, officially the scribes were regarded as the backbone of the state, and great prestige attached to the instruments and symbols of writing. As we have seen, no officer of state, however grand, seems to have felt it beneath him to be portrayed in stone like an ordinary scribe, sitting cross-legged on the ground, with a sheet of papyrus partly unrolled on his lap and a brush in one hand, poised to write.

Political control of the bureaucracy was in practice divided between the capital and the localities. The king had the power of appointment to every position in the state, but prudence and custom normally inclined him to confirm influential families in local offices that were, in effect, hereditary. During the Old Kingdom most 'central' government was controlled by the king or a member of his immediate family. There was a chief minister from early times, now often referred to as the vizier, but even he was usually of

Nubians and Asiatics paying their respects; copy by Belzoni of a painting in the Valley of the Kings. Egyptian artists always made sure that foreigners were easy to identify.

royal blood; the exception was also the most famous of Old Kingdom viziers, Imhotep, who built the step pyramid at Saqqara for the 3rd Dynasty king Djoser.

During the Middle Kingdom the vizier, no longer a relation of the king, acquired increasingly wide powers. He was the chief magistrate; he was ultimately responsible for the collection of taxes and the payment of wages; and his office collected statistics, conducting a biennial census and monitoring the amount of rainfall and the height of each year's inundation. The pharaohs' sons often worked for a time under the vizier, acquiring practical experience of government but perhaps also keeping an eye on the way the minister used or abused his powers. From the 18th Dynasty onwards there were two viziers, one for the north and one for the south of the country; the object of this change may have been to reduce the administrative burden, but it may also have been made to prevent too much power being concentrated in the hands of a single man. At least one vizier (Amenemhet, subsequently Amenemhet I, founder of the 12th Dynasty) is suspected of having raised troops in the king's name and then used them to seize power for himself.

The pharaoh's government could normally rely on the co-operation of the forty-two provinces or nomes. Each of these was identified by its own animal symbol and had its own capital, cult centre and local character. The position of provincial governor, or nomarch, was usually hereditary, held by the chief of one of the leading noble clans. He was responsible for the collection of taxes and, where necessary, for raising troops. The nomarchs lived in style, apeing their royal masters by building large palaces and ensuring they were buried in splendid rock-cut tombs.

During troubled times the provincial governors became more or less independent rulers, collecting taxes on their own behalf and even waging war on their fellow-nomarchs. This 'feudal' disintegration seems to have been most marked after the collapse of the Old Kingdom; the reassertion of royal authority in the Middle Kingdom seems to have been accompanied by new security measures to prevent such a situation occurring again. Later reorganizations probably had a similar aim.

A slave; detail from a relief on the Temple of Ramesses II at Abu Simbel. Most slaves were prisoners of war, although some Egyptians fell into slavery through debt.

Although Egypt could not altogether avoid the fate of other empires – eras of decline, fragmentation, foreign occupation – she enjoyed remarkably long periods of order and stability that testified to the efficiency of the administration and the cohesiveness of Egyptian society.

LAW AND ORDER

The Egyptians lived under a god-king, in a state that has often been described as a theocracy; but the crimes and disputes that occurred were of a kind found in most human societies. Consequently Egypt too had its magistrates and courts, police and penalties.

The king was the fount of justice, able to punish or forgive at will. In one of the most famous Egyptian stories, *The Tale of Sinuhe*, the hero is received by the pharaoh and, after recounting his fantastic adventures in foreign lands, is pardoned for having left his post and is even given great riches; the climax appears to be brought about by the intervention of the pharaoh's queen and his children, who marvel at the stories and plead for Sinuhe, in a scene that is obviously being stage-managed to display the pharaoh's goodness and generosity. In most real cases the vizier would take charge if the issue was important enough, condemning the worst offenders to death or mutilation; the slicing-off of noses and ears was a common punishment, probably because it was inexpensive and did not prevent the culprit from working as a slave or convict. Lesser affairs were probably dealt with by officials in much the same way. In the towns, councils of elders dealt with local matters such as property disputes in the wake of divorce.

No codified set of laws is known before the Late Period, but even if they did not exist, a wealth of precedents could be found in the state archives to supplement common-sense conclusions. From the point of view of the state, the worst offences were failure to pay taxes, avoiding the corvée (forced labour) and deserting from the army. Whether or not the offender could be found, his entire family was often punished. Failure to pay seems to have provoked an early

Prisoners, roped together, shuffle forward awkwardly in this relief detail from the Temple of Ramesses III. In Egyptian art, the country's foes are always dead, prisoners, or in full flight.

Shattered habitation. The Egyptian's 'eternal house' proved all too vulnerable to greedy intruders. Even pyramids and rock-cut tombs, police patrols and terrible curses, failed to deter robbers.

retaliation without recourse to a court: the scribal assessor arrived at the farm with some security men and had the miscreant beaten; the bastinado – beating administered on the soles of the feet – was already known as a singularly effective form of punishment.

A good many disputes were probably resolved by the community, without official intervention. Local oracles were frequently consulted when there had been a minor theft or an argument over property. The oracle may well have served as a mouthpiece for community opinion, pointing the finger at a culprit and perhaps ensuring the return of stolen goods without any need to take matters further. At Deir el-Medina, the village that housed workers employed on the royal tombs, courts were held by the foreman and scribes, who were empowered to inflict surprisingly heavy sentences: on occasion these might range from hundred-stroke beatings to multiple brandings. For much of Egyptian history the police were, in effect, special units of the army. They patrolled the frontiers, kept Bedouin raiders in check, guarded the convicts working in the desert mines and quarries, escorted caravans, and supervised foreign visitors and residents.

Early in the New Kingdom a more distinct state police was formed, mainly from the formidable Medjoi, Nubian warriors who had been taken into royal service during the wars against the Hyksos. They looked after the security of the royal family, policed Thebes and patrolled the royal tombs in the Valley of the Kings.

Protecting the tombs was a losing battle. Lacking a vocal owner in residence and containing quantities of valuable objects, they tempted and fell victim to generations of poor or greedy people. Egypt's tomb-robbers were persistent and ingenious, digging claustrophobic tunnels through rubble, climbing high internal barriers, and nimbly avoiding traps and false passages – although no doubt many operations of the sort were conducted on the basis of inside information that made the difficulties less daunting. The official penalty for these blasphemous burglaries was death by impalement, although we have no way of knowing whether it was regularly carried out. The records of tomb-robbery trials include a major scandal which broke during the reign of Ramesses IX, when Paser, the mayor of Thebes, alleged that the head of the necroplis police, Pawero, was implicated in large-scale violation of the west bank tombs. There is a familiar ring about the subsequent proceedings, in which official denials were followed by the production of surprise witnesses who confused the issue, and further enquiries reached no clear conclusion.

WAR AND DIPLOMACY

Deserts, cataracts and distance protected Egypt from hostile states and allowed the Egyptians to develop a distinctive and long-enduring way of life; by contrast, the Near Eastern cradle of civilization, though equally venerable, was a scene of constant marching and counter-marching, as Sumerians, Akkadians, Hurrians, Assyrians and many other peoples snatched their moments of glory and then disappeared. With the single exception of the Hyksos invaders after the collapse of the Middle Kingdom, ancient Egypt was not seriously threatened by foreign domination for well over two thousand years.

However, the Egyptians had plenty of experience of warfare. The unification of the country occurred at the end of a series of conflicts between Nilotic states, and the victory of the Upper Egyptian rulers does not seem to have been complete, or at any rate secure, until the end of the 2nd Dynasty. The earliest 'political' document, the Palette of Narmer, is dominated by images of violence: the king smiting a foreigner, stricken foes, decapitated prisoners, and a rampaging bull-king destroying a town. The 'smiting' image became a standard way of representing royal power, and even if it is not a literal record of events, there is no mistaking the attitudes and ambitions it expressed.

Nevertheless the five hundred years of Old Kingdom history were remarkably free from wars. Penetration of Nubia seems to have led to some fighting, but the Egyptians were able to undertake mining and trading operations on a reasonably friendly basis without attempting to conquer the region.

During the 5th and 6th Dynasties there were said to have been incursions into Palestine and Syria. They have left little trace and may have amounted to no more than long-distance pursuits of raiders; one of these is recorded on a wall in the tomb of Weni, a counsellor of the 6th Dynasty

A magnificent dagger and sheath from the tomb of Tutankhamun; the king was buried carrying them on his mummified person. The blade is hardened gold, and the handle and sheath of inlaid gold.

king Pepi I, who chased Bedouin marauders into Palestine.

Most of the 'tens of thousands' that Weni claimed to have led into Palestine would have been local levies. There was no standing army in the Old Kingdom, although a royal bodyguard and border patrols must have been kept up. By the end of the period, Nubians, Libyans and western Asiatics were already considered traditional enemies, to be included on the lists of hated beings in 'execration texts'; these were written on pottery jars and then ritually smashed so that those named might suffer an equivalent fate. But when the Old Kingdom fell, the reason was internal decay, signalled by the shift of power – including the power to raise troops – from the king to the governors of the nomes.

Royal authority was gradually re-established during the Middle Kingdom, a period in which military involvement beyond the frontiers began to be more common. Early Middle Kingdom rulers were said to have sent expeditions against the Libyans and into Syria, but a more thorough-going militarist attitude appears with Amenemhat I, the founder of the 12th Dynasty. A usurper, Amenemhat consolidated his hold on power by a show of force, sailing up the Nile with a large fleet to overawe the provinces.

Amenemhat's Asian policy was defensive, entailing the construction of a line of forts, known as the Walls of the Prince, across the eastern edge of the Delta. But more aggressive intentions lay behind the building of a great fortress at Semna, south of the Second Cataract, which marked the beginning of an Egyptian forward policy in Nubia. It was the first of a chain of 12th Dynasty fortresses along the narrowest section of the Nile Valley, dominating the area and giving Egypt undisputed control of the north-south trade route. The fortresses – now at the bottom of Lake Nasser – were remarkably large mud-brick structures, skilfully adapted to the peculiarities of each site. With features such as bastion-towers arranged so that attackers could be caught in a cross-fire, they anticipated many features of much later fortifications.

Nubian soldiers on the march. As these tomb models suggest, Egyptian depictions of Nubians as captives or tributaries do not tell the whole story. The pharaohs were more than willing to recruit their doughty southern neighbours into their armies.

Treading the enemy underfoot. The painted fragment shows a pair of sandal soles whose wearer could triumph at every step over the traditional enemies, an Asiatic and a Nubian.

Buhen was the command centre for Egyptian forces in Nubia. Its mighty ramparts were among the casualties of the Aswan Dam project; they now lie beneath the waters of Lake Nasser.

Following the collapse of the Middle Kingdom, the threat of foreign domination became serious when the Hyksos took control of the Delta. In response, the Egyptians copied their enemies' superior weapons and tactics, fighting back vigorously and finally expelling them. The New Kingdom pharaohs subsequently went on the offensive, driving further south into Nubia and becoming the paramount power in Palestine and much of Syria. This region – the Levant – was a geopolitical crossroads that Egypt would dispute with the empires to the north and north-east for four hundred years.

The biggest technical change took place in weaponry. Until the end of the Old Kingdom, Egyptian soldiers were equipped with bows and arrows, spears and axes; they wore no armour but carried long shields. The axe largely replaced the crude but effective mace, which consisted of a round stone head attached to a wooden haft; surviving early mace-heads are engraved with scenes from the reigns of Scorpion and Narmer, and the mace remained a pictorial symbol of royal authority, much used in smiting scenes, long after it was abandoned on the battlefield.

During the Old and Middle Kingdoms, Egyptian soldiers were infantrymen. The Hyksos employed horse-drawn chariots, whose speed and mobility gave them a tremendous advantage, and the Egyptians may well have adopted this radical new weapon by imitating their enemies. Big, powerful horses had not yet been bred, and Hyksos and Egyptian chariots were light, semi-circular wooden structures, open at the back, which carried a driver and a warrior.

Though armed with spear and shield, the warrior was most effective as an archer; a division of chariots, wheeling and darting backwards and forwards, could pour arrows into the ranks of slow-moving infantry without suffering significant retaliation. The impact made by chariots on the Egyptian mind is apparent in the way they became pictorial symbols of royal domination, appropriate even to a short-lived monarch such as Tutankhamun, who almost certainly never took part in a military campaign.

Weapons subsequently continued to be improved: a longer-range bow was introduced, along with a scimitar-like weapon, the *khopesh*, for hand-to-hand fighting. Armour was worn, in the form of tunics with rows of small bronze plates attached to them.

Once it had to assume the responsibilities of empire, the New Kingdom army developed into a regular professional force, although conscripts made up the numbers on major campaigns and Nubian and other mercenaries were widely employed. It was organized in 5,000-man divisions, each consisting of twenty 250-man companies; the companies were further divided into 50-man platoons. An officer corps came into existence, the key figures being the 'standard bearers' commanding companies. Military service became a career option, probably attractive to those without the taste, ability or opportunity for a scribal career. The expansion of the army created a variety of new administrative posts for scribes, but their writings suggest that they never completely accepted the pretensions of the military.

Nevertheless, in the New Kingdom career officers often played a political role that is not perceptible in earlier periods. During the reign of Tutankhamun, General Horemheb may well have been controlling events, perhaps in partnership with the minister Ay; after Ay's death he became pharaoh, and his choice of a comrade-in-arms as his successor marked the beginning of the Ramesside era. And when the Ramessides began to fail, another ambitious soldier, Herihor, crowned his career by making himself the high priest of Amun at Thebes and, in effect, sovereign of Upper Egypt.

The Egyptians were never entirely comfortable on the sea, and much of their naval expertise, along with their timber, was supplied by the Levantine client-state of Byblos. However, Ramesses III did win a decisive battle against the Sea Peoples, celebrated in action-packed reliefs at Medinet Habu. The fighting seems to have been based on land tactics, with Egyptian archers firing showers of arrows at the enemy and other troops boarding their ships and engaging in desperate hand-to-hand combat.

FAMOUS BATTLES

Two sets of records from the Egyptian high noon of empire tell us something about New Kingdom strategy and tactics. Within a short time of taking power, Tuthmosis III set out to quell a confederation of Syrian city-states led by the ruler of Kadesh. With Napoleonic swiftness Tuthmosis marched up the coast, capturing Gaza en route, and then chose the shortest but most risky route through a narrow pass where an enemy might easily have picked off the Egyptians as they went through in single file. His gamble succeeded: the enemy host was surprised outside its base at Megiddo, and it seems likely that the Egyptian attack broke through the centre before all the enemy units could regroup.

The Syrians fled back to Megiddo, which closed its gates in such haste that the prince of Kadesh was stranded outside and had to be pulled into the city over the walls. According to the official account, written up on a temple wall at Karnak, the Egyptians failed to destroy the enemy completely because many soldiers allowed themselves to be distracted by opportunities for looting. Megiddo held out for seven months before it surrendered to Tuthmosis' besieging army. He launched a further sixteen campaigns in western Asia, so his initial conquest cannot have been complete. Presumably his victories compelled recalcitrant vassals to renew their allegiance, and at the end of each campaign his army returned with quantities of booty, enriching the soldiery and the temples. Tuthmosis is said to have captured hundreds of cities, and the cumulative effect may have been to make Egyptian rule a reality. Syrian princes were held as hostages in Egypt and, at the same time, brought up to be Egyptians in culture and outlook. Eventually an Egyptian viceroy was permanently established in the region, making certain decisions on his own authority and 'advising' the local rulers in a manner reminiscent of the 'residents' installed as advisers to native princes in British India. This was very different from the situation in Nubia, where direct Egyptian rule was exercised for most of the New Kingdom by a Viceroy or 'King's Son of Kush' with extensive powers.

Over two centuries later, the Egyptians were still struggling to hold the Levant. The confederates opposing Tuthmosis had probably been backed up by the great power further north, Mitanni; now, Ramesses II was directly con-

For valour: gold flies were the Egyptian equivalent of a military medal. These came from the tomb of Queen Ahhotep, who is known to have played a significant politico-military role in Egypt's war against the Hyksos.

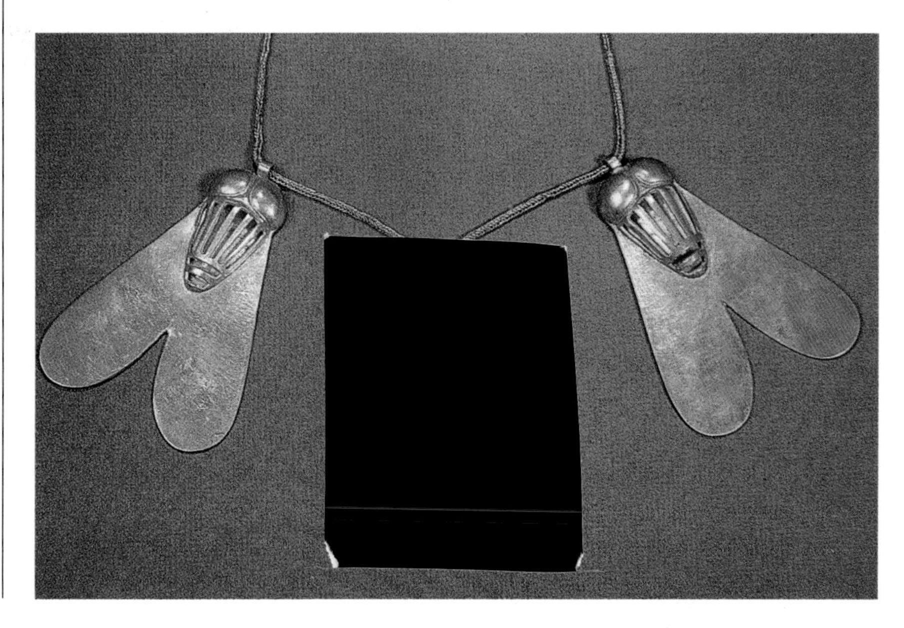

fronted by the Hittite empire ruled by King Muwatallis. Tuthmosis' many campaigns had culminated in the capture of Kadesh, and the city was also Ramesses' objective. He set out with a very large army. A reserve force took the coastal route, while Ramesses himself led four divisions (Amun, Re, Ptah, Seth) directly towards Kadesh.

The campaign that followed was described on a number of temple walls, pictured in reliefs and written about on papyrus. It became the basis of a set-piece account copied out by generations of young students. The Egyptian version of the culminating battle at Kadesh is the first such account in history – and perhaps the first example of 'the Big Lie' as wartime propaganda.

On the march, the Egyptians captured two Bedouin who asked to be taken into the pharaoh's service and volunteered the information that the Hittite army was at least 150 kilometres away to the north. Ramesses believed this false report and confidently went on ahead with the Amun division, camping close to Kadesh in order to besiege it. Then two Hittite spies were captured and revealed under torture that Muwatallis' army was just to the north-east, waiting to pounce. The Hittites, numbering 2,500 chariots and 37,000 men, greatly outnumbered the Egyptians – or so Ramesses' monuments claimed. Before the pharaoh could act on his new information, the Hittite chariots ambushed the Re division on its way to Kadesh. The Egyptians broke and fled in disorder to Ramesses' camp. Thrown into confusion, the army began to disintegrate, but Ramesses mounted his chariot and, almost single handed, cut a terrible path of destruction through his enemies. The Hittite king fled, and when the Egyptian army belatedly reassembled, Ramesses poured scorn upon it – or so the memorials claim. Reading between the lines, it seems that Ramesses was saved by the arrival of the reserve force from the coast; the Ptah and Seth came up later, and an indecisive battle took place the next day. A truce was arranged, and the pharaoh withdrew without having taken Kadesh. The Egyptians had fought the most boasted-about draw in history.

The Hittites at the battle of Kadesh (1274 BC), crushed by the might of Ramesses II. This is the Egyptian version: the Hittites claimed to have won, and historians suspect that the outcome was a stand-off.

A 5th-Dynasty vizier in all his glory: Ptahhotep, the author of an early how-to-succeed manual, is being carried aloft in his palanquin. Painted relief from the vizier's tomb at Saqqara.

5 MIGHTY MONUMENTS

EVERYONE HAS HEARD OF THE PYRAMIDS AND THE GREAT SPHINX AT GIZA. BUT THESE COMPRISE ONLY A SMALL PART OF THE EGYPTIAN ACHIEVEMENT AS BUILDERS OF MIGHTY MONUMENTS. GREAT PALACES AND ENTIRE CITIES HAVE DISAPPEARED SINCE ANTIQUITY, BUT VAST AND NOBLE RUINS STILL COVER THE LAND. PYRAMIDS, TEMPLES AND TOMBS WERE NOT, AS IS WIDELY BELIEVED, THE WORK OF WHIP-DRIVEN SLAVES, BUT THEY WERE CERTAINLY THE RESULT OF ENORMOUS LABOUR AND GREAT SKILL IN THE USE OF BASIC TOOLS AND SIMPLE DEVICES. AS SUCH, THEY REPRESENT ONE OF THE MOST EXTRAORDINARY, LONG-SUSTAINED FEATS IN HUMAN HISTORY.

FROM BRICK TO STONE

The mud brick of Egyptian houses and palaces has crumbled, and they survive at best as ruinous, indistinct versions of their former selves. By contrast, in spite of the decay and destruction of millennia, tombs and temples made of stone constitute Egypt's most highly visible, awe-inspiring legacy.

During the earliest phase of Egyptian history, however, all building was done with mud brick. The importance given to death and the afterlife soon became apparent with the elaboration of a type of tomb known as the mastaba, erected in large numbers at Abydos and Saqqara. The word mastaba, Arabic for 'bench', described the long, low shape of the superstructure (the visible, above-ground part of the tomb), which was rectangular in plan, with sides that sloped slightly inwards towards the flat-topped roof. Beneath the superstructure lay a pit divided into chambers by brick cross-walls; the dead person lay in the largest of the chambers. A chapel and other funerary structures lay close by, and the entire complex was enclosed by a wall.

Mastabas were substantial structures which only the king and members of the nobility could afford to build. The even mightier pyramids developed directly from mastabas, but were for royal occupation only; other high-ranking Egyptians continued to be buried in mastabas, although they soon copied the kings' use of stone as a building material.

The Step Pyramid at Saqqara, built for King Djoser by Imhotep, must have seemed an astonishing break with the past, but it actually began as an unusual mastaba, square and made of stone. It was twice extended before it became the base of a four-step pyramid – or, to put it another way, the bottommost of a series of ever-smaller mastabas. Later still, the north and west sides were built up in order to turn the structure into a six-step pyramid standing about sixty metres high. Fascinatingly, the erosion of part of the Step Pyramid's base has made this sequence of changes visible and comprehensible even to the non-specialist.

Like later pyramids, Djoser's was originally cased in eye-dazzling white Tura limestone. A wall with fourteen gates enclosed the pyramid and other funerary structures. A number of these were associated with the jubilee (*heb-sed*) rituals, apparently mimicking the setting for the king's run and homage; they were obviously not for use (by mortals), since the chapels, like thirteen of the gates into the complex, were dummies, actually made of solid masonry.

The Step Pyramid was not the first burial at Saqqara, which already served as the necropolis of the capital, Memphis. Other pyramid-builders chose the area for the same reason, but selected sites just to the north or south, such as Giza, Abushir and Dahshur. However, the next surviving pyramid after Djoser's was an exception; built for Huni, the last 3rd Dynasty king, it was located at Meidum, much further south. It too reveals the Egyptian builders experimenting and

Opposite: Interior of a mastaba with several chambers. The proportions of such non-royal tombs indicate the effort and planning that Egyptians devoted to the construction of their 'eternal houses'.

Mighty columns from Medinet Habu, the temple complex built by Ramesses III on the west bank of the Nile opposite Thebes. Among other things, Ramesses' temple reliefs celebrate the Egyptians' victory over the Sea Peoples.

The Temple of Seti I at Abydos. Seti restored Egyptian power and made the 19th (Ramesside) Dynasty secure. The carved reliefs on his temples are regarded as masterpieces of New Kingdom art.

learning: changed from a seven- to an eight-step pyramid, and cased to signify that it had been completed, it was converted into a true, smooth-sided pyramid when the steps were filled in. Access to the burial chamber was shifted from the ground floor (where it was located in Djoser's pyramid) to some way up the north face, a security measure imitated by later builders.

The Meidum pyramid was probably finished by the 4th Dynasty king Sneferu, who also built no less than two pyramids of his own at Dahshur. In his southern 'bent pyramid', the angle at which the sides rise towards the apex abruptly changes from 54 to 43 degrees; although symbolic explanations have been offered for this curiosity, a failure of nerve or know-how seems more likely. The sides of Sneferu's northern or red pyramid are also constructed at a modest 43-degree angle, some 9 degrees smaller than the later norm. On the other hand, an increasing confidence is shown by the treatment of the interiors: in the bent pyramid, separate entrances led down to two unconnected chambers, one subterranean and one within the pyramid, while the red pyramid's single entrance went down to no less than three large chambers inside the superstructure. However, Sneferu's works were to be surpassed in size and complexity by his descendants.

THE GREAT PYRAMID

Sneferu's son, Khufu, selected a new site on which to construct the most spectacular of all pyramids. At Giza, just north of Abusir and Saqqara on the Memphite 'necropolis belt', workmen levelled a large area and laid some 2,300,000 stone blocks, each weighing 2.5 tonnes. When completed, Khufu's pyramid occupied an area 230 x 230 metres and rose to a height of 146 metres, dwarfing every known man-made structure. It is now always called the Great Pyramid, but the more poetic Egyptian term was 'the Horizon of Khufu'.

Like most pyramids, Khufu's is entered from the north. But inside the arrangements are so peculiar that they have given rise to all sorts of occult theories, mostly involving the existence of fabulous treasures or mathematical keys to the riddle of the universe. The entrance leads down to a chamber 30 metres below ground level; it was evidently unfinished, since the corridor leading out of it is a cul-de-sac, abandoned before a new chamber was even started. It is reasonable to suppose that the king changed his mind and decided to be buried inside the masonry of the pyramid instead of below ground.

Consequently the roof of the entrance corridor was breached and a new passage was driven into the heart of the structure. But this leads to two very different chambers. At the top of the corridor a horizontal passage terminates in the small 'Queen's Chamber'.

An alternative, higher route from the top of the corridor opens out into the high, 47-metre-long 'Grand Gallery', lined with polished stone, at the top of which stands the 'King's Chamber'. A narrow passage runs from the bottom of the Grand Gallery, deep underground to join the entrance corridor; it was obviously an escape route for the workmen, who would leave after stopping the breached roof of the entrance corridor with huge granite plugs.

The most plausible explanation for the existence of two corridors and chambers inside the pyramid is that Khufu changed his mind again, settling on the so-called King's Chamber as his final resting place – although the redeployment of resources involved staggers the imagination. The King's Chamber is entirely lined with red granite and contains the royal sarcophagus; but like all the other chambers in pyramids, it was empty when the first recorded examination was made. An interesting fact about the sarcophagus is that it must have been put in place while the pyramid was being built, since it is wider than the narrowest point of the corridor. To prevent the chamber collapsing under the weight of the stone above it, five apertures were created over the roof, spreading the thrust.

The most intriguing features of all are two narrow shafts or 'vents' leading upwards in different directions from the King's Chamber and emerging high up on the north and south sides of the Great Pyramid. Their alignment with stars in the night sky makes it almost certain that they had some religious-astronomical function, allowing the king's spirit to achieve union with 'the imperishable stars'. Astronomical calculations played their part in the building of the Giza pyramids, which are aligned with the cardinal points of the compass.

Much more controversial, and difficult to prove or refute, is the claim that the layout of the pyramids as a group was intended to copy the star-pattern of the belt of Orion.

There are two more shafts in the Great Pyramid. These leave the Queen's Chamber and appear to be headed for exits in the sides of the pyramid, in much the same fashion as the shafts described above. But the Queen's Chamber shafts seem to have been abandoned when they were only a few metres long, presumably following the decision to create the Grand Gallery and the King's Chamber. Yet in 1993, when German investigators managed to send a robot camera up one of the shafts, it was found to end in a sealed door – a portal-like formality suggesting that more than stone might lie behind it.

The other two pyramids at Giza were built for Khufu's son, Khafre, and his grandson, Menkaure. Khafre's pyramid, almost but not quite so large as his father's, is the best preserved of the group. Some of the limestone casing has survived at the apex, although it is no longer a dazzling white and any gilding (believed to have crowned all the pyramids) has long since disappeared. Another note of colour would have been introduced by the use of red granite, and some of this also survives round the bases of Khafre's and

Painted scenes in the pillared hall of the tomb of Sennefer, an 18th Dynasty mayor of Thebes; the scenes show Sennefer and his wife enacting the rituals essential to a happy existence in the world to come.

The Great Gallery inside the pyramid of Khufu. The largest surviving pyramid has an appropriately extraordinary interior, of which the 47-metre-long Great Gallery leading up to the 'King's Chamber' is only one item.

Menkaure's pyramids. Both have more traditional internal arrangements than Khufu's, with the burial chamber mainly below ground level, although there have once again been changes of plan involving the digging of alternative passages and chambers.

Each of the Giza pyramids was surrounded by tombs and temples that added further to the king's glory: deeply impressive by any normal human standards, they were as nothing when compared with the mighty royal tombs. Beside each pyramid stood a mortuary temple where offerings were made every day to the dead king. A long covered causeway, decorated with reliefs, linked this building with a near-identical valley temple where funeral rites were carried out (possibly including the actual embalming) and the cult of the king, represented by many statues of him, was celebrated; though most of the contents were pillaged or destroyed, Khafre's temple yielded a magnificent statue of the king, now recognized as one of the masterpieces of Old Kingdom art. On one side of the pyramid stood a number of 'subsidiary pyramids', ten metres or so in height, that have generally been regarded as tombs for the ruler's queens. And at a respectful distance there were a large number of mastabas, put up by the family, officials, courtiers and priests of the king, still huddled close to their master in death in the hope of sharing his immortality.

No fewer than five boat-pits have been discovered around the Great Pyramid. Securely covered by limestone blocks cemented together, the fourth pit was opened in 1954 and yielded a complete boat, dismantled into hundreds of pieces to make it fit the available space. Evidently Khafre, as a new king, begrudged the resources that would have been needed to enlarge the pit; such economies are often found in the final stages of Egyptian royal monuments, imposed by a successor pious enough to finish the job but impatient to get as much as possible of his own monument done during his lifetime. Khufu's boat has been painstakingly reassembled and is now on show in a museum devoted to it at Giza.

Further investigation has indicated that there are also remains in the fifth boat-pit, but in a much less promising condition. The boat that has been excavated may never have been used, serving instead as a 'solar bark' in which Khufu could sail across the firmament. Such boat-burials are known from as far back as the 1st Dynasty, but none have been found beside the pyramids of Khafre and Menkaure.

No other pyramids match those at Giza for size or workmanship, although more than seventy have survived. Many were constructed with rubble or mud-brick cores and have suffered greatly from the inevitable stripping away of the fine stone casings for use as building materials. Much of this was done during the Middle Ages, but even kings of ancient Egypt were not above plundering their predecessors' monuments as an alternative or supplement to quarrying. The Middle Kingdom pharaoh Amenemhat I destroyed much of Khufu's pyramid complex in this way – an act of impiety even if Khufu was already a figure from a remote (600-year-old) past. Pyramid-building had lapsed after the fall of the Old Kingdom, to be revived by the rulers of the Middle Kingdom. The Old Kingdom pyramids had probably been robbed during the confusions of the First Intermediate Period, and the rulers of the Middle Kingdom made strenuous efforts to avoid the same fate. Labyrinthine passages, dead ends, false doors and traps proliferated in the pyramids of late 12th Dynasty kings such as Amenemhat III, but to no effect. Their tombs were robbed in turn, and pyramid-building came to be seen as a counter-productive activity. Apart from decorative miniatures, pyramids were no longer built after about 1650 BC, and the New Kingdom pharaohs chose a radical new approach to the problem. An interesting footnote to pyramid history was supplied by the Egyptianized kingdoms of Napata and Meroe in Nubia, where the pyramid was revived in the 8th century BC in a smaller, distinctively elongated form.

Stonemasons at work, building blocks and a cross-section of a house are shown on this fragment. The schematic representation of the house is filled with vivid little sketches of the furnishings.

THE GREAT SPHINX

The Great Sphinx is the most idiosyncratic sight on the Giza plateau. Although itself a mighty monument (20 metres high and 73 metres long), it cannot compare with the pyramids in size. But its strange, distinctive presence seized the imagination even in antiquity, and most of us think of it as a mysterious guardian figure, watching over 'the pyramids'.

In reality the Sphinx belongs with the pyramid and other mortuary buildings of a single pharaoh, Khafre. It stands beside the causeway leading to the king's pyramid and its face is almost certainly a portrait of the king. The body is that of a lion, already regarded as a royal beast and also associated (like the king) with the sun-god. The making of the Sphinx may have originated with a moment of inspiration, for it was carved from a limestone outcrop left over after extensive quarrying operations: instead of remaining as an eyesore, the rock was shaped into a symbolic figure of then-unprecedented size.

Initially the Sphinx was a more obviously kingly creature. It wore a crown that slotted into its headdress of rock. There was a *uraeus* (rearing cobra) on its brow, now reduced to a vertical lump, and the ceremonial false beard of a pharaoh protruded from its chin.

By the New Kingdom period the Great Sphinx was an ancient monument, evidently neglected and half buried in sand. It was still associated with the sun-god, specifically with the-sun-on-the-horizon, Horemakhet. According to the stele erected in front of the Sphinx, a young prince who was resting in its shade had a dream in which Horemakhet appeared to him. The god promised that the prince would become the next pharaoh if he freed the gigantic figure from the discomforts of the engulfing sand. The work was promptly set in hand and the prince duly succeeded as Tuthmosis IV. Sceptics have speculated that the entire story may have been a propaganda exercise on Tuthmosis' part, intended to strengthen a perhaps shaky claim to the throne. However, it is clear that the first repairs were done to the Sphinx's stonework during this period (the 18th Dynasty), and traces of the contemporary red repaint are still just visible on it. In addition to this refurbishment, a royal statue was set up in front of the Sphinx's chest and a new temple was dedicated to Horemakhet; neither proved to have the staying power of the Sphinx itself.

The sand piled up again, and later attempts to clear it away seem to have been half-hearted. But enough was visible in the 14th century for a religious fanatic to inflict the first really serious injury by destroying the figure's nose.

Nineteenth-century clearances were partial, and the entire figure was only exposed in 1925-6. The effects were not entirely happy. Despite much conservation work, exposure led to a speeding up of deterioration from erosion, which, combined with rising damp, is claimed to threaten the very existence of the Sphinx. The collapse of part of the right shoulder in 1988 prompted the launch of a determined, scientific investigation and conservation programme.

The Great Sphinx at Giza appears to stand guard over the pyramids built by the 4th Dynasty kings of Egypt. The face of the sphinx is believed to be a portrait of King Khafre.

TOMBS IN THE LIVING ROCK

The pyramids at Giza are unrivalled examples of conspicuous display, triumphantly proclaiming their occupants' wealth and power – and consequently inviting the attentions of tomb-robbers. The New Kingdom pharaohs were equally self-assertive in their temples and monuments, but hoped to avoid the fate of their predecessors by creating hidden houses in which they could enjoy eternity among their treasures. Tombs cut into living rock had been made for local governors and nobles during the Middle Kingdom and even earlier, at sites such as Beni-Hassan and Assyut, although the

The village of Deir el-Medina, purpose-built for the artisans who created the rock-cut tombs in the Valley of the Kings. Although ruinous, its general layout is still perfectly clear.

resting-places of these provincials were modest by comparison with what was to come. Having decided to follow their example, the New Kingdom pharaohs chose a promisingly remote spot, now known as the Valley of the Kings, that was nevertheless accessible from the city of Thebes, now entering its greatest period. The Valley of the Kings lay on the opposite (west) bank of the Nile, in the desert. The decision to turn it into a royal necropolis seems to have been taken by Amenhotep I, the son and successor of the first New Kingdom monarch, Ahmose I. Ironically, Amenhotep's tomb has never been identified, and it is just possible that he himself was not buried in the Valley, although his mortuary temple was built on the west bank at Deir el-Bahri. One consequence of burying rulers in rock-cut tombs was that their mortuary temples were separately sited, in a line on the edge of the desert, no longer signalling the immediate proximity of rich pickings. However, although there were no regular temple services in the Valley of the Kings, there would have been a lively human presence in the form of workmen from the village set up by Amenhotep I, more or less permanently at work on one tomb after another over a several-hundred-year period.

So far, sixty-two tombs have been located in the Valley of the Kings. Their occupants were pharaohs of the 18th-20th Dynasties and favoured relatives, courtiers and officials who were permitted to remain near their masters in death. Two of the tombs belong to the viziers Rekhmire and Rahmose; Rekhmire, vizier to Tuthmosis III, had a virtual autobiography inscribed on the wall of his burial chamber, helpfully detailing the responsibilities of his office. The tomb of a high official, Yuya, and his wife Thuya was found intact in 1905, and was rightly regarded as a major discovery, although later overshadowed by the opening of Tutankhamun's tomb. Yuya and Thuya were close to the centre of power as the parents of Tiy, Amenhotep III's queen; they were therefore the grandparents of the heretic pharaoh Akhenaten, and it is also possible that Ay was their son. They remain impressive in death, since they are among the best preserved of all Egyptian mummies.

Eighteenth-Dynasty pharaohs tended to share their tombs in the Valley of the Kings with their Great Wives. But other New Kingdom queens, and a number of princes who never inherited the throne, were buried in the Valley of the Queens, about two kilometres south.

The royal tombs in the Valley of the Kings were on a completely different scale and, when first sealed, quite certainly contained objects of a beauty and sumptuousness that are only hinted at by the contents of Tutankhamun's tomb. The tombs themselves are as extraordinary in their way as the pyramids, comprising a series of long corridors and more or less spacious chambers cut deep into the valley cliffs. The longest, deepest and most complex of all is the tomb of the warrior-pharaoh Seti I, who re-established Egypt as an international power after the decline of the 18th Dynasty.

A hundred metres deep and superbly decorated, Seti's tomb was intended to baffle intruders. At the bottom of the downward-sloping entrance corridor lay a deep shaft; even if the wary thief spotted it before falling in, he was likely to assume that the burial chamber lay at its bottom, far below. In reality there was a door in what appeared to be unbroken wall. It led straight into a 'burial chamber' – but even that was a false one, not Seti's, which could only be reached via a set of concealed steps.

But the robbers did reach it, along with every other tomb except the forgotten Tutankhamun's. With the disappearance of the New Kingdom, the situation became so serious that priests collected the royal mummies and hid them in two tombs where they were only discovered late in the 19th century. Luckier than the pyramid-building kings, they survived physically even though they had been stripped of their wealth and their tombs lay empty.

A spectacular view of the chapel of Hathor, with two great heads of the goddess forming the capitals of columns. The chapel is only a part of Hatshepsut's huge temple at Deir el-Bahri (page 126).

The Temple of Hatshepsut at Deir el-Bahri, on the west bank of the Nile, close to the Valley of the Kings. Set in a bay in the cliffs, the temple, with its long lines of columns and huge ramps, dominates the other remains in the area.

TEMPLES

Immense resources were devoted to building, maintaining and embellishing the temples of Egypt. They had a vital role to play in the scheme of things, honouring (and placating) the gods and helping to ensure that Maat – universal order and harmony – prevailed. Materially, temples were the focus for populous communities of priests, officials and workers (and the families of all three classes), endowed by the pharaohs with vast estates to support them. Around, and sometimes within the precincts of the actual temples, were the offices, granaries, slaughterhouses, storerooms and other facilities needed to run this large-scale enterprise. It seems certain that temples eventually accounted for a high percentage of Egypt's economic activity, making the priesthood a political power to be reckoned with.

Although it was the centre of a community, a temple was not a place of communal worship. It was a house dedicated to the service of the god who dwelt within it. The god's abode was a shrine in the depths of the temple, where he or she inhabited a statue-image that was fed, washed, dressed and cared for by the priests. Other mortals were not allowed inside the sanctuary which held the shrine; indeed, outsiders could go no further than the temple courtyard even during religious festivals, although these might involve the god's image emerging and being paraded up and down on land or water. The temple was a kind of opening where the human and divine worlds met, enabling the pharaoh, or his priest-surrogate, to communicate with the god. By lavishing wealth

on the temple, and ceremonial attentions on the god, a pharaoh ensured the prosperity of the land and asserted his own essential role in the ordering of the world.

One result of this materialistic piety was that Egypt's temples were built, and rebuilt or enlarged, many times over. The older structures were plundered for materials or covered by new monuments, and as a consequence the Old and Middle Kingdom temples have largely disappeared. The most substantial remains date from the New Kingdom or later, often with an accumulation of features added by succeeding pharaohs. Almost all of them belong to Upper Egyptian sites, which suffered much less than the populous north from the re-use of materials for building during and after the Middle Ages.

The best-preserved Egyptian temple is at Edfu, not far from the southern border. Dedicated to the falcon-god Horus, it was started late in the Ptolemaic period, replacing an earlier pharaonic temple from about the mid-3rd century BC. Its relatively modest size and straightforward layout reveal the essential features common to Egyptian temples. It is entered through a pylon – that is, a huge stone gateway resembling linked twin towers, characteristically battered (sloping slightly inward as they rise). The outer face of the Edfu pylon carries reliefs showing the Roman-protected king Ptolemy XII in time-hallowed poses, smiting his enemies, despite his conspicuously poor record in this respect. A wall encloses the temple on all four sides. Through the pylon gateway lies a large colonnaded courtyard. On its far side a processional way leads down the centre of a series of rooms: two hypostyle ('pillar-supported') halls crowded with massive columns, an offering hall and a vestibule. The vestibule is the threshold of the sanctuary, the small room in which the god's shrine stood, holding the divine image.

At Edfu and other temples, the floor rises and the rooms become progressively smaller, lower-ceilinged, and dimmer along the line of approach to the sanctuary. This served to emphasize that the shrine was a holy of holies, to be avoided rather than sought out by all but the chosen servants of the god. But the arrangement also reflected the Egyptian conception of a temple as a microcosm of the original Creation. The sanctuary, the highest point in the temple, represented the Primeval Mound – the earth itself, risen from the waters in the first age. The hypostyle hall, filled with row upon row of columns, mimicked the reed-covered marshy terrain bordering the mound; since this is an Egyptian-Nilotic conception of the world, the columns are carved to represent densely growing lotus or papyrus plants. The hypostyle hall seems to have seized hold of the Egyptian imagination: the visitor encounters two on the way to the shrine at Edfu, and at other temples there were even more. Their overpowering, forest-like interiors were lit from windows high up on the walls, creating a strange, shadowy atmosphere that made a suitable preliminary to an encounter with the god of the sanctuary.

The temple at Edfu is a mighty monument, but it is small and compact by comparison with the vast complex of buildings at Karnak, which the Egyptians knew as *ipet-isut,* 'the most blessed

The Valley of the Kings, celebrated for its 62 rock-cut tombs,' most of them originally housed the mummies and tomb goods of the pharaohs. They were chosen in the hope that they could be guarded against tomb robbers, but none escaped unscathed.

place'. At its heart are three great temples, dedicated to Amun, the principal state god, his wife Mut, and the falcon-headed god of war, Montu. Amun was particularly closely associated with Thebes, and when the city became the capital of New Kingdom Egypt, Amun's pre-eminence was assured – and with it the pre-eminence of Karnak, which was part of Thebes' expanding urban area. At Karnak, even more than at other sites, the pharaohs accomplished amazing feats of self-advertising devotion, adding to the complex from generation to generation while inscribing stone façades with images of their piety and accounts of their glorious victories. As a result, the walls of the temple of Amun enclose a huge area that took in temples to other gods, various chapels, halls and enclosures, and a very large sacred lake in which the priests could perform their ablutions before starting their duties. The main way into the temple leads through no less than six monumental pylons and courtyards, including the most celebrated of all – the Great Hypostyle Hall. This awe-inspiring building was mostly constructed under Seti I, although Seti's son Ramesses II, true to form, claimed most of the credit. The hall is filled with 134 huge columns, carved to resemble papyrus plants, the slightly higher inner rows rising to 23 metres. Now open to the sky, it is awe-inspiring; its impact when roofed and only half-seen by angled beams of light from above, beggars the imagination.

Seeking new ways of pleasing Amun, other pharaohs, notably Tuthmosis III and Horemheb, created another series of pylons and courtyards at right-angles to the main temple layout; combining orthodoxy with economy, Horemheb took his materials from the temple to Aten erected on the spot by the heretic Akhenaten. This second processional way ran from the temple of Amun to that of his wife Mut. The main processional way from Amun's temple was lined with ram-headed sphinxes and led from Karnak to another Amun temple-site, a short distance to the south at Luxor. The relationship between the two became important at the annual festival of Opet. This was a great popular event, held when the inundation was at its height and the people were free to turn out in their thousands.

Amun's temple at Luxor, though not on the same breathtaking scale as his Karnak residence, was fully worthy of the god. It was founded by the 18th Dynasty ruler Amenhotep III and augmented by the hyperactive Ramesses II, who added a large extra courtyard with a pylon in front of it – and, in front of that,

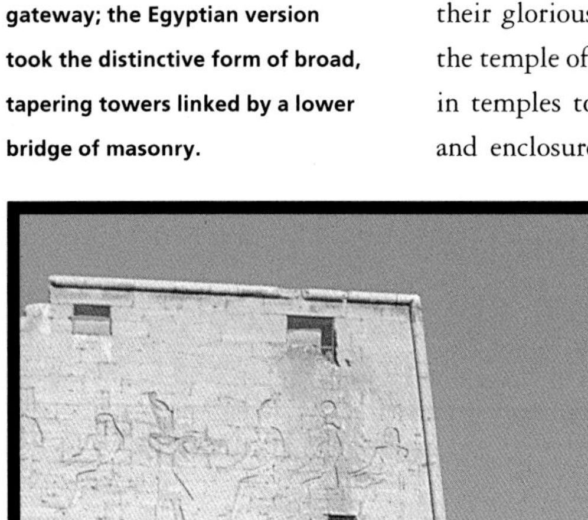

The pylon of the Temple of Horus at Edfu. A pylon is a ceremonial gateway; the Egyptian version took the distinctive form of broad, tapering towers linked by a lower bridge of masonry.

two colossal statues of himself and two obelisks, one of which is still there.

With Thebes, Karnak and Luxor clustered together and the Valleys of the Kings and Queens on the opposite, west bank, this part of Upper Egypt is a prime location for archaeologist and tourist alike. Many of the mortuary temples associated with the pharaohs buried in the Valley of the Kings have virtually disappeared, but the Ramesseum (Ramesses II's temple) and Medinet Habu (Ramesses III's) are huge and splendid ruins. The temple of Amenhotep III, which once stood between them, has vanished – except for the seated figures of the king, misnamed the Colossi of Memnon, described in an earlier chapter. Beyond this line of temples, about a kilometre to the north-west, stands the temple of Hatshepsut, the female pharaoh. It is spectacular in itself and also in its setting, the deep bay of the cliffs at Deir el-Bahri. Its extraordinary colonnaded terraces and ramps are in fact works of architectural revivalism, imitating the nearby temple of Mentuhotep II, built some five hundred years earlier. The decay of Mentuhotep's temple, and the painstaking restoration of Hatshepsut's, have meant that the queen-king's edifice now dominates the scene.

Seti I also built a huge mortuary temple, not in the Valley of the Kings but further north at the ancient sacred city of Abydos; this seems to have been part of a deliberate attempt to secure his dynasty by emphasizing – or fabricating – its links with the past. Among other things the temple is known for its lovely painted reliefs and inscribed list of Egyptian kings. Behind it lay a rather mysterious building, the Osireion (Abydos was the city of the god Osiris). Its interior was laid out as an island surrounded by canals – perhaps the Primeval Mound – and held a sarcophagus that was purportedly Seti's, although he was in fact buried in the Valley of the Kings.

Other well-preserved temples include those of Ramesses and his queen at Abu Simbel in Nubia and striking, though essentially Ptolemaic-to-Roman structures at Esna, Philae, Dendera and Kom Ombo. The reliefs at Dendera are of historical as well as artistic interest, since they feature a scene with Cleopatra VII and her son by Julius Caesar, Caesarion. Kom Ombo was very unusual in being a double temple, jointly dedicated to Horus and the crocodile god Sobek: remarkably, parallel processional ways lead through hypostyle halls and vestibules into the parallel and adjacent sanctuaries of the deities.

The Great Hypostyle Hall in the Temple of Amun at Karnak. Hypostyle halls were filled with rows of columns, intended to create an impression of gigantic reeds growing from primeval waters.

The most familiar of Egypt's public monuments, thanks to European acquisitiveness, is the obelisk. Four-sided and tapering towards a pyramid-form top, these great blocks of granite were quarried, moved and set in place with an accuracy that still astounds engineers. Like the pyramids, they were tipped with gold to emphasize their connection with the cult of the sun. Private individuals sometimes set them up in front of their tombs, and mini-obelisks were popular as amulets.

In New Kingdom times obelisks were usually erected in pairs in front of the temple pylon. Now, not a single pair is left in Egypt. The Romans developed an early taste for obelisks and carried off no less than forty-eight in antiquity, of which there are still thirteen in Rome's public places. Later-comers included France, Britain and

A section of the avenue of ram-headed sphinxes which once linked the great temple complexes at Karnak and Luxor. Images of the gods were carried down this great processional way to visit one another.

the USA. In 1836 an over-generous ruler of Egypt, Mohammed Ali, presented France with one of Ramesses II's obelisks from Luxor, which now stands on the Place de la Concorde in Paris. Britain also acquired an obelisk from the pasha, although 'Cleopatra's Needle' did not reach the London Embankment until 1878. New York followed suit, acquiring its own obelisk in 1880.

THE BUILDERS

Egypt's mighty monuments were the creations of a still-primitive technology. Egyptian workmen had no iron tools, knew nothing of devices such as pulleys, and made little use of the wheel (not entirely without reason, however, since large areas of soft terrain were better suited to transportation by sledge).

The basic tools employed in building were hardstone hammers and copper chisels and saws, and the most sophisticated technical aids were rulers, set-squares and the simplest lifting and levering techniques. But the greatest builders – the pharaohs – did command a huge labour force and the time and determination to learn and succeed. An examination of the pyramids has shown that trial and error played a large part in their creation, and even their alignment with the points of the compass became progressively more accurate.

Because the ancient Egyptians' achievements as builders seem near-miraculous, their feats have sometimes been exaggerated to the point of fantasy. For example, many people believe that the thousands of tonnes of stones needed to build the Giza pyramids had to be brought from far-distant quarries; whereas in fact the workers quarried most of it on the plateau, very close to the construction site. The brilliant limestone for the casing came from Tura, just across the river, from where it could be brought by barge across the Nile and along a canal that ran to the edge of the cultivated area, not far from the plateau. The long causeways linking the valley and mortuary temples may well have served initially as ramps along

Stylized papyri, superbly carved, are captured in this close-up detail from the Temple of Amun at Karnak. The papyri decorate the colossal pillars that once supported the temple roof.

which the stone blocks were hauled up to the site. More complicated arrangements were needed to obtain the granite used to line the pyramids' lower courses and burial chambers; this did have to be quarried far to the south, around Aswan, but it could then be shipped down the Nile in a journey that took about a week. Nowhere in the settled 'Black Land' was far from the river, and this made communications relatively swift and efficient. As in other respects, ancient Egypt was 'the gift of the Nile'.

Still, even when properly understood the Egyptian achievement remains stupendous. Almost every operation was incredibly laborious and had to be carried out under a blazing sun. Quarrying to produce blocks of roughly the same size was probably done by heating and weakening the stone, then patiently cutting long, straight grooves into it; later, a different technique was adopted which involved driving a line of wedges into the stone until it cracked. But efforts were economized where possible. On the Giza plateau the deposits of stone were layered and the cutters were able to ease their task by working along the softer layer to remove the harder material above it. Tura limestone also had helpful properties: it was easy to quarry and work because it was soft, but hardened on contact with the air to become a useful monumental material.

Stone was moved on sledges towed by gangs of labourers. One way of doing this was to cover a rock surface with clay in which a series of transverse wooden ties were embedded; the ties were doused in water or mud and the sledge would slide over the lubricated surface with relative ease. But to build one of the pyramids, the workers had to raise course upon course of stone blocks. They almost certainly set up ramps, hauled the blocks up them, and levered them into place; but just how this was done is a matter of conjecture, since there are no Egyptian texts that describe the operation, and objections can be lodged against every plausible explanation. It is particularly difficult to imagine how the ramps worked – whether they ran along the sides of the pyramid (eventually reaching a hard-to-believe height) or were somehow used internally, exploiting the 'steps' in the partly finished edifice. Pyramid-building efforts by modern engineers, even on a very small scale, and admittedly with limited time and resources, have failed to provide a definitive solution.

The Egyptian time-scale was different. Above the burial chamber in the Great Pyramid, in one of the cavities, a stonemason has scribbled graffiti which includes the date: Year 17 of Khufu's reign. Since work on the royal tomb was begun as soon as the king came to the throne, the Great Pyramid must have been finished during Khufu's lifetime. To have embarked on the project at all, he must have been remarkably confident of his longevity, for it was the pharaoh's life-span that determined the time available for building. Once he died, his tomb had to be ready within the seventy days allocated to embalming and funerary

The Temple of Isis at Philae. This photograph conveys the awe-inspiring monumentality of the main pylon (ceremonial gateway); in the distance stands the colonnade of the courtyard.

rituals. If it could not be finished in time, someone had to decide what could and should be done: the priorities are not always obvious, since some unfinished tombs in the Valley of the Kings were not even cleared of debris before being sealed.

The labour force recruited to build the pyramids brought together professional craftsmen and mostly unskilled labourers who had been conscripted. All Egyptians below the rank of scribe were liable to work on state projects, but it seems unlikely that people were removed from productive employment for long periods. Consequently the most intense work was probably done during the annual inundation, when thousands of peasants had time on their hands. There is no evidence to suggest that they resented being called up, and the absence of any large security force suggests that crowd-control was not seen as a problem. Moreover the ample rations of food and clothing, provided for the labour force by an efficient administration, may have been a positive incentive at a time when farmers were living on grain stored from the previous harvest.

Quite a lot is known about the professional element in the workforce, thanks to excavations at three towns or villages from different periods of Egyptian history. All three were founded by the state and laid out in a series of terraces for worker-occupation. The oldest, Kahun, dates from the Middle Kingdom and housed the builders of Senruset II's pyramid complex; this was of course a less ambitious project than the Giza pyramids, employing mud brick for the core. As well as building workers, Kahun was occupied by priests and officials concerned with Senruset's mortuary cult. The workers probably moved on when their tasks were finished, but Kahun continued to function as a town for about a century, when it

Colossal Osiris figures, each holding a crook and flail across its chest, backing on to pillars; in the foreground, a granite head of Ramesses II. The site is the Ramesseum, the pharaoh's mortuary temple.

was abruptly abandoned, as though struck by disaster; people left behind quantities of their everyday possessions, unintentionally providing archaeologists with invaluable evidence of ordinary Egyptian life.

Kahun was a mixed settlement, never exclusively inhabited by builders. Over three hundred years later, when the New Kingdom pharaohs began to be buried in the Valley of the Kings, a village was founded with the sole purpose of housing the workmen who would excavate and decorate the tombs. Deir el-Medina was occupied for well over four hundred years, until the end of the Ramesside dynasty. There was a short break when the workforce was transferred to a similarly purpose-built village at Amarna, far to the north, where Akhenaten wished to build a new capital and prepare rock-cut tombs in the cliffs. But when the heretic pharaoh died, his capital, Akhetaten, was rapidly abandoned and the workmen returned to Deir el-Medina.

The main settlement there was walled and consisted of about seventy terraced houses. It was run by two overseers or foremen, assisted where necessary by scribes. The inhabitants were not labourers but skilled men such as stonemasons, painters and relief-carvers; when manual labourers were needed, for example to remove excavated rock, they were recruited from the people scattered about the area and were paid less than the artists and artisans. The villagers were generously treated, each receiving a house and animals, a rest-hut close to the workplace in the Valley of the Kings, tools, clothing and sandals from the warehouse, and wages – mainly in grain and other foods – once a month. Their trades were also advantageous in the afterlife; during their leisure hours the artisans were able to prepare very decent rock-cut tombs for themselves and their families. If they had a grievance, it was that their wages often arrived late, especially during periods when the central administration was in trouble. It was non-payment lasting for months that led to the first recorded strike in history during the reign of Ramesses III. The outcome is not known, but the men must have been adequately looked after, since they and their descendants remained in business for at least another eight reigns.

This unfinished colossus still lies in the granite quarries of Aswan. If completed, it would have been the largest known obelisk, but it developed a fault (visible in the photograph) and was simply abandoned on the site.

Obelisk raised by Ramesses II outside the Temple of Amun-Kamutef at Luxor. It is one of a pair; the other stands in the Place de la Concorde, Paris.

6 ARTISTS AND CRAFTSMEN

MOST SURVIVING EGYPTIAN ART WAS MADE FOR A PURPOSE, USUALLY CEREMONIAL OR RELIGIOUS, AND GOVERNED BY CONVENTIONS QUITE DIFFERENT FROM OURS. AT FIRST SIGHT IT APPEARS ALOOF AND HIERATIC, BUT IT IS ALSO THOROUGHLY HUMAN-CENTRED AND IMPLICITLY OPTIMISTIC, PICTURING A WORLD IN WHICH THE GODS ARE FRIENDLY AND ABUNDANCE LIES AT HAND, READY TO BE ENJOYED IN THIS LIFE AND THE NEXT. THE SHEER MASTERY OF ARTISTS AND CRAFTSMEN, WORKING WITH PRIMITIVE TOOLS AND MORE OFTEN THAN NOT ON INTRACTABLE MATERIALS, IS ONE OF THE NEVER-ENDING WONDERS OF THIS ANCIENT SOCIETY.

ART WITH A PURPOSE

In modern times the distinction between arts and crafts – between 'fine' arts such as painting and 'applied' arts such as weaving – has often come under attack. To the Egyptians the distinction would have meant little or nothing, since every image or object was made for a specific purpose and the concept of a special kind of art being called an artist did not exist. Painters and weavers, like sculptors and carpenters and potters, were craftsmen, set to perform definite tasks, working side by side in the same studio, and all treated in much the same way by their employers. A few of them signed their productions, or became known for their exceptional skills, but their labours were essentially anonymous, often

submerged in a large collective effort such as the creation and decoration of a tomb.

The craftsman's work was highly valued, but not for its originality or as a vehicle for personal expression. In the arts, as in most things, the Egyptians were a deeply conservative, tradition-loving people. With the exception of the heretic-dominated Amarna period, traditions and conventions, once established, were faithfully adhered to for millennia, with only slight and subtle changes. In Egyptian eyes, the finest artists and craftsmen were those who most effectively deployed the conventions and carried on the tradition.

The generally formal, hieratic poses in Egyptian art were not adopted because they were the only way that the artists could see the world (lively sketches and cartoons on ostraca prove otherwise), but represent a deliberate choice, not just by their makers but by society as a whole. Art was, among other things, an expression of Egyptian values and the social order.

As all of this implies, there was no such thing as art for art's sake in ancient Egypt. The Egyptians were far from insensitive to beauty, but aesthetics were subordinate to function. Just as pots were made to be receptacles, so statues, reliefs and paintings either existed to glorify kings and gods, expressed piety in the form of votive objects, or populated tombs with scenes and figures that would magically come alive, enabling the dead to re-experience the joys of the upper world: the joys but not the pains and perils, which Egyptian art ignores unless they are inflicted on Nubian or Asiatic foes, presented as caricatured racial stereotypes.

Such works were a way of fixing and mastering reality, a magical operation that many societies have sought to accomplish by the naming or picturing of objects. In their thorough way the Egyptians did both, attaching inscriptions to their sculptures and paintings so that there could be no doubt as to what they represented and why they had been carved or painted.

With its conventions and formulas, and its organization of scenes into strip-like registers, Egyptian art often resembles a form of writing, conveying information through imagery that could instantly be 'read'. In this it is not very far removed from the hieroglyphs – themselves stylized pictures – that reinforced its message.

The continued use of such a beautiful but laborious and over-elaborate script suggests that the Egyptians were conscious of its aesthetic appeal, and in fact inscriptions were laid out with conscious attention to overall design, sometimes to the point of using the same text twice over on a surface for the sake of symmetry. So strong was the association of pictures with writing in Egypt that the same term, *sesh*, was used for a scribe and a painter or draughtsman.

Opposite page: Interior of the 5th Dynasty tomb of Ptahhotep at Saqqara. The extraordinary skill of Egyptian art-workers, and the number of man-hours expended on funerary art, still has the power to astonish.

Left: Relief carving in the Amarna style associated with the heretic pharaoh Akhenaten. This is obviously a trial sketch or model that was intended as a guide for the craftsman who executed the work.

Below: A jewellery-making workshop. The craftsmen bore holes in beads, some of which are being polished and assembled as a broad collar. At the bottom right a metalworker is using a blowpipe to stoke up his brazier.

Akhenaten's daughters by Nefertiti; the elongated heads are a feature of the curious Amarna style. The dense ornamental background is reminiscent of oriental carpets. Painted stone fragment from Amarna.

WORKERS IN STONE

Despite the huge number of Egyptian artefacts that have been found and conserved, even more have been lost. Obviously the looted tombs of the pharaohs contained spectacular works of art, perhaps finer than anything now known. But the recovery of other items – for example, paintings that decorated the walls of noble or affluent families – might arguably be of more value in widening our understanding of Egyptian culture. At the moment, an over-high proportion of the Egyptian art that has survived was made for the tomb, the royal family or the great cult temples; and, through accidents of politics and climate, most of it comes from Upper Egypt (which is dry and relatively remote) rather than the Delta.

However, new discoveries are unlikely to do more than slightly modify the prevailing conviction that the production of works of art was highly organized and conducted on a large scale. The most important workshops and studios were attached to royal palaces and temples, and the most ambitious enterprises could only have been undertaken by the pharaohs, whether for their own benefit or to honour their families and favourites. The Overseer of All the King's Works was responsible for construction projects and, presumably, any art-work closely associated with them, such as inscriptions and reliefs on buildings and obelisks. Other ministers may have had a hand in the provision of furnishings, which in the case of royal tombs would have entailed the production of everything from ships to sarcophagi. There was also a Chief Sculptor, a title that is most likely to have concealed an efficient administrator, perhaps with an acknowledged capacity for judging good-quality work. He was certainly not a worker in stone who wielded a mallet and chisel; in fact, the examination of unfinished figures found in the remains of studios has revealed that they were designed by a master and actually carved, under supervision, by a humbler operative. Incidentally, 'Chief Sculptor' was one of the titles held by Imhotep, who is credited with designing the first pyramid; his other titles – Chancellor of Egypt and High Priest of Re at Heliopolis – emphasize the closeness of the connections between religion, scribal administration and the arts.

The existence of a tradition-based art, produced by a craft-trained workforce, must have made it relatively easy for an official to organize and direct most projects. In view of the collective and bureaucratic way in which such projects were carried out, the quality of Egyptian art, maintained over such long ages, is quite astonishing.

The Egyptians carved, modelled or moulded a wide range of materials, including stone, wood, metal, clay, glass and ivory. But the most ambitious and prestigious works were carved in stone, a material which Egypt possessed in abundance and great variety. Much of it was close to hand or easily available; and, more than any other medium, its strength and durability seemed to promise that the individual it celebrated would live forever in human memory.

Both very hard and relatively soft types of stone were quarried along the Nile, in the eastern desert or in Nubia. Throughout the pharaonic period the main soft rocks, limestone and sandstone, were used for building and sculpture on a huge scale. But the Egyptians also acquired impressive skills in working hard stones as early as Predynastic times, when quantities of basalt vessels were produced. Among the other hard stones used were granite, speckled diorite, quartzite and schist; even quarrying them was a tricky business, since the stone had to be heated, doused with water and pounded to remove it from its bed, a process which could easily damage the hard-won material.

Soft stones were worked with simple tools: wooden mallets and copper or bronze chisels, saws and adzes (axe-like implements with the blade set at right-angles to the haft). Hard stone had to be pounded with equally hard stones, often in the handy form of balls of a naturally occurring material, dolerite. Grinding, smoothing and polishing was done with the help of quartz sand; hard stones took a particularly high polish which enhanced

Seated statue of Bedjmes the shipbuilder; an early example of a small statue intended for a private tomb. He carries an adze over his shoulder, indicating the nature of his calling. Red granite, c.2650 BC.

Three scribes of the 25th or 26th Dynasty. Figures of this type, block statues, were particularly economical to make and left ample space for the inscriptions which, for the Egyptians, were as important as the images.

and lightened their distinctive and massy appearance. Remarkably, despite the extreme difficulty with which they were worked, hard stones were used for some of the finest examples of Egyptian statuary; an early example is the magnificent life-size seated statue of the pyramid-builder Khafre, made of diorite imported from Nubia. Quartz sand was also used as an abrasive in drilling, an operation for which the Egyptians used a metal bit that was rotated with a bow.

Sculptures consisted of more or less three-dimensional figures – statues and stauettes – and relief scenes cut into stelae (inscribed slabs) or panels. Three-dimensional subjects included figures of human or animal gods, individual portraits, and husband-and-wife or family groups. Some of the best-known figures are colossi like the 'Memnon' figures or the huge seated portraits of Ramesses II outside the king's temple at Abu Simbel, but in fact there are not many of these vainglorious objects. Against them can be set the many affectionate domestic groups in which a man and his wife sit or stand beside each other; sometimes, as in the double portrait of Menkaure and his queen, the woman's hand is carved in relief so that it appears to be sneaking lovingly from behind round her husband's waist or arm.

If Egyptian statuary nevertheless makes an impression of extreme formality, it is because of its stiff frontality and restricted range of poses. With a few exceptions such as recumbent animal-figures, a statue was generally designed to be seen from the front, as if standing or sitting with its back against a wall. And in fact standing figures were not carved completely in the round but always rested against a pillar; this may have been a convention, or may simply have been a way of making sure that the figure was adequately supported. Looking at a group of Egyptian statues creates a strong sense of the stone block from which each of them has – but only just – escaped. Single standing figures are commonly shown with arms held straight against their sides and the left leg slightly advanced – one of only a few significant departures from a rigid at-attention pose. (Incidentally, the area of stone behind the advanced leg was not removed, since that too stood at an angle from which the statue would not be viewed.) There were practical advantages to these restrictions. A tight, contained figure could be carved with less effort, and from a smaller block, than a figure that, for example, stretched its arm out into space. It seems unlikely that the pharaohs would have economized if they had not preferred formal, hieratic images, but such material considerations probably reinforced artistic conservatism in the intractable medium of stone. Significantly, somewhat more varied poses were rendered in wood carving.

Seated figures were also posed frontally, sitting bolt upright with one arm held close to the chest or both hands placed in front of them on their legs; the back of the seat or throne was another flat, unworked area. High officials were portrayed as scribes, cross-legged on the ground with a partly unrolled papyrus book across the knees. In an alternative version, the block statue, the scribe sat with his knees drawn up, draped in a long robe. The result was an extremely compact sculpture, its origins in a block of stone still clearly visible. The smooth surfaces created by the draped robe give these figures a distinctive, stylized elegance and, from their subjects' point of view, had the advantage of leaving large empty surfaces that could be filled with hieroglyphic inscriptions.

The present appearance of most Egyptian statues is deceptive, since they have lost their once-bold colouring. Limestone and other soft-stone figures were plastered, then painted or gilded and provided with rock-crystal eyes. Works in hard stone were treated with more restraint, only details such as the eyes and lips being coloured, probably because their brilliant polished surfaces were thought sufficiently effective in their own right. Where the original colours have survived on figures, the effect is quite startling: Prince Rahotep and his wife Nofret, despite their formal seated poses, seem intensely alive, as if the promises of their religion have been fully kept. They also display one of the major conventions of Egyptian art in an almost dramatic form: Rahotep, as a man, has the red-brown skin colouring of the individual who lives and works much in the open air, whereas his wife's pallor indicates her sex and the indoor existence implied by it.

The figures of Rahotep and Nofret are clearly

Prince Rahotep and his wife Nofret; from their 4th Dynasty tomb at Meidum. Unlike most Egyptian statues, these have not lost their painted surfaces. The prince's skin is much darker than his wife's, a convention that emphasizes their different outdoor-indoor roles.

true portraits, not depictions of conventional types, although it is perfectly possible that the sculptor flattered them a little. Some other statues are even inscribed 'carved from the life', presumably conveying the artist's pride in capturing a likeness. However, tomb figures often portray the subject as he or she might have been at some chosen time in the past, when suitably mature and vigorous, or as a series of figures at different stages of life. Portraiture was an aspect of Egyptian art in which fashions did slowly change, depending on whether, at any given time, there was a preference for idealized or for more down-to-earth images of the living and the dead.

RELIEF CARVING

Reliefs created a very different impression from sculpture in the round, and embodied a different set of conventions. Reliefs were essentially pictures carved on stone surfaces such as palettes, stelae and the walls of tombs and temples. Unlike free-standing statues, they were effectively two-dimensional, although a little closer to three-dimensionality than paintings done on a flat surface. The relief probably developed from a type of simple engraving – the incising of lines on a stone surface to create an outline picture. In the relief proper, the carver cut away the entire picture background surrounding the figures and objects so that these stood out from the surface and could then be internally modelled. The Egyptians usually restricted themselves to low relief, in which only a thin background layer is removed and the modelling of the relief areas is quite shallow. (By contrast, figures in high relief may stand out so boldly that they are nearly three-dimensional.) But they also devised an alternative technique known as sunk relief, practised hardly anywhere outside ancient Egypt. It involved scooping out some material on the inside of the contours, so that the modelled areas within them appear to rise up from some unseen surface underneath. Both forms of relief are less labour-intensive than carving in the round, and are well-adapted to decorating large areas. Sunk relief has a very distinctive appearance and interesting light-catching properties that make it highly effective on the

A workman adds the finishing touches to a large metal vessel, using a mallet and chisel. Wall painting from the tomb of Rekhmire, vizier under two pharaohs of the 15th century BC.

Colossal statue of Alexander the Great, found at Luxor. Alexander is shown as a pharaoh, but the hieratic style of the carving has been modified by the naturalism of Greek art.

outside walls of temples. Even more economical than low relief, it was used on a large scale by Akhenaten when he was building his new capital, Akhetaten, and needed to make it habitable in short order. Though reliefs are primarily associated with stelae and walls, superb examples of the technique were created on the large ceremonial palettes made at the very beginning of Egyptian history. The earliest palettes are covered with animals and corpses in apparently wild confusion. By contrast, the Narmer Palette might well symbolize the emergence of a new, disciplined culture; even if it does not literally record the unification of Egypt, it is something of a landmark in the development of the Two Lands.

In fact, most of the idiosyncratic features of two-dimensional Egyptian art are already present on the Narmer Palette. Whereas Egyptian statuary is, in a general sense, realistic, reliefs and paintings are governed by a set of conventions designed to make certain points about what they were showing. Narmer, the triumphant smiter of his foes, is larger than the other figures, since status, not mere appearances, would henceforth determine size. (Consequently there is no sense of perspective, and when an Egyptian artist wished to indicate that one object was closer to the viewer than another, he had to do it by showing the two as overlapping, so that the fully-seen object was interpreted as being in front.) The action is clarified by separating the scenes into registers, framed strips in which the base line serves as the ground on which the figures stand. Narmer and his followers are all facing to the right, as the majority of two-dimensional figures would do on reliefs, paintings and papyri for the rest of ancient Egyptian history. And they are shown standing in the anatomically impossible poses that have proved so puzzling to generations of people brought up on the western tradition of fidelity to outward appearances: the head is seen in profile, with a full-frontal eye set in it; the shoulders are turned to face the viewer, while the legs and undifferentiated feet also appear in profile.

Needless to say, this arrangement was a matter of deliberate choice. To make an image worthy to last forever, and to exploit to the full the magical, life-giving properties of art, the carver or painter selected the most significant or characteristic aspects of his subjects. The convention seems to have taken on a moral value, as the only dignified way in which a human being ought to be represented. At any rate it was always employed when the subjects were persons of any consequence, and was also commonly applied to lesser folk; but in their case it was relaxed when the scene called for pictures of physical activities such as food being served by a maid, carpenters sawing or dancers shimmying.

Detail of a relief showing figures bearing different types of produce; from the temple site at Kom Ombo in Upper Egypt. Carved in the Ptolemaic period, the reliefs show the persistence of traditional Egyptian art.

PAINTING

Reliefs were widely employed as tomb and temple decorations. Like statuary in the round, they were painted and therefore both colourful and durable. Painting alone – done on a flat, uncarved surface – was regarded as a second best, acceptable on the perishable walls of palaces and houses, but not durable enough for the 'eternal houses' of gods and men.

Fortunately for us, some people could only afford the cheaper form of decoration, and others had to put up with it on sites where the rock was too soft to carve properly. This was in fact the case at the necropolis sites on the west bank of the Nile opposite Thebes, including the Valley of the Kings. But for such accidents, few paintings would survive beyond those on papyri and coffins. The loss would be great, for Egyptian painting, though as formal and conventional as reliefs, has passages of greater fluency and, on occasion, a lively approach to everyday and natural scenes that make its labourers, musicians and dancers, animals, birds and plants, heaps of fruit and bouquets of flowers, a particular delight not found elsewhere in Egyptian art.

The preparatory work on paintings and reliefs was carried out in much the same way. A master-draughtsman made an outline drawing of the figure or scene on a white-plastered board, and his design was then transferred to the wall surface on a larger scale. This was done by 'squaring-up', a method that is still used by artists for purely mechanical copying. A grid of squares was superimposed on the original drawing. A proportionally identical grid, in which the squares were much larger, was marked out on the wall with a taut length of twine that had been dipped in red paint; then assistants copied the design, square by square, on to the wall. By breaking down the design into relatively small framed units, squaring-up simplified copying and ensured that the proportions of the original were accurately reproduced. Even so, the copying did not always satisfy the artist in charge; there is visible evidence of this in the masterful strokes, correcting the original, which appear on some unfinished works.

Portrait of a boy wearing an amulet. This is one of the celebrated encaustic (wax and pigment) portraits produced during the Roman period; they were positioned over the face of the deceased in the coffin.

The Egyptians also used the grid to create human figures according to a fixed canon of proportion. Each square corresponded to the width of the figure's clenched fist, and the figure itself stood exactly 18 squares high from the sole of its foot to the hairline of its forehead; similar square-measures determined the size of other parts of the anatomy.

Among the many innovations of Akhenaten's reign was a new 20-square canon, producing a longer figure. It was abandoned on Akhenaten's death, but in later times the Egyptians adopted an even more elongating, 21-square canon.

When the squaring-up was done, and had been corrected by the master, the carver or painter got to work. Like the stonemason, the painter was not independently creative, but worked under direction, filling in the outlines with appropriate colours. These were water-based and were generally applied flatly, without any significant attempt to convey shading or texture, although an ultra-thin layer of white might be expertly applied over flesh tones to convey the transparency of fine linen during periods when that was fashionable. Greater licence seems also to have been allowed in rendering natural objects such as birds and plants, which are among the most appealing of all Egyptian painted subjects.

STYLES IN ART

Work in progress: a master-sketch (left), complete with guide-lines, and an unfinished relief beside it. From the tomb of Horemheb in the Valley of the Kings.

No brief account of Egyptian art can chart its development satisfactorily, since the changes that occurred were not big and bold but slight and subtle, for example in the balance between realism and patterning in the portraiture of each age.

The paramount influence of the pharaohs on Egyptian culture is shown by the way in which the arts rose, decayed and were renewed in parallel with the fortunes of the monarchy; hence the Intermediate Periods between eras of strength and unity generally witnessed an artistic as well as a political decline.

Old Kingdom art tended to be formal and solemn. Royal portraits were lofty idealizations, intended to inspire awe in the presence of divine majesty. However, this generalization is partly contradicted by the amiable-seeming portraits of Menkaure (singularly appropriate to his reputation as a ruler), so different from those of his father Khafre.

A century or more of confusion followed the fall of the Old Kingdom, but a less formal art emerged with the stabilizing of the Middle Kingdom. In painting, colour was used more freely and everyday scenes became more varied, notably in the tombs at Beni Hassan in Middle Egypt. The facial expressions on royal portraits became less remote, and from the time of Senusret III (1874-1855 BC) kings often looked reflective or even careworn.

For much of Egypt's third great era, the New Kingdom, the arts reflected a pronounced elegance, refinement and luxury, influenced by new contacts with the Aegean and the Near East, and paid for by tribute and plunder. Royal portraiture now conveyed a rather bland, smooth, youthful image, sometimes sharing the tactile, even sensual, element often found in other types of statuary. During the 18th Dynasty (that is, the Hatshepsut-Tuthmosis-Tutankhamun era) painting was at its most relaxed and lively; banqueting scenes were particularly popular, evidently catering to a taste for scenes of opulence and entertainment, featuring revealing female costumes as well as virtual nudity. There is no way of knowing whether this reflected changes in reality or only in artistic convention; whichever may have been the case, it seems to have provoked a reaction during the following (Ramesside) dynasty, perhaps associated with the counter-attack of orthodoxy against the accursed Akhenaten and all his works.

This would not have been surprising, for the only really dramatic innovations in Egyptian art are associated with the heretic pharaoh and the Amarna period. Opulence and sensuality remained important elements in these works, but they were integrated with new subjects and a number of new stylistic features. Portraits of

Head of Queen Tiy, the wife of Amenhotep III and mother of Akhenaten. One of the more strong-minded women in Egyptian history, she seems to have played an important political role even after her son's accession.

Akhenaten himself are like no other representations of pharaohs from the beginning to the end of Egyptian history. There has been endless speculation about their strange, epicene characteristics – the long face, the wide, heavy-lidded eyes, the fleshy lips, feeble upper torso and bloated belly. This is either warts-and-all realism or a mysterious new artistic convention. Akhenaten's father, Amenhotep III, was portrayed from early in his reign as possessing almond-shaped eyes and very full lips – but were these real characteristics, inherited by Akhenaten, or does their presence merely show that the new convention was already present, though not fully developed, in the earlier reign? More convincing as evidence of new conventions are candid portraits showing an elderly Amenhotep and his lined and rather disagreeable-looking queen, Tiy; these do suggest that realism had come into vogue, although they hardly prepare us for the apparent abnormalities of Akhenaten's physiognomy.

However, whether or not Akhenaten's portraits reflect his actual appearance, there is no doubt that their distinctive features were transferred, with modifications, to other subjects sometimes including his queen, Nefertiti, and their children. Akhenaten's chief sculptor created a pot-bellied self-portrait and declared that the king himself had taught him how to make statues – a discreet way of declaring that the dominant convention had been imposed by royal decree.

Amarna art makes a curiously mixed impression. Strangely endowed and proportioned, the members of the royal family are shown in scenes of extraordinary intimacy, the adults cuddling children who climb all over them. Human feeling mingles with the religious ecstasy evoked by the omnipresent sun-rays pouring down, suggesting that what we are looking at is a new Holy Family who share in the divinity of the Aten. But there are also precise, realistic elements, such as properly articulated hands and differentiated feet, that are only exceptionally found elsewhere in two-dimensional art. An atmosphere of exaltation, sensuous depictions of pleated garments clinging to the half-naked female form, passages of visual realism – these hard-to-reconcile features make the art of Armarna peculiarly fascinating and enigmatic, to a degree that is perhaps beyond its aesthetic merits. In direct contradiction of that proposition, its masterpiece is a portrait bust of classic simplicity – one that was never seen even at Akhenaten's court.

The famous painted bust of Nefertiti was found among plaster casts and half-finished works in the studio of the chief sculptor; it has been interpreted as a trial piece or (perhaps more likely) a master portrait intended to serve as a pattern for the journeymen sculptors who would produce the quantities of carvings needed to satisfy royal demand.

The reaction that followed Akhenaten's death was artistic as well as political and religious, and like many reactions it swung over-hard in the opposite direction. Not only the Amarna style but many characteristics of earlier New Kingdom art were repudiated, and there was a partial return to the more formal styles of the Old and Middle Kingdoms. The tomb of Akhenaten's successor, Tutankhamun, contains evidence of the change taking place. The ivory-veneered lid of a box carries an intimate garden scene in which Queen Ankhesenamun offers Tutankhamun bunches of lotus and papyrus, the emblematic plants of Upper and Lower Egypt; both husband and wife are obviously very young. The more famous panel-picture on the back of Tutankhamun's throne is even more tender and animated. On this, the queen anoints the seated king (whose pose is so relaxed that it could be described a slouch) while the benevolent rays of the Aten pour down on them. The figures continue the Amarna-style representation of hands and feet, with the fingers and toes accurately shown – except that the designer of the throne-panel made one slip, misplacing the thumb of Tutankhamun's right hand. These reliefs are evidently early pieces, made before the return to orthodoxy, or perhaps during some period of uncertainty preceding the complete victory of Amun; in fact an inlaid cartouche on the throne identifies its owner as Tutankhaten, the -aten name by which the king was known before he was induced to switch to the -amun form. Another item from the tomb, the canopic shrine which held the dead king's viscera, also followed the conventions introduced by Akenhaten, for example in being guarded by four gilded goddesses clad in clinging pleated materials and proportioned according to the 20-square canon.

In sharp contrast to these 'Amarna' pieces, the faces of Tutankhamun's human-form coffins and his celebrated gold mask have stylized features and the formal, impersonal expressions associated with Old Kingdom statuary. The only wall paintings, in the Burial Chamber, are also conventional in style and based on the old 18-square grid.

Ka-aper, a 5th Dynasty notable. This splendid wooden statue is still sometimes known as 'Sheik al-Balad', the name given to it by workmen who claimed that it resembled their village headman.

Hesire, 'Greatest of Physicians and Dentists', sits in front of an offering table stacked with loaves of bread. His scribe's equipment is slung over his shoulder and he grips a long staff.

Elements of the Amarna style lingered for a few years under Ay and Horemheb, but rapidly disappeared under the new Ramesside dynasty. During the reign of Seti I the main tradition displayed considerable vitality, especially in the delicately drawn reliefs showing the king worshipping the gods or smiting an enemy. The introduction of the horse and chariot at the beginning of the New Kingdom had provided a variation on smiting, the deadly chariot pursuit, which was now zestfully carved and painted to the greater glory of Seti and his son Ramesses II. Statuary of very high quality continued to be produced under Ramesses, although modern taste is perhaps less enamoured by the Abu Simbel colossi than by the more reflective figure of the king in the Museo Egizio, Turin, where he sits on a throne with tiny figures of his chief wife and son on either side of him. Curiously enough, while monarchs boasted of their martial prowess, apprehensions about the afterlife seem to have spread, at least if the content of tomb paintings is anything to go by: the scenes of feasting and fun largely disappear, and men and women tremble before the gods and depend more heavily on magic spells to take them through the perils of the underworld.

The quality of Egyptian art became less consistent in the latter half of the 20th Dynasty, as the successful reign of Ramesses III was followed by a rapid decline in royal authority. Over the next few centuries the arts decayed, flourished and decayed again, in line with the fluctuating fortunes of the monarchy. Politically the old confidence was never fully restored, and a significant artistic development was the rise of antiquarianism, in the form of past styles revived and reinterpreted with considerable skill and varying degrees of nostalgia.

Nevertheless the distinctive character of Egyptian art was maintained to an extraordinary extent, even when Assyrians, Persians and Greeks became masters of the country. Under Alexander the Great and the Ptolemies, Egypt became part of the Hellenistic world, but Philae, Edfu and other fine temples were built in accordance with Egyptian tradition, and on the pylon at Edfu the pharaoh Ptolemy Auletes still smites the enemy in traditional fashion, however feebly. Indigenous Egyptian and implanted Greco-Roman arts coexisted and sometimes fused, for example in classical-style Serapis figures and stelae carrying elements from both cultures.

However, the only fusions of real artistic significance occur in the funerary items produced during the first four centuries of Roman rule. The heads of some mummies were covered with painted plaster masks, a few of which are startling in their force, whether or not they are true portraits. An alternative way of pro-

Akhenaten and his family worship the life-giving rays of the Aten, which terminate in hand-shapes. The size of the figures conveys their relative importance. Sunk relief from Amarna; the clinging pleats and distorted forms are those of the Amarna style.

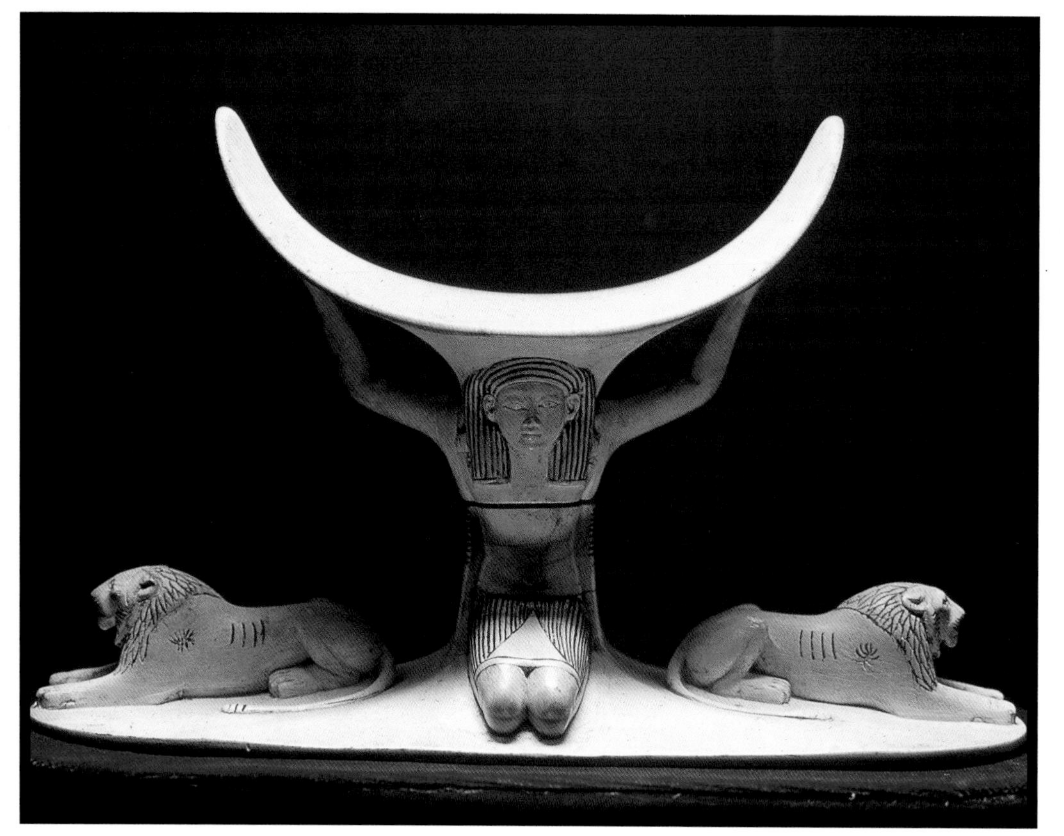

A beautifully crafted luxury object. The upper part of the headrest is supported by a kneeling slave who is flanked by two lions.

viding a mummy with a 'face' was even more significant, becoming the medium for truly great works of art. These are portraits of the deceased, painted on thin wooden panels, which were recovered from burials in the Fayum region and, less plentifully, in other parts of Egypt. Most of them were done with a mixture of beeswax and pigment, and are therefore known as encaustic paintings. The wax base accounts for the rich, glowing effect, but not for the extraordinary sense of a living human presence that is conveyed by the best of the paintings; appropriately, in a land where the afterlife was taken so seriously, these men and women seem not only alive but half-aware that they are being looked at. The subjects are unmistakably individuals, not types, and it has been suggested that they may have been painted long before the subject's death and even hung as portraits in the family home until needed for their ultimate purpose. Shown from the front or slightly to one side, and painted with inspired realism, encaustic portraits are far removed from the old Egyptian tradition; but they are unique, and would have vanished from the earth if they had not been associated with one of the most characteristic aspects of ancient Egypt.

WOOD AND METAL

Egyptian woodworkers fashioned a variety of objects including doors, panels and furniture, chariots and ships, statues, statuettes, reliefs, tomb models and toys. They discovered most of the now-standard techniques of joinery and carpentry, as well as developing the carving skills needed to create works of art. However, since Egypt was not well-supplied with timber, the cannibalizing and adapting of earlier pieces was very common, greatly reducing the number of objects which have survived. The native species of palm were used for basic construction purposes, with sycamore and tamarisk reserved for more detailed work; but high-quality timbers such as cedar or ebony had to be imported from Lebanon or Nubia.

Although they understood the characteristics of various woods, the Egyptians generally carved in the conventional style largely formed by the unyielding nature of stone. Some masterpieces in wood, especially relief scenes, strongly resemble stone carvings and did to some extent serve as substitutes; since the wood, like stone, was plastered and painted, the illusion must in many cases have been complete. However, large wooden figures were usually carved in a single piece but without arms; these were attached later, a fact that evidently encouraged small experiments in pose such as the lector-priest Ka-aper, who holds his arm out, gripping a staff that adds a sense of motion to the conventional left-foot-forward stance. Coincidentally or otherwise, the figure is wonderfully life-like, with a facial expression that seems to change subtly according to the angle at which it is seen.

Discovered by the French Egyptologist Auguste Mariette in the mastaba of a 5th Dynasty courtier at Saqqara, Ka-aper was given a still-current nickname, 'Sheik al-Balad', by Mariette's workmen, because of his close resemblance to their village headman.

All metals were regarded as more or less precious in ancient Egypt, and each was assigned a fixed value by which other commodities were judged. Consequently recycling was even more common than in the case of wood as well as being more effective, since the metal could be melted down and re-used without any constraints imposed by its previous form. As a result, relatively few figure-works survive from all but the final phases of Egyptian history.

The earliest metalworking was done with copper. By the Early Dynastic period, Egyptians were regularly using copper tools and utensils, and the earliest copper statue is said to have been made during the 2nd Dynasty. The earliest to have survived is a life-size – but broken and corroded – figure of the 6th Dynasty king Pepi I; a smaller figure, found inside Pepi, may be his son Merienre.

This statue was made by hammering sheets of copper on to wooden 'formers'. More sophisticated techniques could be adopted once the Egyptians had begun to use bronze instead of copper. Bronze was an alloy of copper and tin that was both easier to cast and, when finished, tougher than copper alone. Although it was introduced during the Middle Kingdom, it was only used on a large scale during the 18th Dynasty; as so often, New Kingdom imperialism led to new wealth entering the country, in this instance bronze, gold and silver, exacted as tribute or acquired by way of trade.

For their metal statuary the Egyptians used the cire perdue ('lost wax') technique. The figure was modelled in a quartz-based substance and coated with a thin layer of beeswax. The fine detailing

Above: Three Apis bulls and a Hathor cow, with headgear appropriate to their divinity; the Apis bull was identified with Osiris. Bronze, 7th-6th century BC.

Figures of Osiris, the king of the dead. The bases of such objects were containers which held either the penis of the dead man or a devotional roll of papyrus. The small figure on the right represents the ba, one aspect of the soul.

Large objects of gold and silver have suffered the same fate as bronzes, except of course for the gold treasures hidden in Tutankhamun's tomb for three thousand years. Until the Middle Kingdom, gold was regarded as less valuable (because less rare) than silver, since Egypt possessed no silver deposits. Egyptian objects made from these precious metals, and from their natural alloy, electrum, are mainly small but of exquisite, meticulous craftsmanship.

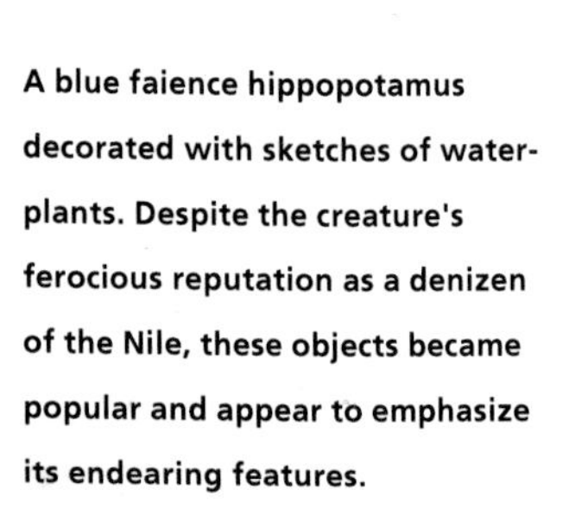

A blue faience hippopotamus decorated with sketches of water-plants. Despite the creature's ferocious reputation as a denizen of the Nile, these objects became popular and appear to emphasize its endearing features.

EGYPTIAN CERAMICS

Pottery is a paradoxical material, easily broken but virtually indestructible: potsherds, whether dumped in a tip or swept out of sight, may last for thousands of years, to be collected and analysed when archaeologists investigate a site. Then, even where they are too fragmentary to be of aesthetic interest, such wares may become important sources of historical evidence.

In the course of their work, archaeologists record the level at which sherds are found, along with observable changes in the way the pots have been made or designed. This provides information that is especially valuable when it comes from a society without written records, which means that it has left behind no dates, lists of rulers, accounts of contacts with other cultures, or similar pieces of direct information. Without these, it is often impossible to determine the stages by which a society developed, or relate finds on different sites to one another. But if pottery found at different levels can be arranged in a chronological sequence, other sites can be 'dated' by placing their artefacts within the framework that has been established.

This was exactly how the prehistory of Egypt was first brought into focus; and in fact the British Egyptologist Flinders Petrie was a pioneer figure in the analysis of pottery remains to establish 'sequence dates'. Using the technique, he was able to identify and name a number of Predynastic cultures, and although adjustments have inevitably been made to his original scheme, it was the basis of all subsequent work.

As this implies, relatively large amounts of pottery survive from ancient Egypt, by no means all of it merely fragmentary. Interesting vessels, deceptively modern in appearance, were produced in the Badarian period (5500-4000 BC), before Egyptians used any kind of potter's wheel. These owe their distinctive appearance to the fact that they were thrust upside down into the ashes of an open fire. The ware burned red where it was exposed to the air, but the buried area around the rim turned black, creating an irregular, rather stylish two-tone effect.

During the next Predynastic phase, pottery was incised or painted with a variety of human, animal and geometric designs. But then there was an 'anti-artistic' development of an unusual kind: decoration disappeared from the wares of the Dynastic period, and Egyptians seem to have lost interest in pottery as an art form, although they presumably continued to appreciate the imported wares which arrived in great quantities from Crete, Cyprus and Syria.

The main exception to the utilitarian character of the native ware was the pleasing blue-painted decoration, often in the form of plant-inspired patterns, introduced during the reign of Amenhotep III. Perhaps obliquely related to the Amarna style, this type of decorated ware was made until the end of the 18th Dynasty, after which purely utilitarian pottery again became the rule right down to the Roman period.

Among the brightest and best-known of Egyptian ceramics are the so-called faience wares, modelled from a kind of sand paste and covered by a glass-like glaze in a variety of blues and greens. (It is so-called faience because true faience is a type of earthenware, whereas strictly speaking 'Egyptian faience' is not pottery at all.) The result was a cheap but attractive product, often mass-produced from moulds, that was popular because it was not too unlike turquoise and other stones beyond the reach of most people.

Many attractive examples of faience amulets and similar objects survive, although in some of them the colour has faded or darkened. Among the most charming figures are little hippopotami and quantities of *shabti*, the figures of 'workers' that were placed in tombs.

Other objects were carved or modelled from ivory, terracotta and glass. The rarity of glass before the New Kingdom suggests that it developed only when manufacturing techniques, and perhaps foreign craftsmen, were imported. Glass-blowing was unknown under the pharaohs, but some very attractive glassware was produced. As well as a variety of small items, some elegant and colourful vessels were made by rolling molten glass round a plug of mud and sand, and then shaping it. Details were worked with pincers, and threads of different-coloured glass could be trailed through the main material. When the piece had cooled, the plug was laboriously chipped out. As has so often been the case, their rather primitive technical resources did not prevent craftsmen from fashioning beautiful and sophisticated objects.

Of the other arts, weaving was perhaps the most important. In ancient times Egyptian textiles were famous for their quality, and both men and women were engaged in home or workshop production. During the Old Kingdom, the professional workshops may have employed only women, but the situation was reversed under the New Kingdom, when the horizontal loom was replaced by a more efficient vertical device. Pleated shirts, loincloths, and mummy wrappings and bandages survive, inevitably in a condition that no longer has much visual appeal; but the sight of such intimate objects, in which a human presence seems still to linger, makes a powerful appeal to the imagination.

Tuthmosis III in the form of a half-human, half-lion sphinx, very much a royal beast; bronze. Tuthmosis (1492-1479 BC) was an appropriately aggressive ruler, re-establishing an extensive Egyptian empire.

7 REALM OF THE GODS

MYTHS OF PRIMEVAL WATERS AND THE SEPARATION OF EARTH AND SKY; A HOST OF GODS IN HUMAN AND ANIMAL FORM; A SEMI-DIVINE RULER, VAST TEMPLE COMPLEXES, A POWERFUL PRIESTHOOD AND FIRM PROMISES OF IMMORTALITY – THESE THINGS WORKED TOGETHER TO MAKE RELIGION ONE OF THE CARDINAL FACTS OF EGYPTIAN LIFE. ALL OF THE GODS HAD TO BE GIVEN THEIR DUE, BUT THE EGYPTIANS' EMOTIONS WERE PERHAPS MOST DEEPLY TOUCHED BY THE STORY OF THE MURDERED OSIRIS, WHICH REPRESENTED THE CYCLE OF LIFE, DEATH AND RENEWAL THROUGH WHICH THEY TOO WOULD HAVE TO PASS BEFORE ENTERING ETERNITY.

IN THE BEGINNING

The Egyptians worshipped many gods and goddesses. These divine beings were credited with a bewildering variety of attributes, and were pictured in many different forms, human, animal and hybrid. In early times most of them were probably associated with particular places and were mainly called upon to use their powers in specific situations such as childbirth. But beliefs and practices changed over thousands of years, often in response to new political conditions; the best-known example is the rise of Amun, a minor deity whose fortunes were initially tied to those of the Theban princes who became masters of Egypt during the Middle and New Kingdoms. Unrecorded changes of this kind must have been

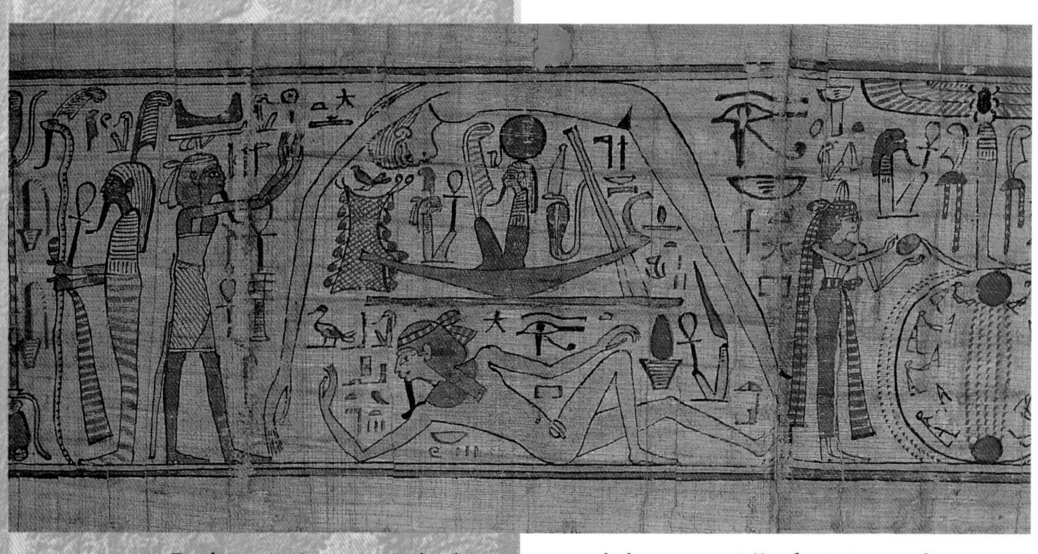

Left: The Creation according to Egyptian myth. Geb (the earth) is separated from his wife Nut (the sky). From the papyrus of Nespakashuty, 11th-10th century BC.

common even in Predynastic times, as rival rulers brought more and more of Egypt under their control. In the process some local deities may have disappeared altogether; but it was probably more common for gods to be organized into triads – families of father, mother and son – or to merge or co-exist so that they became aspects of a single god, with characteristics that were not always logically compatible with one another. In time, the many, many gods of Egypt numbered intimate household spirits, local deities with specific gifts, and universal state gods. The latter, though linked with the earthly kingship of the pharaoh and the maintenance of the cosmic order, also manifested themselves in several different aspects and patronized all sorts of activities: Hathor, for example, was the merry goddess of music, dancing and sexuality; a nurse and healer; the 'Queen of the West' who received the setting sun and protected the dead – and a bloodthirsty avenger, more than willing to destroy the human race on the whim of her father Re!

According to the Egyptian version of the Creation, in the beginning there was nothing but Nun, the watery chaos. Then the Primeval Mound rose above the waters, bearing the sun-god Atum; the mound-image was a potent one for Egyptians, reflecting the emergence of the silt-rich land after the Nile flood. Atum proceeded to make Shu, the god of air, and Tefnut, the goddess of moisture. This act of creation was described with a curious logic: since Atum was solitary, his act of creation could only be accomplished by masturbation; his hand was consequently regarded as essentially feminine, and is sometimes represented as a separate, divine partner.

Shu and Tefnut coupled and gave birth to Nut, the sky-goddess, and the earth-god Geb. He is shown in Egyptian art as lying on his back, while the naked goddess is arched above him. The children resulting from their union were gods vital to the well-being of Egyptians: Osiris, who became the king of the dead, and his siblings Isis, Seth and Nephthys.

This relatively neat scheme was not typical of Egyptian mythology, which never developed a coherent set of characters and stories comparable with those of the ancient Greeks. The most consistent feature of the Egyptian world-view was the pre-eminent role of the life-giving sun, although the name and aspect of the god underwent many changes and elaborations. With the ascendancy of the falcon-headed Re during the Old Kingdom, Atum was not replaced but became Atum-Re, representing the creative and protective aspects of the god. A number of other deities were absorbed by Re or linked with him. Horus, the sky-god identified with the living pharaoh, became in one of his aspects the god of the sun as it appeared on the horizon, while Horus-pharaoh became known as 'son of Re'. Other gods were associated with dawn, noon and night, the stages in Re's journey across the sky in his solar bark, followed by his passage through the dangers of the underworld. Re was eventually fused with a new supreme god, Amun of Thebes, whose origins are obscure and who seems to have had little mythological baggage of his own;

Opposite: One of the animal-headed judges of the underworld. The dead person made a perilous journey through the nether regions, seeking eternal life; from the tomb of Nefertari in the Valley of the Queens.

Below: The goddess Sekhmet; she was shown both as a woman and, as here, in lion form. An appropriately ferocious deity, Sekhmet was the wife of the god Ptah.

instead, as Amun-Re, he took over many of his predecessor's attributes and past exploits.

Even the religious revolution brought about by Akhenaten was solar-based, making a single aspect of the sun – its disc or orb – the exclusive object of worship. In the very distinctive art of the Amarna period, the sun's rays end in hands that reach out to the pharaoh and his family, and it seems possible that Akhenaten's revolution was intended to identify the pharaohs with the godhead; already divine, the king would henceforth brook no rivals. If this interpretation is correct, Akhenaten's often-praised 'monotheism' may in fact have been an expression of megalomania. On the other hand, the text of the *Hymn to the Sun*, said to have been composed by the king himself, contains passages reminiscent of Psalm 104 in the Old Testament – one of many interesting parallels between Egyptian and Hebrew religious beliefs and practices.

Whatever the intention behind Akhenaten's monotheism, its scope appears to have been restricted: the workers who built his new city Akhetaten were not prevented from worshipping their own cult images, and it is likely that the king was concerned to establish worship of the Aten as the state religion but did not attempt to interfere with popular and local cults.

With the death of Akhenaten and the religious counter-revolution, Amun regained his supremacy and ruled unchallenged down to the Ptolemaic period, when he coexisted, and was equated, with Zeus, chief god of the Greek pantheon. Much earlier, the god Ptah had also figured as the world-creator in a rival set of myths associated with his native city of Memphis. He

Re-Horakhti seated at tables laden with offerings. In one of his aspects, the sun god Re merged with the god Horus and was known as Re-Horakhti. The painting is from a papyrus dated c.1000 BC.

was subsequently demoted in favour of Re, but remained important as the patron of artists and craftsmen. Ptah is usually depicted in mummified human form, but he was also one of the few gods who was believed to live on earth as an actual physical being. He was incarnated in the Apis bull, an individual animal specially selected for its markings, which had its own sanctuary at Memphis. When it died, a search was begun for its successor, while the dead Apis was embalmed and buried in a huge granite sarcophagus in the Serapeum at Saqqara.

Hathor, more than any other Egyptian deity, showed many faces to the world and played many parts. In early times the consort of a bull-god, she was represented as a cow and also as a woman, sometimes with cow-like ears, sometimes wearing a distinctive headdress of horns enclosing a solar disc. She was later regarded as the daughter of Re and the wife of Horus in at least one of his manifestations; her name actually meant 'House of Horus'. However, one of a pharaoh's titles was 'son of Hathor', and the pharaohs – incarnations of Horus – were often shown suckling from Hathor in her cow-form.

Egyptians must have had some sense of Hathor as a comprehensible presence, if only as a summation of femininity in all its variety. Some other gods were less enigmatic, clearly personifying a single idea. Maat, often described as the goddess of truth, embodied the principles of cosmic order and harmony, which almost every pharaoh would claim to have restored, however prosperous the reign of his predecessor. In the underworld Maat was closely involved with the judging of the dead. She was portrayed as a winged woman who wore in her hair an ostrich feather – the feather of righteousness – against which the heart of the dead person was weighed. By contrast with the near-abstract conception of Maat, Hapi personified an annual event, the vital Nile flood. Combining male and female elements, he was represented as a bearded being with a woman's breasts, wearing a papyrus-plant headdress.

Animal or animal-headed gods are among the most familiar members of the Egyptian pantheon. Ptah's consort was the lion-headed Sekhmet, a ferocious goddess whose breath was the hot desert wind. The cat goddess Bastet represented a more benign version of the feminine principle. Sobek was a crocodile god, whereas Thoth was variously shown as a baboon and a sacred ibis. As the god of writing and learning, Thoth often appeared as an ibis-headed man using the writing equipment of a scribe to record the judgements made on the dead in the underworld.

Anubis, a dog or jackal, was originally the god of the dead, but was demoted in favour of Osiris. Here, as the god of embalming, he guards a canopic chest.

Another subterranean deity, the snake Apophis, was the enemy of men and gods, even attempting to ambush Re as he sailed through the nether regions in his solar bark. It was because the underworld was such a dangerous place that the god Anubis compelled deep respect. Strikingly pictured in funerary art, he is usually described as a jackal-god, but it is not certain that he was anything more than a large dog with pricked-up ears. He looks formidable, but as embalmer, guide through the underworld, and the benevolent hearer of pleas and prayers, he was popular throughout ancient Egyptian history.

To judge from surviving charms and fragments of wall paintings, the common people felt

Above: The falcon-headed god Horus was closely identified with the king of Egypt; on this relief he wears the double crown of Upper and Lower Egypt.

Below: Horus as a falcon; his various incarnations included sun god, child of Osiris and Isis, and reigning pharaoh. When a pharaoh died, it was said that 'the falcon has flown to the horizon'.

closest of all to lesser gods such as Bes and Taweret, who helped them through everyday difficulties. Significantly, Bes, Taweret and other popular deities had no temples dedicated to them, and it seems likely that they were specifically gods of hearth and home, thought of as permanently in residence. Bes was grotesque – a lion-faced dwarf with a protruding tongue – but he acted as a guardian who kept snakes from the house and assisted women in labour. The hippopotamus goddess Taweret was even more closely linked with childbirth; her image, visibly pregnant, was often used to decorate beds.

Most of the Egyptian gods were native born, reflecting a deep belief that Egypt was the heart and centre of the universe, needing nothing but a few material goods from other lands. But during the New Kingdom, Egypt's contacts with the Near East did lead to the import of Syrian deities such as the war-goddess Astarte and the more enticing, Venus-like Ashtoreth. Both were comfortably absorbed into the Egyptian pantheon. More challenging influences appeared during the Ptolemaic period, when Greek gods and religious ideas were introduced by the dynasty. Excavations at Alexandria have revealed that Egyptian and Greek statues and temples co-existed almost side by side in the city. However, Alexandria was the cosmopolitan capital of the Greek-speaking Ptolemies, and probably untypical of Egypt as a whole. One new deity did emerge from the meeting of the Hellenistic and Egyptian cultures: Serapis, who is generally interpreted as being a hybrid of Osiris, Apis, Zeus, and elements derived from several other Greek gods. He became surprisingly popular, especially outside Egypt; he and his consort Isis, seen primarily as fertility gods, became prominent in the Greek mystery cults that spread throughout the Roman world in the centuries before the triumph of Christianity.

THE DEATH AND LIFE OF OSIRIS

Most Egyptian gods and goddesses were magical beings, apparently unconcerned with moral and ethical matters. From the point of view of a human petitioner, offerings and rituals were more likely to be effective than virtue in appeasing a god or winning his favour. (The pantheons of most other ancient peoples, including the Greek Olympians, operated in much the same way.) The concept of Maat was a partial exception, invoking imperatives of order, good government and piety, but these were mainly binding on the king, who was expected to bring them about by the exercise of his authority. At this level, his subjects were required only to be humble and obey.

In reality the Egyptians were perfectly familiar with concepts such as honesty, just dealing and the protection of the unfortunate, but these were generated from sources such as community custom, wisdom literature and the law. However, religion and personal conduct did come together in one crucial area – the underworld, where every individual could expect to be judged by Osiris, the god of the dead, and found deserving or undeserving of eternal life. A command of magical spells always eased the way through the underworld, but in the course of time the actual judgement of the individual seems to have been increasingly based on his or her righteousness.

This alert cat, adorned with earrings, is one of many delightful animal studies by Egyptian artists. Inevitably there was a cat goddess, Bastet, whose popular shrine once stood at Bubastis. Bronze, c.600 BC.

Their fervent belief in an afterlife made such matters of vital, personal interest to Egyptians; so it is hardly surprising that the most powerful and coherent of their myths centre on the emblematic death and resurrection of Osiris and the link between the god and the upper world.

Osiris himself was said to have been the first king of Egypt, and as such to have created the entire Egyptian way of life: he gave laws to the people, taught them to worship the gods, and showed them how to grow crops and make wine. The fate that subsequently befell him was part of a divine family drama involving his sister-wife Isis, his evil brother Seth, and a fourth sibling, Nephthys, who was also Seth's wife.

Seth was furiously jealous of Osiris and hatched a plot to destroy him. He discovered Osiris' bodily measurements, employed craftsmen to make a magnificent chest that would exactly fit him, and then invited his brother to a banquet. During the festivities Seth announced that he would give the chest to the person whom it fitted best. Many of the guests – all of them Seth's henchmen – tried it out and proved to be too large or too small. When Osiris stepped into it, Seth slammed the lid shut, bolted it and sealed it with molten lead. Fearing Isis' magical powers, he was determined to get rid of his brother's body for good, so he ordered his confederates to throw it into the Nile. The current carried the chest – or coffin – for a great distance, until it became entangled in the branches of a tree. After many adventures the devoted Isis found the body of Osiris and hid it in the marshes of the Delta until she could arrange its burial. But while she was absent Seth recovered it and adopted a new stratagem, dismembering the body and scattering the pieces all over Egypt. Isis resumed her search, finding one piece after another of her husband's body. According to one version of the story, she buried each piece where she found it. This enabled a number of cities to claim the honour of being an Osiris burial-site; Abydos, where his head was said to have been interred, became the god's principal cult city, a place to which all Egyptians hoped to make a pilgrimage, in body or spirit, to be united with Osiris. The alternative, co-existing version had Isis binding together the scattered parts, thus creating the first mummy. Thanks to her magic, Isis was able to conceive a child by Osiris – even in a curious version which states that only the god's penis was not recovered (it had been swallowed by a Nile carp) and that Isis had to fit him with an artificial member. Dead but not dead, Osiris went down into the underworld as its king. Isis subsequently gave birth to Horus, who engaged in an eighty-year struggle with Seth to avenge his father's murder and establish his own right to the throne of Egypt. The struggle provided excellent opportunities for story-telling, and the 'Contendings of Horus and Seth' are particularly lively. Some versions portray the gods as vain and quarrelsome, in a manner usually associated with Greek myth-makers rather than the pious Egyptians. During the contest between Horus and Seth, Re, the king of the gods, is shown as bad-tempered and petulant, but although prejudiced against Horus he was unable to come to a final decision.

While Re and his fellow-immortals failed to make up their minds, a series of encounters took place. Asking for Seth's opinion about an imaginary injustice, Isis lured him into giving judgement against himself; Horus and Seth changed themselves into hippopotami and fought in the river; the two rivals even tried to impregnate each other. Although the mighty Seth tore out Horus' eye, which was fortunately restored by Hathor, Horus triumphed whenever the situation required cunning. One of his most entertaining tricks brought him victory in a boat race against Seth: he plastered the outside of his vessel so that it looked as though it was made of stone; Seth, not to be outdone, made his own boat of stone – and on launching it went straight to the bottom.

Finally the gods referred the matter to Osiris;

Serapis and Isis on a sardonyx cameo fashioned in the 2nd century AD. Its gold frame was added in the 16th century, along with the mistaken inscription identifying the couple as the Roman emperor Antoninus (Marcus Aurelius) and his wife Faustina.

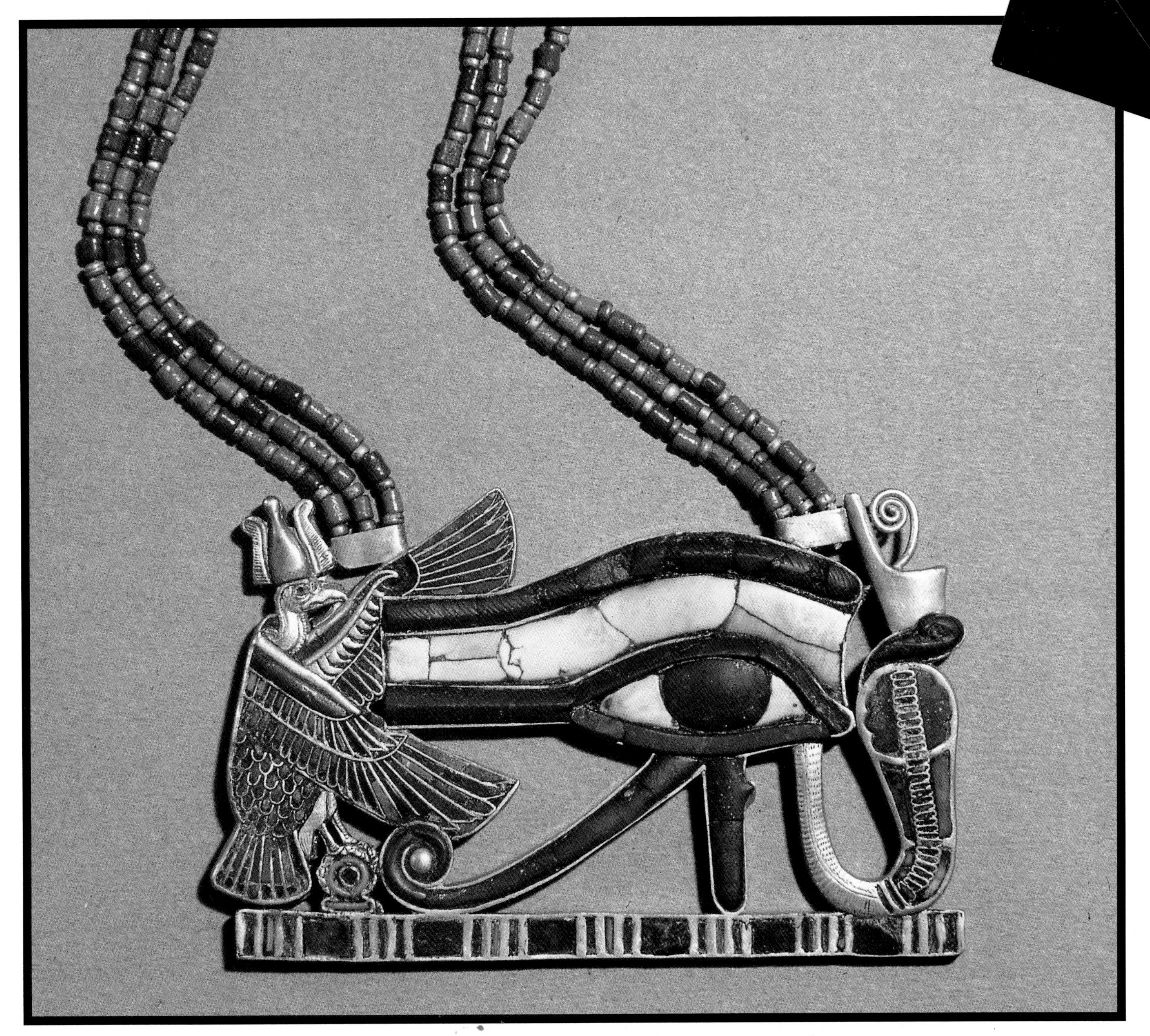

in true Egyptian fashion they sent him a letter, written by Thoth. Predictably, Osiris found in favour of his son; a point of some interest is that when Re showed his irritation, Osiris' sharp response carried the implication that ultimately he was more powerful than even the king of the gods. As a result of the judgement Horus became the living king, just as his father had become the dead king; and Egypt's pharaohs would take each role in turn. It seems likely that the Egyptians' faith in a renewal following death was suggested by the cycle of the agricultural year in which plants ripen and die, only to be reborn at a later season. Osiris, the god of death and resurrection, was in fact also the god of vegetation. The link is even more strikingly manifested in the 'Osiris beds' found in some New Kingdom tombs including Tutankhamun's. The 'bed' was a kind of frame, shaped to resemble the god, which had been filled with rich soil and sown with barley; for once, the magical-symbolic purpose of the object is unmistakable. Paintings of Osiris show him as a king, wearing a double-plumed version of the white crown and a pharaoh's false beard, and holding a crook and flail in his hands despite being swathed in white mummy bandages; but in other scenes he is shown as earth-black or plant-green. Although his part in the mythical narra-

Pendant from the tomb of Tutankhamun. The main components of this splendidly designed object are a healing eye of Horus, the vulture goddess Nekhbet, and the snake goddess Wadjet. It afforded its wearer powerful protection.

tive was essentially passive, Osiris was a popular deity whose annual festival at Abydos rivalled the celebration of Opet at Karnak and Luxor; at Abydos, the god took to the river in his bark, and his story was played out in a series of dramas or tableaux. His sister-wife Isis, whose heroism and cunning had saved both Osiris and Horus, became the ideal of Egyptian womanhood (that is, devoted wife and mother), largely ousting Hathor as the nursing mother of each Egyptian king. She is pictured with a headdress shaped like a throne, or with a set of horns and a disc, also usurped from Hathor.

The falcon-headed god Horus wears the double crown symbolizing the unity of Egypt; it is a composite of the white and red crowns of Upper and Lower Egypt. Sunk relief from the Temple of Philae.

The struggle between Horus and Seth appears to have been a distant echo of real conflicts between the followers of the two gods during the Early Dynastic period. This suggests that Seth was not always an evil character, and probably explains why he is sometimes the antagonist rather than the ally of the evil snake-god Apophis. However, Seth's defeat by Horus made certain that he became associated with all that the Egyptians suspected or disliked – disorder, desert places and foreign lands. Nephthys, although Seth's wife, became devoted to Osiris and is shown side by side with Isis in the underworld, standing immediately behind their seated lord. One result of the connection was that Nephthys became the mother of Anubis by Osiris; since dog-headed Anubis had been the ruler of the underworld until displaced by Osiris, this was doubtless a kindly way of keeping the dog in the family.

The incorporation of Horus into the Osiris story strengthened its connection with the Egyptian monarchy, although Horus underwent a startling transformation in the process, from sky- and sun-god into first a helpless infant and later the youthful contender for the crown. Consequently he appears in Egyptian art in widely different guises, as the protective-combative falcon, a falcon-headed man, a winged sun-disc, and a child with the forelock of youth and a finger in his mouth.

THE PRIESTHOOD

Egyptian priests formed a visibly distinct group within the general population. They dressed in white linen robes and wore papyrus sandals. Their heads and bodies were completely shaven. They had to be circumcised and they were obliged to bathe four times a day. All these were necessary because priests served the temples and, being directly or indirectly in contact with the gods, had to be physically pure; for some this also involved abstaining from certain foods, notably pork or fish.

Priests were also expected to lead fairly respectable lives; but no special sanctity or sense

Bronze figure of a priest at prayer. The Egyptian priest was essentially a servant of the god, not an intermediary between the god and the people at large.

of vocation seems to have been attached to their office as such. Many were in fact part-timers, alternating between service at the temple and working at a profession, on a one-month-on three-months-off basis. They married and had families, and generally speaking a priest's oldest boy succeeded his father in his calling, just as sons did in other social groups.

The high priest of each cult certainly bore a heavy responsibility, since his task was to act on behalf of the king himself in tending the image of the god. However, even this office seems to have required few definite qualifications, for when the temples of Amun reached the height of their wealth and power the high priesthood was assumed by Herihor, an ambitious military man, whose exercise of religious authority seems not to have been regarded as scandalous.

Apart from the high priest and those who assisted him inside the god's sanctuary, there were many others with lesser responsibilities who probably saw the divine image no more often than the common people did. The lowest grades of the priesthood performed routine tasks which might be ritual or might have more to do with estate management than religion. Others developed special skills. Some taught writing, and perhaps other subjects, in the House of Life, or made copies of important texts; some became experts in reading the sky, correcting the calendar and identifying the lucky and unlucky days to come in the course of the year. Priests with special functions might be identified by distinctive additions to their costumes, notably the leopard skin flung over the shoulder of the sem-priest who officiated at funerals and the sash of the lector priest who recited sacred texts during ceremonies; this was an important office, since words and names could only work their magic if the text was delivered without the smallest mistake being made.

Female deities were served by priestesses, although the chief priest in any temple was generally a man. Women played a part in music-making at the temples of both gods and goddesses, especially as singers and dancers, wielding the sistrum and tambourine; and women of the upper class often boasted in tomb inscriptions of holding the official 'Songstress' title.

The wealth and influence of the temples made it likely that they would become involved in politics, and this certainly happened at some critical moments in the New Kingdom and later. The most dramatic was Akhenaten's attempt to promote a new god, the Aten, and suppress the cult of Amun. A later development in the priestly hierarchy was probably also political in its motivation. During the Third Intermediate Period, when the high priests of Amun had established themselves as semi-independent rulers based at Thebes, the pharaohs revived a position known as the God's Wife of Amun. This had been intermittently held during the New Kingdom, most often by the pharaoh's wife, and reflected the belief that the god Amun, disguised as the reigning king, impregnated the queen; consequently each new king was literally the god's child and possessed a title to the throne that was beyond dispute. In its revived form the title was settled upon one of the king's daughters, in combination with another potent office, that of Divine Adoratrice. The holder of these titles was not allowed to marry and would in time adopt another royal daughter as her successor, ensuring that the office would always be loyal to the pharaoh. Residing at Thebes, the God's Wife of Amun exercised great authority within the city, keeping the high priest's ambitions in check.

The crocodile god Sobek enthroned, receiving offerings. For a time, during the 18th and 17th centuries BC, he was so popular that pharaohs regularly named their children after him.

8 BEYOND THE TOMB

LIKE MANY PEOPLES, EGYPTIANS BELIEVED PASSIONATELY THAT THEY WOULD LIVE AGAIN AFTER DEATH, AND THE PREPARATIONS THEY MADE, AT FIRST SIGHT BIZARRE, WERE ACTUALLY PRACTICAL AND HARD-HEADED. SINCE THE SOUL AND THE PERSONALITY NEEDED A BODY TO INHABIT, EMBALMERS DEVELOPED TECHNIQUES THAT WOULD PRESERVE IT FOR ALL TIME, AS A MUMMY. THE FUNERAL WAS ALSO MOVING DAY, WHEN THE GOODS OF THE DECEASED WERE DELIVERED TO A NEW ADDRESS. FOR ANYONE WHO COULD AFFORD IT, THE TOMB BECAME A FINE AND PRIVATE PLACE WHERE AFTER-LIFE COULD GO ON JUST AS IT HAD BEFORE, NOT IN TIME BUT IN ETERNITY.

TO LIVE ON

'Pass the day happily and do not grow weary of it. Think: no man may take his belongings with him [into death] and none that has gone before may return.' These sentiments from *The Song of the Harper* are typical of a pessimistic vein in Egyptian literature whose scepticism is at odds with the apparently profound belief in a happy life after death to which the entire culture was committed. Such contradictions are hard to resolve when they occur in modern societies, so we are never likely to have much insight into the tension between doubt and faith, present sorrow and promised joy, as it was experienced in ancient Egypt. But it is worth bearing in mind that rituals and funerary texts and tomb paintings do not necessarily tell the whole story about the Egyptians' view of reality.

Nevertheless the Egyptians did take extraordinary measures to survive into the afterlife and live comfortably there. Quite apart from anything else, they arranged for themselves to be elaborately embalmed, and built the finest 'eternal homes' – tombs – that they could afford, ranging from quite humble mastabas to mighty pyramids. They took dying (or not-dying) so seriously that most scholars find it necessary to insist on the merry, life-loving nature of the Egyptians. They argue that the older picture of Egypt as a gloomy, death-obsessed land was a distortion created by the accidents of survival (stone pyramids, rock-cut tombs) and discredited by the gradually accumulating evidence about everyday life. In fact, it is claimed, the Egyptians enjoyed themselves so much that they wanted nothing more than to go on as they were for ever. Though useful as a corrective, this view perhaps underrates the extraordinary nature of the Egyptians' preparations for death and the resources they were prepared to devote to them.

Like other peoples, the Egyptians probably glimpsed the possibility of a life beyond the grave by observing the cycle of the seasons, in which plants vanish and are reborn from the seemingly barren earth. In Predynastic times the dead were buried with grave-goods, so a belief in a future existence must already have been present. At some point its imagined character was deeply influenced by a new observation. When the bodies of the poor were consigned to simple pit-burials on the edge of the desert, the sand absorbed all their natural fluids, making it impossible for decay-creating bacteria to live or breed on them. The dead became nature-made mummies and, thanks to the lack of rain in Egypt, they were capable of surviving, desiccated but perfectly preserved, for the duration.

This discovery almost certainly lay at the root of the Egyptians' belief that the physical body was an important, perhaps an essential, element in individual survival – a belief that eventually led them to develop an elaborate procedure for artificially preserving it. This emphasis on the physical does not mean that they lacked a concept of the soul: on the contrary, they held that every person

A cosmetic disaster. The skin of the priestess Henttawy's face was packed to give it the fullness of living flesh; but later shrinking caused the packing to break through, defeating the object of the exercise.

Opposite: Professional mourners earning their pay by beating their breasts and pouring dust over their heads; wall painting from the tomb of the vizier Ramose, who served both Amenhotep III and Akhenaten.

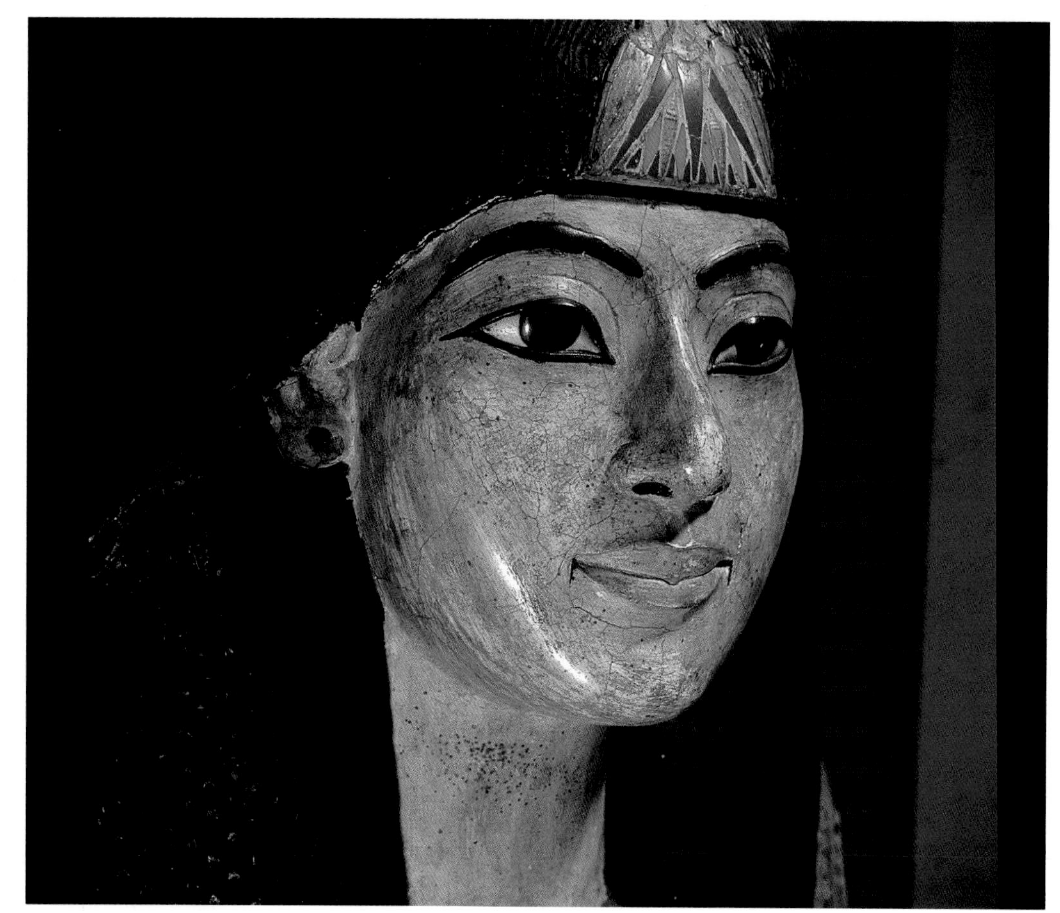

Mummy mask with boldly stylized features, a heavy wig and a lotus ornament above the forehead. Such masks were more or less portraits, assisting the identification of a mummy at the embalmer's, and its recognition in the tomb by its soul-elements.

was composed of several physical-spiritual components, all of which had to remain intact if he (or she) was to survive death without diminution. Apart from the physical body, the individual had three soul- or personality-forms, the *ka*, the *ba* and the *akh*, as well as a shadow and a name, which were also potent. They could all be preserved with rituals and spells, and in earlier times the Egyptians may have felt that a body was not indispensable to a future existence. But evidently the prospect of direct physical survival, once entertained, had an irresistible appeal.

The importance of drying-out the corpse must have been realized when it became apparent that tomb burials failed to prevent the deterioration which had been kept at bay by humble sand-pits. Yet it was natural for the affluent to want a comfortable, respectably furnished dwelling for eternity. Only artificial means of preserving the body would enable it to be suitably housed without forfeiting its chance of immortality.

Few early mummies have survived, but the evidence suggests that it was a long time before a fully successful technique was developed. During the Old Kingdom, a kind of imitation mummy was created; the oldest-known example is a man named Waty, who died around 2400 BC. He was tightly wrapped in resin-soaked bandages which moulded themselves to his features and form. Black paint was used to pick out his features, including the moustache that some upper-class men sported at this time. The treatment of Waty's flesh, if any, was unsuccessful – there are only bones inside his bandages – but a kind of cast or shell corresponding to his physical form remained, presumably endowed with life and energies that were infinitely preferable to extinction.

MUMMIES

During the Old Kingdom period, only the pharaoh had a clear title to immortality, shedding his Horus-self when he died and becoming one with Osiris. Being housed in a pyramid was appropriate to his divine status, and even in death others gathered about him – his queens in their mini-pyramids, courtiers and priests in their mastabas – hoping for a humble part in his afterlife. An important change took place during the First Intermediate Period, perhaps because the collapse of the Old Kingdom altered the Egyptians' perceptions of kingship. From this time, any individual could hope for immortality and achieve a mystic union with Osiris. The king's importance was not necessarily diminished, for he now became the semi-divine intercessor with the gods and the guarantor of the cosmic order, on which the fate of all Egyptians depended.

For the great majority this new conviction, however consoling, made no difference to the way in which they buried their dead, since all they could afford was interment in the desert sand on the edge of the cultivated area. Natural mummification remained the norm. But there must have been a greater demand for embalmers on the part of the court and provincial elites and the official classes. By this time, the basic secret of efficient dehydration had been discovered, although technical improvements continued to be made for another thousand years. Mummy-making was becoming a craft, imbued with a sense of religious awe and run by a closed corporation. The disposable incomes of the embalmers' clients differed widely enough for them to devise treatments of varying sophistication, which were accompanied by a sliding scale of fees. In the example that follows, an imaginary citizen of Thebes during the 18th Dynasty – perhaps a wealthy official such as the mayor – dies and begins the long journey, via the embalmers' tent and the terrors of the underworld, to the security of the tomb.

The citizen's death was greeted with extravagant displays of grief in which the women of the household tore their hair and rent their clothing. This intensity may have been related to the climate, which necessitated a rapid removal of the body: any impression of unseemly haste was contradicted by the hectic emotional scenes that preceded its departure. It was carried across the Nile to the west bank; the dead were said to have 'gone into the west', like the setting sun, and cemeteries were usually to the west of any settlement.

On arrival, the body was taken to 'the place of purification', where it was washed in a solution of natron, the Egyptians' all-purpose sodium-based cleaner and disinfectant. This hygienic precaution also had a symbolic significance, plunging the dead man into the waters as a preliminary to his sun-like rebirth. Every operation that followed had a similar ritual meaning and was accompanied by the reading or chanting of incantations and spells; without these, the merely technical preservation of the body would not have been efficacious. Curiously enough, artistic representations of this first washing might be either symbolic, showing a living person sitting under a beneficent shower, or realistic, with an obviously still defunct corpse laid out beneath it.

The place of purification was essentially a large tent, and so originally was the encouragingly named 'House of Beauty' where embalming was done. These light, presumably temporary structures must have been all that was needed when

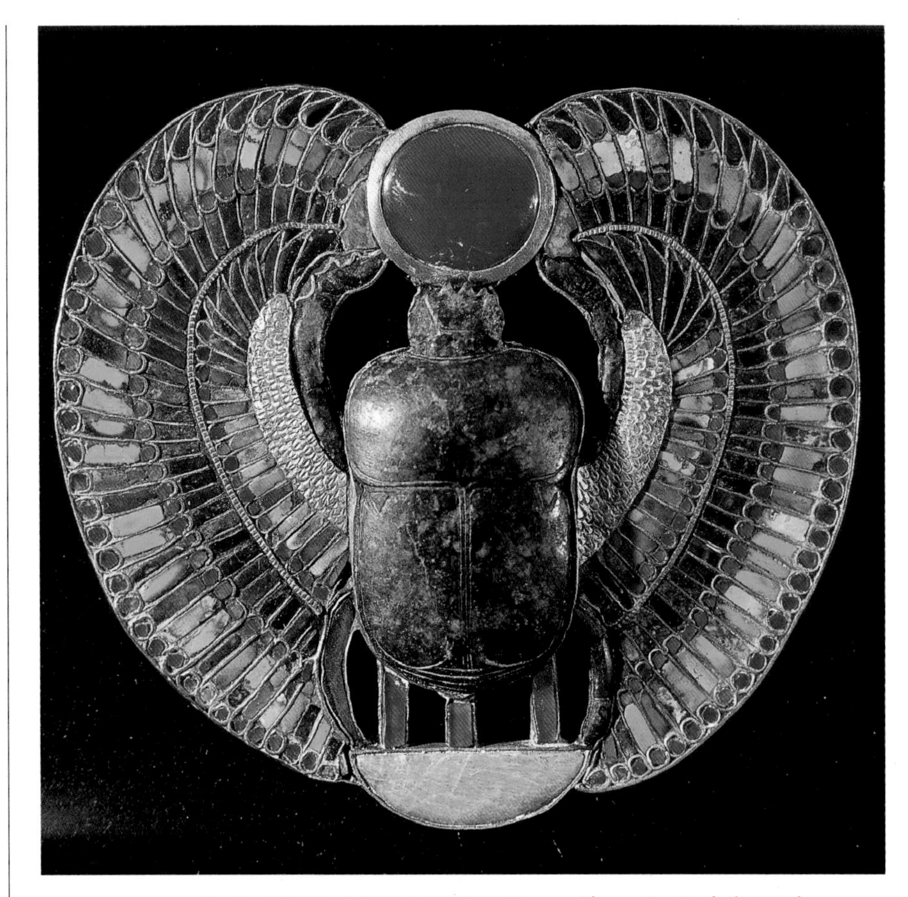

Above: An amuletic scarab pectoral from the tomb of Tutankhamun; gold, brilliantly inlaid with glass and semi-precious stones. The scarab is shown pushing a solar disc.

A scarab pectoral from the tomb of Tutankhamun, hanging from a chain consisting of inlaid plaques; these show the royal uraeus (cobra) as well as more scarabs and solar discs.

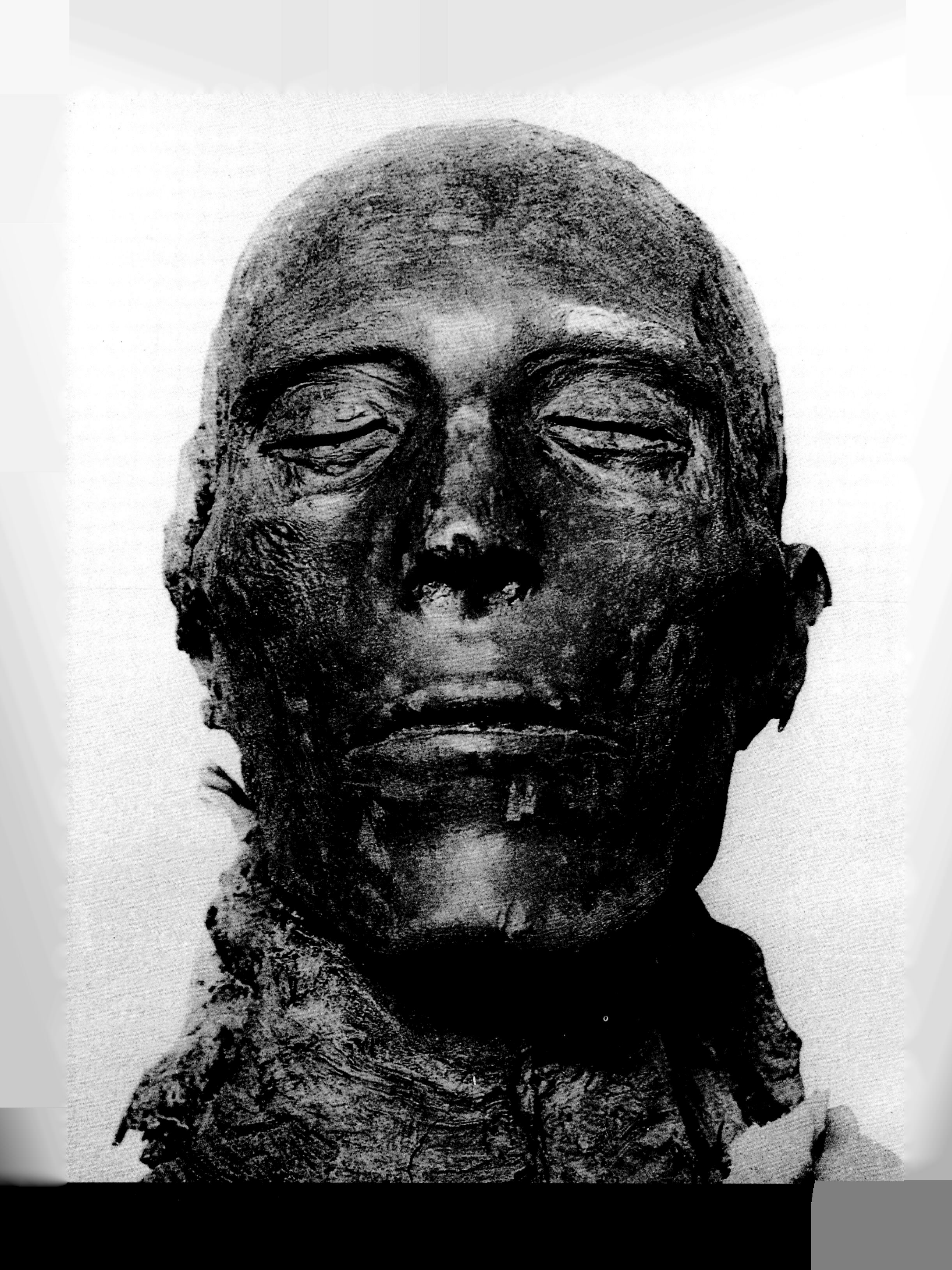

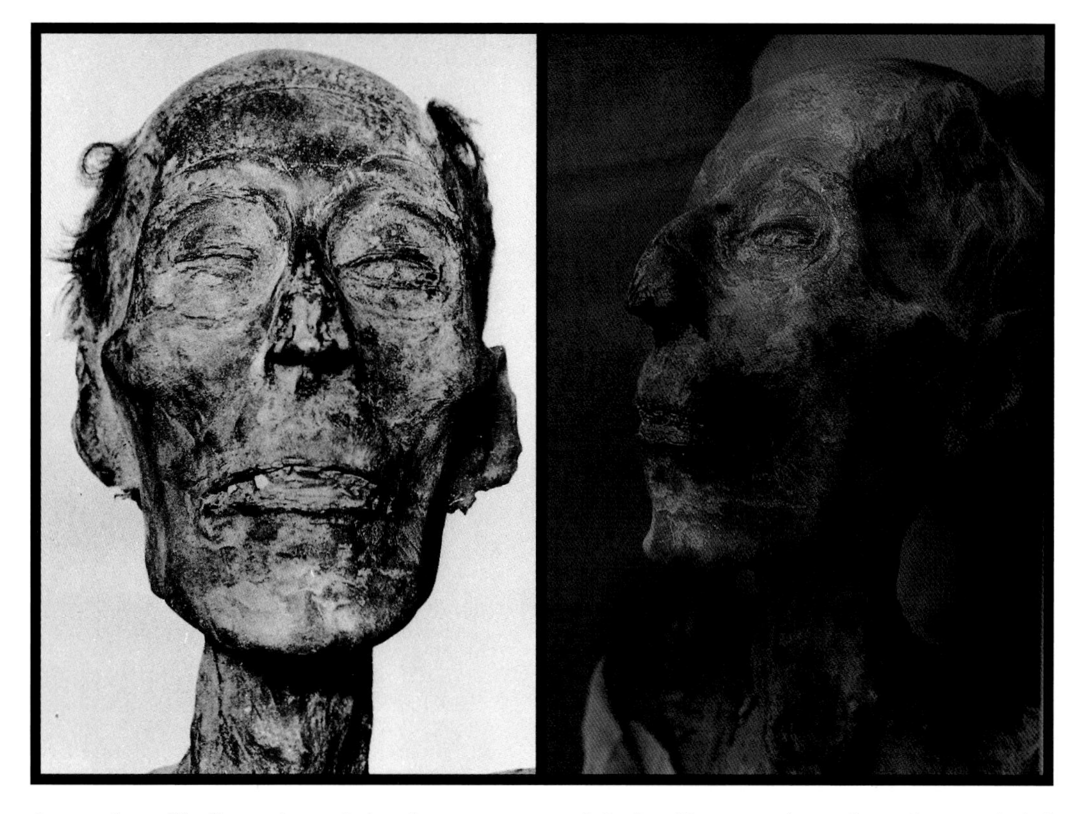

Two views of the mummified head of Ramesses II (1279-1213 BC). He was the son of Seti I (Opposite), whom he closely resembled. Two large caches of mummies, including those of Ramesses and Seti, were discovered in the late 19th century, providing evidence of first-class Egyptian embalming practice and fascinating human material for researchers.

the number of bodies to be embalmed was very small. Egyptian conservatism kept them in use even when demand increased, and there may have been something to be said for doing work of such a kind in airy conditions; but eventually – certainly by the Late Period – the house of beauty became a permanent brick structure.

Here the corpse was attended to by a large staff. Its chief was the Overseer of the Mysteries, who on occasion wore a dog-headed mask that identified him with the embalmer-god Anubis and implied that the dead man was to be restored to life as Osiris. His second-in-command, the God's Seal-Bearer, was in effect chief surgeon, and a Lector Priest was on hand to recite the requisite spells and incantations. All the other operations were carried out by assistants rather grudgingly known as 'bandagers'.

At the house of beauty the corpse was again washed and all its head and body hair was removed. Then the internal organs – the parts most liable to rapid putrefaction – were taken out. A long hooked instrument was inserted into the nasal passage and forced through the bone into the brain, whose contents were spooled out or possibly just allowed to leak away. Since the Egyptians believed that the heart was the centre of the intelligence and emotions, they concluded that the brain served no useful purpose and made no attempt to preserve it.

The most momentous part of the proceedings began when an incision was made in the left side of the deceased and the intestines, stomach, liver and lungs were taken out. The instrument used was not a metal blade but a knife made from obsidian, a glass-like stone which does not even occur naturally in Egypt and must have had ancient magical associations. Moreover, according to one account (by Diodorus Siculus) the 'ripper' who made the incision was subsequently driven from the scene with curses and stones. This was presumably the ritualized punishment for an act that, however necessary, was also impious.

The viscera were not discarded, but dried, coated in resin, bandaged and stored away. Like every non-fluid part of the body, they were essential to survival and had to be preserved. In earlier times they had been kept in a compartmented chest, but from the Middle Kingdom it became customary to store them in a set of four canopic jars (the name, based on a misunderstanding of a Greek legend, is irrelevant to the function of the jars). At some point in the 18th Dynasty, the stoppers of the jars began to be fashioned to rep-

Alabaster canopic jars from a 7th-century BC tomb. They were used to preserve the internal organs of a dead person; the guardian heads at the top represent a falcon, a human being, a jackal and an ape.

resent the heads of the four 'sons of Horus' who would protect the viscera: the falcon Kebehsenuef (intestines), the jackal Duamutef (stomach), the human Imsety (liver) and the baboon Hapi (lungs). Despite their mortuary purpose, these jars, made from a variety of materials, are among the most attractive of Egyptian artefacts. Later on, the viscera were no longer put in jars, but were wrapped in linen packets and put back inside the body or (later still) placed between the mummy's legs. Figures of the Sons of Horus were included in the packets, but canopic jars continued to be made for the tomb, sometimes in dummy form (that is, solid all the way through); this combination of traditionalism and common-sense economy is characteristic of the ancient Egyptians.

Meanwhile the drying qualities of natron were put to full use in treating the body. Its cavities were rinsed out and partly stuffed with linen, leaves and similar materials, surrounded by bags of natron; the bags absorbed internal fluids, while the stuffing helped to maintain the shape of the body during the operation to come. This began when the dead man was laid on a stone table, carved in an elongated lion form, and entirely covered with natron. The internal and external action of the natron would ultimately wring every drop of fluid from his body, assisted by the slight slope of the table which drained away any excess.

After forty days the body was blackened and sticklike, but completely dried out. The stuffing was removed but, because it had been so intimately connected with the body, kept for burial with or near it. Cleaned up and doused in spiced and perfumed wine, the cadaver was re-stuffed, the head filled with resin and/or sawdust, and the skin rubbed with oils to restore as much of its suppleness as was possible. In later times a form of plastic surgery was also practised: small cuts were made in the skin, which was subcutaneously packed to create the full-fleshed look of a living person. (The 11th-century BC priestess Henttawy has become a notorious example of the possible drawbacks, since the stuffing eventually broke out through her skin.) A final coat of resin waterproofed the body. The nails were tied back on with thread and artificial eyes were put into the vacant sockets. The lips of the wound in the side were pulled as close as possible and covered with a protective *wadjet* plaque. Finally cosmetics were applied to the face, a wig was placed on the head, and the body was decked out in the owner's jewels. The result was no doubt a masterpiece of the embalmer's art.

The masterpiece was not created for the benefit of the living, since the dead man would now be placed in a shroud and swathed in bandages from head to foot. The operation was a complex one, lasting from fifteen to seventeen days and, like the actual embalming, accompanied by meticulously performed rituals. The head, torso and limbs, and each of the fingers and toes, were wrapped separately before a wider bandage was used to bind the body into a single object. Further layers of bandages and shrouds and yet more bandages were added before the process was finally done. In total, several hundred square metres of materials went into the wrapping of a mummy. With their oddly hard-headed attitude towards sacred matters, the Egyptians mainly used cast-offs – old household linen for most people, but for the rich the garments used to dress cult-images of gods in their shrines.

At every stage in the bandaging, little figures of gods and a range of amulets were placed on the body at precisely designated points, and bound in; they were made of various materials, depending on the income of the deceased. Amulets protected the dead from human violation, helped the mummy to live, or assisted the soul's passage through the underworld; understandably, dozens or even hundreds of these useful objects might find a place among the wrappings. The most important of all was the heart-scarab, which magically restrained the heart of the deceased from revealing guilty secrets to the tribunal sitting in judgement down in the underworld.

Scarab beetles were popular as symbols or charms in many contexts because of their association with miraculous rebirth and the sun cult. Like the re-born, the beetles appeared to emerge spontaneously from the dung in which they had been laid as eggs; and the adult beetle tirelessly rolling a ball of dung was seen as an earthly counterpart to the heavenly scarab that drove the sun across the sky. Amulet forms included the dramatic *wadjet*, representing the falcon-eye of Horus stolen and injured by Seth, and the *djed*, a pillar with four horizontal bars representing stability. Less often found, despite its omnipresence in Egyptian society, was the *ankh*, the hieroglyph representing life, which consisted of a cross with horizontals like a *djed's*, surmounted by a curious loop. The origin of the *ankh* sign is unknown, but as an image of life – and eternal life – it had great potency.

When the mummy was fully prepared, a mask was placed over the dead man's head and shoulders. A pharaoh such as Tutankhamun had a mask of pure gold, but even the upper classes were normally content with an article made from cartonnage. This material consisted of linen or papyrus that had been stiffened with plaster; it served as a substitute for wood, which was always scarce, and was consequently also used for coffins and other funerary containers. Cartonnage masks were painted or gilded with features that probably gave an idealized view of the dead person, but presumably one that his grieving relatives would accept and his fugitive soul, the *ka*, would recognize when it sought him out in the tomb.

In practice, of course, there were variations in procedure over the centuries, and in the care and reverence with which the body was treated. By the Greco-Roman period the outward trappings were more splendid than ever – the corpse laid out inside a gaudy, gilded coffin, in neatly criss-

A mummified cat, one of many creatures embalmed by the Egyptians. At ancient Bubastis, the cult centre of the cat goddess Bastet, huge vaulted cat cemeteries have been uncovered.

crossed bandaging, with a plaster head or wax portrait over its face – but the embalming was slapdash and most of the bodies had decomposed long before they were unearthed. It would be hard to find a better image of a religion in its final phase, still splendid on the outside but no longer sound within.

THE FUNERAL

When the seventy days were up, the funeral procession crossed the Nile, took charge of the body, and travelled still further west towards the necropolis. The journey is shown in a number of paintings on tomb walls and in papyrus manuscripts. It resembles a sorrowful emigration, with a host of servants carrying furniture, chests, clothing, sandals, game-boards, heaps of food, jars of wine and unguents, and everything else that was needed to lead a normal (after-) life. The scribe took with him his palette, the warrior his weapons and even his chariot. In fact the dead person was literally moving house.

The mummy itself lay in a shrine supported by a flower-decked bier which was sometimes made to resemble a boat; the bier stood on a sledge that was drawn along by a team of oxen. In funerary scenes the shrine is shown as open so that the mummy is visible: as the chief actor in the drama it was appropriate that he should appear, although during the real procession a screen concealed the interior of the shrine. Behind came a smaller sledge carrying the canopic chest. Priests were much in evidence, chanting and waving censers; the leading role was taken by the leopardskin-clad *sem*-priest. Friends and colleagues walked together in sober fashion, but paid mourners wailed and bared their breasts, while half-naked girls performed a ritual dance, *muu*, which was an indispensable item on such occasions for several thousand years. Two women enacted the roles of Isis and Nephthys, wheeling and crying over the mummy, now a candidate-Osiris. Funeral scenes also show a figure in shroud or sack, seated on a sledge; the function of this real, or possibly only symbolic being, the *tekenu*, is still a mystery.

When the cortège arrived in front of the tomb, the mummy was placed in its coffin, which was stood upright on the ground. After ritual preliminaries and a eulogy of the deceased, the male heir – or, in his absence, the *sem*-priest – performed the

A scene from *The Book of the Dead* of Hunefer. The dead man's heart is weighed while a green-faced beast waits to devour him if he fails the test; then, having passed, he is led before the enthroned Osiris. Papyrus, c.1300 BC.

fateful Opening of the Mouth ceremony which was designed to restore the dead person's senses. When this was accomplished the mummy became a suitable vehicle for the dead man's wandering *ka* (soul or life-force), which would take up residence again. Statues and other images of the dead might also have the ceremony performed on them, for if the physical body was destroyed they could act as substitutes.

The Opening of the Mouth involved seventy-five separate operations, including the touching of the mouth, eyes, ears and nose with a set of symbolic implements; among these were a forked object of great antiquity, the *pesesh-kaf*, a model adze and a snake-headed rod. Since the mummy was now capable of consuming them, offerings of food and other goods were made with the appropriate rituals. Finally, despite the lamentations of the womenfolk, the priests carried the coffin into the tomb, which had been furnished during the Opening of the Mouth and was ready to serve as the dead man's 'eternal house'. When the coffin

Osiris, wearing the double crown of Egypt, sits with Isis and Thoth as the dead man approaches, ready to deliver the formulaic responses which should ensure his immortality; wall painting, c.2850 BC.

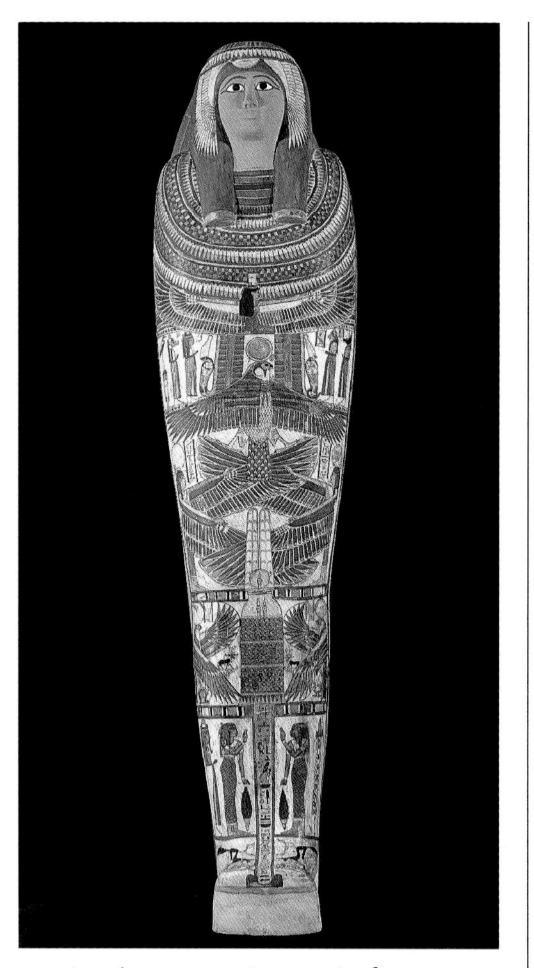

Anthropoid (human-form) coffin, containing the mummy of the Theban priestess Shepenmut; it is made of cartonnage, a composite linen- or papyrus-based material that could be painted or gilded. The painted detail is of great intricacy.

was in place, protective magic figures were arranged round it. Any threatening object or symbol – a weapon or a 'dangerous' hieroglyph – was disabled. The door was sealed and the mourners settled down to a funeral feast just outside the tomb itself.

IN THE TOMB

After his burial, our Theban citizen would only encounter a living human being if his wife died and the tomb was opened for her to join him – or if he received an unwelcome visit from tomb robbers. If his memory was properly honoured, relatives would come to the chapel above ground, deposit letters for him (usually begging for some favourable intervention on their behalf) and leave him food and drink on an offering table held by a seated figure representing the deceased. Realistic enough to know that no one is remembered for ever, Egyptians often arranged for images of foods to be carved on the table so that it would never be completely empty. This kind of magical substitution of image for physical reality, so widely practised by the Egyptians, was obviously regarded as an important fail-safe; and yet it must have been a second best, in view of the great efforts made to secure the 'reality' of an actual body and foods grown in the soil. It would be interesting to know just what effect it was believed to have on the quality of the afterlife if a dead person's spirit was forced to take up residence in a statue and survive on painted offerings.

Food, flowers, carvings and paintings brought victuals and other good things from the outside world into the tomb itself, along with wood and pottery models representing activities that ranged from sailing a ship on the Nile to baking and brick-making, each operation being carried out by useful worker-figures. In addition, the tomb was fully furnished and all the deceased's favourite possessions were thoughtfully buried with him.

Even more than the tomb, the coffin was the 'eternal house' of the dead person. Whether for this or for magical reasons, many coffins are remarkably colourful and elaborate. Their size, their often crowded decoration, and their wide distribution among the world's museums have made them some of the most familiar of Egyptian artefacts. A relatively simple rectangular type was in use from the Old Kingdom era. (Before then the dead had been buried in square coffins with arms and knees drawn up.) During the Middle Kingdom the well-known anthropoid (human-form) case developed, at first as an inner coffin made of cartonnage. In the course of the New Kingdom it became the standard type, and by Ramesside times nests of such coffins became quite common. But the ultimate protection – great stone sarcophagi – remained the preserve of the royal family and a few great nobles. Fashions in coffin decoration came and went over the centuries – the figure might, for example, be completely gilded, or shown in everyday dress – but most were finished off with registers of paintings, filled with useful magical spells and images of the gods, or scenes set in the nether regions or the world of everyday. For the dead person, the coffin, covered with sacred words and pictures, provided another shield against evil.

His restoration to life meant that the deceased was reunited with his spirit-double, the *ka*, which now possessed a kind of primacy in the tomb: Egyptians described dying as 'going to your *ka*'. The *ba*, shown as a human-headed bird, was not confined to the burial chamber but could wander freely during the day; but it had to return at night, on pain of extinction. The fate of the *akh* is less clear – perhaps to represent the deceased in the underworld, or to join the imperishable stars.

However, all the earthly ceremonies that had been performed were not enough to ensure that life would be resumed after death. For that to be certain, one last journey had to be undertaken.

THE FINAL TEST

After dying, every individual travelled through the night, arriving in the underworld the following morning to face judgement and negotiate a perilous passage through to the Fields of the Blessed. Earth logic suggests that these momentous events must have taken place long before the body was ready to leave the embalmer's. But illustrations to *The Book of the Dead* tend to show the funeral and Opening of the Mouth as happening at a very early stage; and since the book itself, an indispensable guide through the underworld, was placed in the coffin before the tomb was sealed, it seems reasonable to assume that the journey did not begin until the deceased could consult it. Ordinary notions of time were no doubt irrelevant in the divine scheme of things.

Spells and guide-notes for posthumous use are known as far back as the Old Kingdom 'pyramid texts' carved on the walls of the burial chambers of Unas (2375-2345 BC) and some of his successors. Later these were selected and compressed into 'coffin texts'.

Then, early in the New Kingdom period the texts were written on papyrus, with much new material, and mass-produced with many variations as *Sayings for Coming Forth by Day*, misleadingly named *The Book of the Dead* by the German scholar Lepsius; this misname, however, has stuck. There are about two hundred spells and declarations in *The Book of the Dead*, plus many vignettes which, though not always of good quality, give a vivid picture of the dead person's trials and triumphs in the realms of Osiris.

The most fraught moment, often illustrated with a sense of drama, occurred when the heart of the deceased was weighed against Maat's feather of truth. This was as close as the Egyptians came to the concept of a Final Judgement. The proceedings were supervised by the dog-headed Anubis and recorded by the scribe-god Thoth, while Ammut the Devourer, a hybrid crocodile-lion-hippopotamus, waited to pounce. If the deceased passed the test and was declared 'true of voice', he or she was led by the falcon-headed Horus into the presence of the enthroned Osiris. In *The Book of the Dead*, which is after all a do-it-yourself manual, the test is always passed; but there must have been those who failed. It is a striking feature of Egyptian art and religion that it never represents damnation or destruction: Ammut never gets a meal.

Outer coffin of the priest Ken-Hor, c.750 BC. Nests of coffins were commonly prepared for those who could afford them. The decoration is relatively restrained; the lean, dog-like form of Anubis, guardian of the dead, lies in a prominent position, on the alert.

There were many more gods to be placated and questions to be answered as the journey continued; even the doorways from one chamber to the next were capable of refusing ingress until they had been correctly identified. At various points the deceased identified with Re, Horus, Osiris and other deities, sometimes speaking out with a real or assumed boldness. A Protestation of Innocence or Negative Confession had to be made before forty-two gods, all addressed by name, denying the commission of a long list of anti-social and blasphemous acts. This, like the weighing of the heart, suggests that personal righteousness had become necessary to 'salvation'; on the other hand it can be argued that what mattered was not righteousness but magical keys such as the 'words of power' supplied by *The Book of the Dead*, an amulet to prevent the heart from revealing its shameful secrets, and so on. What seems beyond doubt is that, despite the absence of pictured hells, the spells were composed in deadly earnest, their texts revealing deep fears of mutilation, decapitation, being reduced to eating excrement and the final horror of 'a second death'. The successful petitioners received the Freedom of the Underworld and assurance of eternal life. Precise in their magic formulae, the Egyptians appear to have held contradictory ideas about the afterlife. At various times it appears to have entailed reincarnation as a star (perhaps for the *akh* alone?), sailing across the sky with Re in his solar bark, and living in the Fields of the Blessed where grain and flax grew to human height and fruits hung down in superabundance; how any of this related to the life that continued in the 'eternal house' is hard to imagine. The Fields of the Blessed were most favoured in New Kingdom papyri and wall paintings, where dead but happy couples are shown harvesting. Presumably their labours are purely symbolic, since they will certainly have brought hundreds of *shabti* into the tomb with them to do any work required by the gods. In *The Book of the Dead* the petitioner for admission to the Fields takes no chances, specifically asking to be able to eat and drink, make love, and hold a position of authority, not servitude. In their practical way, the Egyptians made provision for an eternity of well-insured home comforts.

The amenities of the tomb. In a well-furnished room such as this one, with plenty of food and blankets to hand, the Egyptian hoped to spend eternity in comfort.

9 THE LEGACY OF ANCIENT EGYPT

WONDERFUL TREASURES HAVE BEEN SALVAGED FROM THE RUINS OF THE EARLIEST CIVILIZATIONS, BUT THERE ARE FEW OF THEM AND THE GENERAL HISTORICAL RECORD IS DISTRESSINGLY FRAGMENTARY. BY CONTRAST, DESPITE ALL THAT HAS BEEN LOST, ANCIENT EGYPT LIVES ON IN MANY FORMS, INCLUDING THE TEMPLES, TOMBS AND ARTS THAT ARE STILL ON THEIR ORIGINAL SITES. BUT TIME, PROGRESS AND POLLUTION INCREASINGLY THREATEN THIS HERITAGE. SO FAR, DRAMATIC CRISES HAVE BEEN TACKLED WITH SOME SUCCESS BY LARGE-SCALE INTERNATIONAL EFFORTS; BUT THE UNOBTRUSIVE BATTLE AGAINST SLOW, DAILY DECAY IS ARGUABLY BEING LOST.

A great civilization is a splendid thing in itself and, directly or indirectly, an influence on the peoples and cultures that come into contact with it or take its place. Egyptian arts and customs, words and ideas, passed into the melting-pot of the eastern Mediterranean, influencing such historically momentous phenomena as Greek sculpture and Hebrew scripture. As interpreted by later generations, things Egyptian had an impact on Roman art and religion, became the subject of a Renaissance vogue for occultism and obelisks, contributed images to France's Empire style and thrilled British visitors to Belzoni's shows and the Egyptian Court at the Great Exhibition of 1851.

The discovery of Tutankhamun's tomb in 1922 was, among other things, a major cultural event, fuelling the Art Deco style in art and architecture and giving rise to the long-running 'Mummy's Curse' genre. A study of modern popular culture might do well to examine perceptions of Egypt, which vary from the highly sympathetic illustrated children's book to the kind of film (*Land of the Pharaohs*, *The Ten Commandments*) in which the pyramids are built by slave labourers toiling under the lash.

Much of ancient Egypt's enormous material legacy is distributed all over the globe yet, with a few exceptions, superb examples of every type of artefact and monument are still to be found in their place of origin. Many wonderful things were unearthed by adventurers and explorers who deserve credit for saving them and, all too often, censure for the heavy-handed way in which they wrenched finds from their contexts and blithely carried them out of the country. In this respect, the collectors and connoisseurs of the past were often little better than more obviously unsavoury treasure-seekers.

Treasure-seekers and thieves are always with us, but attitudes in more reputable circles have changed dramatically in the last hundred years. The foundation of the Egyptian Antiquities Service helped to instil a respect for the rights of the Egyptian state and people, and science gradually replaced swashbuckling. A problem of a new kind arose at the beginning of the 20th century when plans were made to build a dam at Aswan, flooding many Nubian sites; scholars responded by conducting a frantic, wide-ranging survey of the area to learn as much as possible about it before it disappeared for good.

Saving Abu Simbel. When it became clear that the Aswan Dam project would drown the area, UNESCO mounted a rescue operation on a scale worthy of the pharaohs, raising entire temples to a new site.

The extent of international awareness and technological progress was revealed when the same problem arose, on a much greater scale, some sixty years later. The building of the Aswan High Dam and the creation of Lake Nasser entailed the flooding of a huge area, including the sites of world-famous temples such as Abu Simbel and Philae. From 1960, co-ordinated by UNESCO, the international community financed and carried out a magnificent engineering feat that saved over twenty temples and other buildings. The centrepiece of the drama was undoubtedly the removal of the rock-cut temples of Ramesses II and Nefertari to higher ground at Abu Simbel, above the level of the lake. The tem-

Philae under threat. This wonderful temple was actually flooded before UNESCO engineers succeeded in removing it from its ancient site to a different island.

ples were literally dismantled – sawn up – and hoisted block by block on to the new site. The temple of Philae was moved by similar means to a nearby island. In both instances, care was taken to find new sites in which the orientation of the buildings remained unchanged so that, twice every year at Abu Simbel, the sun continues to strike deep into the heart of the temple and light up the sanctuary. This extraordinary rescue operation must rate as the ultimate expression of the high value put on Egypt's legacy by the world.

Meanwhile, the work of recording and conserving went on with no sign of slackening. Epigraphers copied the seemingly inexhaustible wealth of inscriptions, while archaeologists directed more of their efforts to excavations that revealed something of the lives of ordinary working people rather than the owners of grand tombs; as is often the case, a new emphasis led to re-evaluations of previously known evidence. Advances in forensic investigation also produced insights into Egyptian life, as scientists accumulated evidence from mummies, examining their teeth, identifying their ailments (smallpox, polio, arthritis), assessing their general health and seeking the cause of death. A new sensitivity, and a realization that the number of surviving mummies was strictly limited, led to the almost exclusive use of non-destructive techniques such as endoscope viewing of the interior via the throat, CAT scans and DNA sampling. A destructive investigation (in effect a belated autopsy) is now a rarity, permitted only when the mummy is held to be in a state of terminal decay. Strenuous efforts may be made to save an endangered corpse, especially one of royal birth (or death). In 1975 Ramesses II was flown to Paris for an urgent operation to remove fungoid growths; he is said to have been issued with a passport giving his occupation as 'king (deceased)', and to have been met off the plane by an official guard of honour.

In spite of its technological achievements, modernity has posed new problems, many of which remain unsolved. The Aswan High Dam has benfited modern Egyptians, but now that the Nile no longer floods every year, salt deposits accumulate on monuments and eat them away. At the same time, expanding urban developments approach the Giza pyramids, bringing with them a variety of pollutants and other problems.

The sheer scale of tourism creates environmental difficulties even when the tourists behave with exemplary correctness: among other things, the breath of thousands causes bacterial decay on wall paintings, and traffic and passing footsteps generate vibrations that undermine the mightiest works of stone. Since emerging fully from the sand in 1925-26, the Sphinx has deteriorated, and in 1988 lost part of its right shoulder. By 1980 the royal mummies in the Egyptian Museum, Cairo, were also decaying so alarmingly that they were withdrawn from public exhibition; it was not until 1994 that a group was put back on display in sealed cases. Meanwhile, the condition of the tombs in the Valley of the Kings began to cause concern as rock movements flaked painted surfaces and conservationists worried about flash flooding. . .

These were not unique problems, but they were probably present in Egypt on a greater scale than in any other country. In future the technological difficulties will no doubt be formidable, but finding the money to put the solutions into practice may be harder still, especially where decay is gradual and there is no easily identified point of no return; as in other human affairs, it is easier to raise funds for a spectacular emergency than for long-term purposes. Like so many aspects of the human heritage, the legacy of ancient Egypt continues to face an uncertain future.

INDEX

A

B

C

D

PHOTOGRAPHIC ACKNOWLEDGEMENTS

Front jacket; bottom right; Bridgeman Art Library/Louvre, Paris, bottom left, Werner Forman Archive/Egyptian Museum, Cairo, background: Michael Holford/Ashmolean Museum, Oxford.
Back jacket: Werner Forman Archive/British Museum, London.

Ancient Art and Architecture Collection 24t, 90, 120, 143, /Eric Hobson 114 /Mary Jelliffe 36, 99, /R. Sheridan 9t, 23, 24b, 31, 65, 72, 116, 135b, /John P. Stevens 8, 28, 110, /Brian Wilson 98.
AKG London 12, 14, 21, 48, 51, 95, 153t, 170, /Henning Bock 117, 134, /Egyptian Museum, Berlin 38t, 39, 45, /Egyptian Museum, Cairo 47, 151, /Israel Museum, Jerusalem/Erich Lessing 49, /Erich Lessing 54, 55, 57, /Egyptian Museum, Cairo, Erich Lessing 60, /Erich Lessing 62, 73, /Museo Egiziano, Turin, Erich Lessing 79, /Erich Lessing 83, 85, 107, 119, 123, 142, 152, 153b, 154t, 155, 166, 167, /Museo Egiziano, Turin/Drovetti Collection 111, /Egyptian Museum, Berlin 179.
Axiom Photographic Agency James Morris 30, 38b, 40l., 52 , 105 , 106/107, 118, 122, 154b, 157b, 160t, 168.
Bridgeman Art Library 80, 130, /British Library, London 41, /British Museum, London 9b, 15, 59, 82, 176, /Stapleton Collection 10, 13, 17, 182 , /Egyptian Museum, Cairo 87, 109, 146, 171t, 177, /Fitzwilliam Museum, University of Cambridge 50, 75t, /Giraudon 42, 53, 101, /Kunsthistorisches Museum, Vienna 162, /Louvre, Paris 27t, 27b, 67, 102, 140, 157t, 164, 174, 175, /O'Shea Gallery, London 104, /Royal Albert Memorial Museum, Exeter 178, /Royal Geographical Society, London 16.
Peter Clayton 33, 46, 56t, 81, 88, 97, 108, 112, 139, 169, 172, 173 r, 173 l, 180/181, 185.
By courtesy of the Committee of the Egypt Exploration Society 89.
Robert Harding Picture Library 58, 69t, 77, 137t, 160 b.
Michael Holford 131, 135t, 138, /Ashmolean Museum 2/3, /British Museum 44, 71b, 91, 158, 161, /Museo Prenestino/Palestrina 11.
Hulton Getty Picture Collection 18, 19, 20t, 20b.
Images Colour Library Limited 22, 124/125.
Caroline Jones 129, 144.
Kobal Collection 25.
Robert O'Dea 132, 165.
Ellen Rooney 64, 126, 127.
Stadt Hildesheim /Pelizaeus-Museum 94.
United Nations 183, 184.
Werner Forman Archive endpapers, chapter openers & hieroglyphic backgrounds, 86, 92, 115, 128, 133, 136, 147, /Ashmolean Museum, Oxford 29l, /British Museum, London 74, 75b, 137b, /Cheops Barque Museum, Egypt 96, /Dr E Strouhal 35, 70, 81, 100, 156, /Egyptian Museum, Cairo 3 tr, /Egyptian Museum, Berlin 29r, 148, /Egyptian Museum, Cairo 6, 26, 32, 34, 37, 40r, 56b, 63, 68, 76, 93, 103, 113, 141, 149, 150, 163, 171b, /Egyptian Museum, Turin 66, /El-Minya Museum, Egypt 121, /J. Paul Getty Museum, Malibu 145, /Louvre, Paris 7, 61, /Metropolitan Museum of Art, New York 78, /Museo Egizio, Turin, 84, /Private Collection 69b, /Egyptian Museum, Cairo, /St Louis Art Museum 43.